'Life is not what one lived, but what one remembers and how one remembers it in order to recollect.'

Gabriel Garcia Marquez

For Dave

'The secret of love is greater than the secret of death'

GOETHE

Noel Tovey

littleblackbastard

a story of survival

HODDER

Photos are from Noel Tovey's collection. Thanks are also due to the *Sydney Star Observer*, the Royal Far West School and Michael Broughton.

The author also acknowledges the assistance of the Aboriginal and Torres Strait Islander Board of the Australia Council in the writing of this book.

A Hodder Book

Published in Australia and New Zealand in 2004
by Hodder Headline Australia Pty Limited
(A member of the Hodder Headline Group)
Level 17, 207 Kent Street, Sydney NSW 2000
Website: www.hha.com.au

National Library of Australia
Cataloguing-in-Publication data

Tovey, Noel.
Little black bastard : a story of survival.

ISBN 0 7336 1798 0.

1. Tovey, Noel. 2. Male dancers - Australia - Biography. 3. Choreographers - Australia - Biography. 4. Aboriginal Australians - Biography. I. Title.

792.8028092

Text design and typesetting by Bookhouse, Sydney
Printed in Australia by Griffin Press, Adelaide

Contents

Acknowledgements

I would like to thank the following people for helping me to tell my story: Cali Vandyke-Dunleavy, Fitzroy Boulting, Bruce Sims, Kathleen Mary Fallon, Michelle Brown and the staff of the Royal Far West School, John O'Toole, staff of the Mitchell Library, staff of the Australia Council for the Arts, Liz Jones and the staff of La Mama Theatre, Robina McKellar, Greta Morton, Fran Bryson, Libby Gleeson, Department of Human Services in Melbourne, Matthew Kelly, the Victorian College of the Arts.

Note: The names of a number of characters in this book (including that of my elder sister) have been changed to protect their privacy.

Prologue

I'm not a writer. The only craft and related skills I know are the ones that I have been practising in theatre for fifty years. They are the ones that I have used to tell my story. That's what I am—a story teller—and I have written a monologue. The tram ride at the beginning of my story is also a metaphor for the journey my life has taken. There have been many stops and starts in all kinds of weather and conditions on the way and sometimes I've fallen off the tram. Falling off wasn't important but getting up and back on again was and thankfully I was always able to pick myself up and continue the journey. Where I haven't been able to remember certain incidents in my early life I have reprinted letters and official documents. Getting them has been very difficult and there are some that I am still not allowed to access. 'Freedom of information' doesn't mean exactly what it says. I have the right to ask but that's as far as it goes. Someone sitting in a cosy government office has the power to release my papers only if they see fit. It hasn't been easy for me to keep going back to the past in my mind. In fact, it has been very painful and several of my old anxiety-related illnesses returned during the process.

What I've tried to do is tell my story to you—the reader—as though we were having 'a bit of a yarn' in my living room. Every now and then I'll stop and hand you a paper and say, 'read this', or sometimes I might say, 'Can we pause here for a minute, this really is upsetting me'. I purposely didn't go to my sister, Bev, and ask her for her memories. I just wanted to write down my own recollections.

So come with me on my favourite tram and share the journey of my early life . . .

Part One

Little Black Bastard

One

I hadn't thought about returning to live in Melbourne for more than forty years, until 1997 when I was invited by the Canadian Consulate to a theatre conference at the Playbox Theatre. In the morning newspaper, I saw an advertisement for a flat in Parkville that is for sale. I like Parkville so I decide to go and have a look at the flat before the conference began.

I caught the number 57 West Maribyrnong tram in Elizabeth Street. Even as a kid I loved riding on the trams. They are the heart, the soul of the city. The tramlines were my songlines. Sixty years ago the trams were quite different to the one I've just boarded. In those days at either end of the tram there was a closed-in compartment for ladies and non-smokers, and the middle section was open on one side to all the elements. It was freezing cold in the winter. In the hot summer months the windows and doors would be opened and the blinds on the outside area rolled up to catch any passing breeze. The air was filled with a mixture of smells—perfume, exhaust fumes and cigarette smoke. I purchased a ticket from the faceless vending machine and settled down to enjoy the long circuitous route I have chosen.

The tram travels a short distance up Elizabeth Street and stops. I'm oblivious to all the shouting and traffic noise. I'm staring idly out of the window thinking of other tram rides in other times. My gaze wanders above the canopy of 57 Elizabeth Street and I'm surprised and thrilled to see still intact a window with a gold and black silhouette portrait of the legendary 1930s musical comedy star Stephanie Deste painted on it. Gone are the words 'Stephanie Deste—Salon de Beaute', they have been replaced simply by the word 'Hairdresser'. Stephanie had been a dancer and leapt to fame with her stunning performance as Wanda the Indian temptress in the 1937 production of *Rose Marie*. She was now the beauty guru to every Melbourne housewife and had a weekly radio program. Her signature tune was the Totem Tom Tom Ballet that had made her famous. Her daughter Toti, named after the opera diva Toti Dal Monte, and I were good friends in the late fifties.

Suddenly, I'm a little boy again. Now I see only the ghosts of buildings that were once real to me. Collins Book Depot where I worked when I was fifteen was a small double-fronted shop with windows displaying all the latest best-sellers. *The Big Fisherman* by Morris West and *Little Boy Lost* by Marghanita Laski were very popular. The manager's name was Charles Dickens, a strange coincidence, I thought at the time, and it was there I met Chesca, who became my soulmate and introduced me to the ballet.

Next door was the London Hotel. I sold newspapers outside the public bar when I was twelve and two prostitutes I knew, Patsy and Jill, always made their sailor boyfriends give me a tip. Gone is the building that was Robertson & Mullens bookstore where John Muirhead worked. Mary Hardy and I would go there at lunchtime to meet him. The three of us were inseparable, and besides, John was the only one who always had a regular job and money for lunch.

As the tram crosses Bourke Street I see a refurbished McGills bookshop. In a lane at the back of the main shop was the storeroom where I applied for my first job as a newspaper boy when I was twelve years old. Luckily one of my mates had warned me about the boss. He liked to grope you as he adjusted the straps on your leather moneybag and used phrases like, 'Aren't *we* big for our age?' The bag had two sections, one for silver coins and the other for pennies. The evening newspaper, the *Herald*, cost twopence and if you had a good day the bag got quite heavy. I suffered the groping and feigned innocence and pleasure and got the job.

On the other side of Elizabeth Street is Pellegrino's Catholic Bookshop with an array of missals, rosary beads, scapulas and other necessities for a suitable entrance into heaven displayed in the window. It was there that I bought my favourite holy card of Jesus baring his chest and showing his bleeding Sacred Heart. On the first floor above the shop was the Borovansky Ballet Studio. I spent many happy hours there.

The majestic old *Argus* building where I worked as a galley boy after my trial still stands sentinel on the corner of La Trobe Street. My trial was big news in those days. One of the most enduring memories I have of that period of my life is seeing a newspaper billboard outside the newsagents near our house in North Melbourne that proclaimed NORTH MELBOURNE BALLET DANCER ON SERIOUS CHARGE. I doubt if a 'gay' trial would even make the back page today.

There is a lot of noise at the next stop. Everyone's pushing to get on and off the tram. It's the Queen Victoria Market and market day. My sister Bev and I would come here on Saturday mornings when we were very young and hungry because we knew we could get broken biscuits and spotted fruit for nothing, and if we had a penny we could buy a jam doughnut. Bev was two years older than me, and taller, with a mop of dark curly hair.

The tram turns left into Victoria Street. The Central Hotel on the corner is the beginning of what I now think of as Mumma's way home. Mumma was barely five feet tall; she had had polio as a child, which left her with one leg considerably shorter than the other, and she walked with a decided limp. She had short straight dark hair and a small pretty face.

Her drinking habits had changed considerably during the time Bev and me were living with the Challengers in Burren Junction. She was now a periodic alcoholic, which meant two to three weeks of total alcoholic oblivion and one week of feeling crook and drinking endless bottles of lemonade that I bought for her on tick from the corner shop. This was followed by weeks of recriminations and alcoholic remorse and promises. Every day she would say, 'No more drink for me, Noely boy.' It was during these periods of sobriety that our lives were comparatively normal. I made a big effort to go to school and Mumma made a bigger effort to stay sober. She worked at Parker Toys in West Melbourne and she always went to the market on payday. I spent my North Melbourne years dreading Fridays. If I walked into the house after school on a Friday afternoon and got this strange inexplicable feeling of emptiness then I knew Mumma had busted on her way home and was doing the pubs in North Melbourne. The British Hotel was a particular favourite. Women weren't allowed to drink in the public bars of hotels in those days. They drank in the Ladies Lounge, usually small glasses of beer called ponies, or sherry, or port and lemonade.

The tram rattles its way up Victoria Street passing the Victoria Hotel and St Mary's Star of the Sea convent where Mumma went to school. As we turn right into Errol Street I can see that the Three Crowns Hotel on the corner is now a restaurant and the Town Hall Hotel has been tarted up in blue and pink paint. The old picture theatre where I went on Saturday mornings has gone but not the memories. I loved Westerns and always wanted the Indians to win. I thought there must have been millions of them because no matter how many were killed each Saturday morning there would be just as many the next week and the week after that.

The tram turns left at the Town Hall, passes the Court House Hotel and swings down Queensberry Street into Abbotsford Street. Crossing Arden Street, I can see the North Melbourne football ground. I was footy mad. North Melbourne was the first team I barracked for. After all, I was a North Melbourne boy and very territorial. The captain, Les Foote, was our idol. He looked like Captain Marvel, the hero of my favourite comic, with his flowing blond hair, feats of athleticism and prowess with the football. I sold drinks and lollies there on Saturday afternoons and made enough money to take Betty Pollock to the pictures in Newmarket on Saturday night. Two tickets, two Peter's dixie ice-creams, two Polly Waffles at interval and two hamburgers with the lot on the way home. I was desperately in love with Betty Pollock.

We pass the Northern Star and British Hotels, and in the distance there's the North Melbourne swimming baths. I think I can see my mate Clarrie still bouncing up and down on the end of the diving board. Clarrie was small and very athletic, with a great body. In the vernacular of my day he was 'a good sort'. All our mob—Chooka, with his large freckled face topped by flaming red hair, Duddy, small and round like a pudding, Sparrow, tall and thin with a bird-like beak for a nose and little Wally—are there, as usual, cheering him on. Clarrie would spend hours bouncing up and down on the end of the board going higher and higher each time and then when everyone was looking he would do a one and a half forward somersault in the pike position into the pool as we all shouted and applauded. Clarrie and I were the same age and we both thought he looked like Cary Grant, especially in his Wesley College uniform. Clarrie was the only real friend I had in those days. Yet no two boys could have had more different home lives. He once jumped into the creek at Ferntree Gully and pulled me to safety after I had fallen out of a tree chasing a possum.

The tram slows down in the traffic opposite Miss Alice Cullen's house. It is one in a terrace of typical small brick working men's cottages. Supported on granite to compensate for the incline in the road, it has an ornate wrought-iron trimmed verandah and front fence. Miss Cullen taught me elocution at St Michael's when I was eleven. Old habits die hard and unconsciously I start reciting out loud a little poem based on the vowel sound 'A'. The man sitting opposite me says 'Pardon?'. I pretend I didn't hear him and that I am perfectly sane.

I knew from the first day Bev and me arrived back from Burren Junction that I would get out of North Melbourne, just as I had known we would get out of Carlton and Burren. Call it instinct or sixth sense but for me it was the ingredient that cemented the protective walls I was building around myself. Maybe I would go to America and join the Indians or become a film star but wherever I went I knew I didn't want to be or to sound Australian so I practised everything Miss Cullen taught me. I would stand under the mulberry tree in the back yard before an imaginary audience and three cats and recite all her exercises for the voice: 'Ann met an ant, and an ant met Ann. Hello said the ant, hello said Ann. Boys' boots are big so when boys jump, boys' big boots go bump bump bump.' One Saturday morning when I had finished my recital, I heard applause coming from inside the outside dunny, which was near the back gate. It was Mrs Molloy. Later she said to Mumma, 'Geez, Win, Noely boy has a lovely speaking voice.' That was the day I invented Rohan Scott-Rowan, my alter ego. He was a blond-haired blued-eyed suave matinee idol. He stayed with me for many years. As I grew up so did he. He told me that one day we would be rich and famous and buy all our clothes at Buckley & Nunn and have plenty to eat all the time.

The tram terminates at the corner of Flemington Road and Abbotsford Street opposite my old school St Michael's. There are so many bad memories here. I had a crush on a girl named Betty. I think she was pretty. Some of the other boys had girlfriends and we all used to line up in the back lane and kiss the girls. When it was my turn to kiss Betty the boys teased her so much about having an Abo boyfriend that she ignored me and joined in the collective laughter and abuse of me. Even though I was quite bright, I always had to sit at the back of the class and I can still feel the burning of the broad leather strap on my hands after getting six of the best from Sister Mary Isidore for being late.

I was a devout Catholic in those early years of my life. So was Mumma. Drunk or sober, she always gave me a 'threepenny bit' to put on the collection plate for the poor at mass on Sunday. I always took a penny change for an ice cream. I figured I was as poor as anyone else. Religion saturated everything I did. I could recite all the catechism by heart, sing the mass in Latin and I always went to benediction on the first Friday of the month. I was fascinated by the ceremony and drama of the occasion. When the altar boys walked down the aisle swinging their incense-laden censers the smell was intoxicating and seemed to bring me face to face with God and the Devil. They were everywhere, they fought monumental battles for my soul. I wanted to be an altar boy myself but I was never asked.

When things were really bad at home I would sit in church and ask God to explain my life to me. I couldn't understand why everyone got drunk and became violent and why I was always being called a little black bastard and being beaten up by the other boys. One time I had my nose broken. But God never did answer my questions. Sister Mary Louis, who taught Mumma at St Mary's, was still teaching Grade Three at St Michael's in her late seventies. She made the only memorable statement I can recall from my brief time at school. She said, 'Now children, I want you to remember that you were all born to die, and when you do Jesus will be waiting for you at the gates of heaven.'

I crossed Flemington Road and got on the Parkville tram. I'm still thinking about St Michael's when the tram driver announces that the next stop will be the Zoo. Opposite the Zoo is where the Royal Park Welfare Depot for Children was. I think part of it is still there. I can hear voices from the past—Bev's voice, my voice. I'm crying, it's raining, I'm cold and I don't know where we are. Bev is saying, 'I'm here, I'm here, everything's gonna be all right,' but everything wasn't all right. I have never been frightened as much again as I was by the unknown that night.

The tram finally arrives in Parkville. I got off at Park Street. I'm disturbed by some of the memories I've been having and I'm asking myself if I'm ready to live in Melbourne again. I went to see the flat but it was too small. I needed some time to think, so I crossed the road, sat in the park, where I discussed my situation with some magpies who are nearby. This is not an unusual thing for me to do. Magpies are my totemic self and I have always believed that they are the embodiment of my ancestral spirits.

It is a beautiful day; the old feller gum trees are whispering in the wind about me to each other and the maggies are singing and asking me to come home. I knew then and there that Melbourne is indeed where I want to live. I don't think I ever really left there. For all the thirty-five years I lived overseas Melbourne was always only a thought or memory away. I am part of Melbourne; I know every nook and cranny of the place. It is something that has been missing from my life for many years.

I also know that today is the day for me to springclean the memories of my youth and exorcise the ghosts of the past. I walked down Park Street to Sydney Road and jumped on the East Coburg tram to Bell Street. I want to stand outside Pentridge Gaol again. I was an inmate there after my trial fifty years ago and two of the most traumatic experiences of my life took place inside those walls.

Looking out of the tram window as I ride up Sydney Road is like watching a travel documentary. I don't think the road was designed to carry this much traffic. There is a cacophony of sound—cars honking their horns, the tram clanging its bell and people wearing a variety of ethnic clothing and yelling at each other in a variety of languages. This is the first time I have ridden a tram up Sydney Road. When I was a boy my areas of activity were North Melbourne, Newmarket, Ascot Vale and the city. Sometimes I'd go to the Zoo in Royal Park. Now, I doubt if there is a more multicultural area in the whole of Australia. The names of the restaurants and shops are so evocative: the Sri Lankan Village, a cheap and popular café with an idyllic jungle scene painted on wooden fan in the front window; the Mediterranean Delicatessen—the best place in Melbourne to buy pasta and other Italian specialities—takes up almost a block; the Muslim Women's association; Sartorial Manduca, a splendid Continental tailor; and the Pummakale Bakery, offering pide bread and other Turkish delicacies. The old Mechanics Institute, built in 1868, is now a community theatre.

Halfway up Sydney Road, I got off the tram: all those Middle Eastern and Italian food stores demand to be investigated. I am instantly struck by the friendliness of the people. There is an air of village and community life here and, compared to Sydney, where I've been living for ten years, the cost of food is very cheap. I went into a Lebanese grocer's and bought some dates, bread and beans. The young girl behind the counter says thank you in her best English when I pay her and I reply, 'Shukrun', in my best Arabic and we both smile.

Sandwiched between the Sun Yee Cafe and La Massaia Trattoria is Herbert's Home-made Pie Shop. It is obvious from the facade that it was there long before the multicultural invasion of Sydney Road. Displayed on old-fashioned trays in the window are vanilla slices, apple slices, rock cakes, lamingtons, fairy cakes, custard tarts and (joy of all joys) real coffee scrolls. Now I know I'm home in Melbourne. I spent so many years of my early childhood being hungry that I am now a compulsive food shopper and even though I have eaten in some of the finest restaurants in the world there are times when I still crave for the taste of a fresh hot meat pie and tomato sauce at the footy, crisp fried chip potatoes from the Greek fish and chip shop in North Melbourne, the big scones and Irish stew that Mumma made for us when she was sober and a coffee scroll straight out of the oven of the pastry shop that used to be in Swanston Street. The coffee scroll is to be enjoyed with your morning coffee and is, as the name implies, a scroll of delicious sultana and mixed-spice-laden dough which has the consistency of a bun and finished off with a dollop of very soft pale pink icing on top. There is an art to eating a coffee scroll; first order your coffee, then start uncoiling the scroll from the outside. This releases the intoxicating aroma of cinnamon, and you gradually eat your way to the centre and finally savour the piece with the pale pink icing on it. I can't resist, so I go in and buy a scroll and then set about looking for a coffee.

Almost by accident I find Mariella's Coffee Shop. It is hidden in a narrow walkway to a car park. I smell the coffee first before I see the shop, which is very small with a few baskets of coffee beans in the window. Inside, there is a 1950s' espresso machine and several shelves of jars filled with sweets all labelled Maria's Lollies. There are a couple of red plastic tables outside to sit on so I asked the young woman behind the counter for 'un cappuccino per favore'. 'Lei Italiano?' she asked. 'No, sono Australiano,' I reply. 'Ma mi piace molto Italiano.' By the time she's made the best cup of coffee this side of Naples, I have told her that I lived in Rome in the 60s and that I have forgotten most of my Italian. She has told me her name is Mariella and that I can come any time and practise my Italian with her.

Feeling that my emotional batteries have been recharged by the friendliness of the people and the enjoyment of the coffee scroll ritual, I begin the walk up the hill to the gaol. When I arrive at the corner of Bell Street and Sydney Road, the first thing I see is a huge real estate hoarding that says WELCOME TO PENTRIDGE VILLAGE. The most exclusive new residential precinct in Melbourne. I don't know whether to laugh or cry. I walk a little further and see the gaol. It has been closed for some years and is soon to be redeveloped as a 'holiday resort for poltergeists'. I arrived here on a very wet night when my trial began and I was taken to the courthouse in a closed van on the day I received my 'good behaviour' bond. When the city fathers of Melbourne had Pentridge designed in 1856 they instructed the architects to build them a replica of an English mediaeval castle in bluestone. Today it looks like the set for the local amateur musical society's production of *Camelot*.

I go searching for someone who may be able to let me have a look inside. When I turn the corner I see the roller spikes on the end of the wall—and I am instantly in my cell again. It was probably even smaller than I remember it. There was no bed. I was given four blankets and slept on the floor. These had to be folded each morning in a particular way. There was a toilet with a tap over it in one corner and a small window that was too high up to see out of. I still suffer very badly from claustrophobia, which began in that cell, and it was there that I contemplated suicide for the first time.

I was sent to Pentridge Gaol at the beginning and end of my trial in 1951. That was the year they executed Jean Lee for her part in the brutal murder of an old bookmaker. She was the last female to be hanged in Australia. Late one evening after lights out, I thought I heard the guards erecting the gallows somewhere near my cell. I could hear them practising the mechanism of a trap door. I don't know how long the rehearsal lasted, but in the silence that followed I decided that I wanted to end my life. I felt doomed and worthless and I wanted to die. Usually in the past I had been able to rise above whatever situation I found myself in by laughing it off or getting angry, but that night I couldn't laugh or get angry. I was just a scared little boy. I felt like one of the animals I had seen waiting to be slaughtered at the abattoirs in Burren Junction. Every time I heard a noise outside my cell door I thought it was someone coming to get me. I started crying as seventeen years of my life passed before my eyes in a torrent of bad memories.

This was the very first time I had consciously thought about my life and how I was living it. I didn't like what I saw and I thought I would be better off dead. I'm sure my sobbing would have echoed throughout the world had not the walls of my cell been deliberately made to absorb all human emotion. I cried and cried until I had no more tears. Then I just sat there, dazed, unable to think of anything other than death. As the early morning light came through my window I thought I heard the trap door again. I panicked and had difficulty breathing. Then something in the cell grabbed me and I heard voices yelling at me from inside my head: 'Did you ask to be born in the slums of Carlton? Did you ask to be born black? Did you ask to be raped and abused by Uncle Josh and Arthur Challenger from the age of four? No!' They said, 'you didn't.' The voices got louder and I thought I was going mad. My head was spinning. Eventually I passed out.

When the banging on the cell door by the guard woke me up, I lay for a few minutes thinking about the voices. I knew they were voices of my ancestors and I had been given my first lesson in survival? By the time I walked into the exercise yard for my breakfast of 'burgoo', prison porridge, I knew that what they had told me was true. None of this shit was my fault. There had to be a better life for me somewhere out there in the world and I was determined to find it when I got out of Pentridge.

This morning I stood looking at those spikes on the gaol wall for some time and I shook my head in disbelief at the brutality of the system fifty years ago. I have a strange feeling of achievement as I walk down Bell Street to catch the tram to Carlton. These memories are mine and I've earned the right to live with them.

I got off the tram in Lygon Street. I bought a notebook, and sat in the nearest coffee shop and wrote down the experience of the tram ride and the disturbing memories it had provoked. At last I had found a way to write my autobiography. When I received the Commonwealth Indigenous Fellowship from The Australia Council for the Arts in the year 2000 the idea of writing anything was a frightening and daunting task considering the little schooling I'd had. Now, feeling excited by the prospect of actually writing a book, I went for a walk around the streets where I had spent my early childhood in search of my past.

The up-market and yuppy Carlton of today with its pinball parlours, all night delis and transient population of mixed ethnic and Australian students is not my Carlton. Nino Borsari's bike shop no longer sells bikes. It is one of the many chic Italian restaurants that proliferate in Lygon Street, although the original neon sign with Nino riding his famous bike into Olympic history is still there high above the restaurant. The 'Bug House', our nickname for the Carlton picture theatre when we were kids, is to my amazement and delight still standing even though it is now closed. It was there that Bev won a green and yellow scooter, which she fell off on her way home and cut her hand open on a broken beer bottle.

My father was short, black, very dapper and always wore

pearl grey spats and matching derby hat. He was a street singer and entertained the picture crowd that went to the Bug House at interval. He carried a small three and a half octave organ on a strap across his shoulder which he would set down on the pavement. He taught my brother Freddie some routines and together they would perform 'Shoe Shine Boy' or 'Me and My Shadow'. The University Hotel on the corner of Lygon and Gratan Streets, where he busked while Bev and me dressed in clown suits collected pennies from the crowd, is now a bank.

I think the only clear memories I have of him are his beautiful singing voice and the clothes he wore. He was well known in the Carlton area, particularly by the local police. On one of my papers it says, 'Father known to the police as a dope peddler'. There was always a mob of people at our house and I never did understand why some of them had white powder on their noses. Many years later Mumma told me about the white powder. She said my father first used cocaine when he was performing in vaudeville.

He had an interesting history. When Mumma was drunk she would often say to me, 'You didn't come from shit, Noely boy. Your father came from a very famous family.' She told me that he had been educated in London and spoke several languages. My grandfather was part of a well-known negro vaudeville act, the Royal Bohee Brothers, and had been taken to Buckingham Palace to give the young Prince Edward lessons on the banjo. These were all wonderful stories and I wanted to believe them but if they were true how come my father died a drunk and a pauper in the St Vincent de Paul Hostel on Flemington Road, North Melbourne, while Bev and me were being violated by Arthur Challenger in Burren Junction?

The unravelling of this saga is due entirely to my niece Greta Morton who, in searching for her own black identity within our bizarre family structure, remembered my sister telling her the stories Mumma had told us about our grandfather being part of a famous negro vaudeville act called the Royal Bohee Brothers. From Paris, where she lives, she obtained my father's birth certificate and his wedding certificate and contacted genealogists and musicologists in America and England. They verified Mumma's stories.

My father was the illegitimate son of James Bohee, one half of the famous Bohee Brothers a popular vaudeville act, and a white woman named Matilda Farquhar. She was married to a tobacconist named James Farquhar. My father was born in London on 29 December 1888 and educated at St Martins in the Fields school. We have no exact date of his arrival in Australia. When he enlisted in the 5th Squadron, 2nd Remounts at Holsworthy in New South Wales in 1915, he was twenty-six years old and he gave his mother's name as Mrs Matilda Morton of Clarence Gardens Gate, London, and on another paper he gives her name as Mrs Matilda Farquhar of the same address. On his marriage certificate in 1918, to Tasmanian vaudeville artist Kathleen Irene Morton—a strange coincidence (or was it?) marrying a woman with the same surname as his and who he was still married to when he met Mumma—he gives his father's name as James Boher Morton, born in the USA. The name Bohee is often spelt differently. Sometimes it it spelt Boher or Bohe but the researchers I have spoken to all prefer the spelling Bohee. This confusion is not strange, as my great-grandfather was in all probability an African slave and the practice of the day was to adopt the name of the plantation owner or just make one up. I have not been able to source any official birth certificates or records of my great-grandfather.

My grandfather, James Douglas Bohee was born in New Brunswick, Canada, on 25 March 1857, one of ten children. In 1859, the family moved to Boston and lived in the African settlement on Beacon Hill. He and his brother, my great-uncle, George Beverly Bohee, were self-taught musicians and singers, and early in their careers, they ran a concert saloon in Washington Street, Boston Massachusetts. In 1881 they joined Haverley's Coloured Minstrels and sailed to England. This is a description of the show from a contemporary paper.

> It is a troupe of all coloured people and when the curtain went up on opening night it disclosed on stage sixty-five real Negroes both male and female ranging in shades of complexion from the coal black Negro to the light brown Mulatto or Octaroon. They were all ages, from ancient Uncle Toms and Aunty Chloes, smart young coons and wenches, down to the little piccaninny a few months old nestling in its mother's lap.

The Brothers were immensely popular, and toured the provinces extensively, reaching the peak of their fame in the late 1800s. They made many songs popular with their rendition of them. The best known of these was 'As Dainty as a Rose' composed by Miss Helen Charles. Great-uncle George was the first person to sing 'A Boys Best Friend Is His Mother'.

The following are extracts from a letter written by Mrs E. Morritt, wife of the great showman Charles Morritt and founder of the Birkenhead Banjo Band.

> On one memorable occasion we received a letter from Sir Arthur Sullivan (famous for his collaboration with W.S. Gilbert) who was giving a party at his home in Queen Anne Mansions, at which His Royal Highness The Prince of Wales (later Edward the Seventh) was to be present. We [*The Morritts*] were to give our thought-reading act. That night will live in my memory forever. Jim and George Bohee surpassed themselves on that occasion. After several selections, including the wonderful arrangement of 'Home Sweet Home', someone jokingly suggested they should honour their host by playing one of his

> compositions, no doubt sharing the general assumption that the banjo was a very limited instrument. However, The Bohees immediately responded with a magnificent harmonised version of 'The Lost Chord' and at the conclusion Sir Arthur Sullivan himself was so overcome his eyes filled with tears as he tried to thank them. His Royal Highness was so impressed he invited Jim Bohee to give him lessons. It was as a result of that experience that I made up my mind that I would do all in my power to further the cause of the banjo.

My grandfather opened his studio for teaching the banjo under Royal Patronage at 7a Coventry St London in 1882. He designed and sold his own banjos for the unheard of sum of fifty pounds each. He was aiming at a society clientele. The banjo had become very popular among the upper classes. His banjos were marked Champion. They had carved ivory pegs inlaid with garnets, gold-plated brackets, a German silver rim and hand-carved neck base and fingerboard inlaid with mother of pearl. They were mostly made by Alfred Weaver. From that time on my grandfather and great-uncle were billed in Vaudeville as the Royal Bohee Brothers.

It was in 1889 that the Bohee Brothers Operatic Minstrels opened their season at the International Hall. In his book *Black People: Entertainers of African Descent*, Rainer Lotz says: 'The Bohee Brothers were the first Afro-Americans to have their music recorded. Sadly, these cylinders do not appear to have survived.' My grandfather loved the good life and gambling. He died penniless in the County Hotel, Ebbw Vale, Wales, on 8 December 1897 aged fifty-three, and is buried in the Brompton Cemetery in Fulham.

When I lived in London, I often took a shortcut through the cemetery. It was my favourite place to go when I had to study a script.

It is not known when or where Great-uncle George died. He was last seen by a friend 'in straitened circumstances' in 1926. In newspaper reviews of their work the Brothers are often referred to as mulattos or octaroons, which suggests that they had white genes as well as African ones. They were in all probability Creole, a mix of French and African. New Brunswick, Canada, where they were born is where the French Acadians settled and the Cajuns originated.

I have often thought about my strange family tree and the 'strange fruit' that it bore—Aboriginal, African, French and the variations of Celtic. I wonder how my life might have been different if my father and Mumma hadn't been cast adrift by their families.

Two

There have been so many gaps in my life that it's difficult to give you a complete picture. The one person who could have filled them in was Mumma and she didn't like talking about the past. Only when I pressed her did she tell me that my father arrived in Australia as a young man and that the first job he had was with an all-black minstrel show. In 1912, he joined the chorus of the now famous Oscar Ashe production of *Chu Chin Chow* at the Princess Theatre in Melbourne.

The following information is from his official papers, which I now have. On 13 October 1915, when he was twenty-six years old, he enlisted in the 1st Australian Imperial Force at Holsworthy, New South Wales. At the time there was a recruiting drive to enlist more men to fight on the side of the British in World War I. He was shipped out to the Middle East with the 2nd Australian Remount Unit and learnt to ride while he was stationed in Egypt. He wanted to join the Light Horse Brigade but was rejected on medical grounds because he had a slightly withered hand. Instead, he played the piano and sang in the Anzac Hostel, the officers' mess in Cairo. His career in the army was very stormy. The following is an extract from the proceedings of a General Field Court Martial held on 7 September 1916 in Moascar, Egypt:

> When on active service, disobeying a command given by his superior officers in that he at Moascar, Ismailia [a town] left camp on 28/8/1916 when ordered not to. Pleaded not guilty . . . Found guilty [given] 4 months I.H.L active service committing an offence against a person of inhabitation of the country in which he was serving in that he at Ismailia in Egypt on 13/8/1916 assaulted No 10046, a native policeman Abel Hamed. Guilty . . . Found not guilty. D.A. hospital Synovitis left knee, discharged to Moascar, marched in details Camp Moascar medically unfit 23/12/1916. Discharged. Unit disbanded. Services no longer required.

He was discharged without his medals the 1914/15 Star, the British War Medal and the Victory Medal, which were restored in 1920.

Mumma never spoke much about her own life to me. She took virtually all of her family secrets to the grave. I know she went to St Mary's in West Melbourne and when she left school she worked as a maid for a Jewish family named Goldberg in St Kilda. They were strictly kosher and Mumma learnt to speak Yiddish fluently from them. She knew all about the Shabbat and holy day rituals. Her father Thomas Tovey came from a well-known family in Christchurch New Zealand. There is a Tovey Street in Christchurch named after one of Mumma's illustrious relatives who were among the first settlers to arrive in Lyttleton. Her mother Elizabeth McCann died when Mumma was quite young. Mumma's grandparents on her mother's side were James

McCann and Margaret Carmody, an Aboriginal woman from South Australia. There is no birth certificate for my great-grandmother but there is a lot of oral history. There are hundreds of Carmodys listed on the Aboriginal index in South Australia and I haven't tried to contact any of them. Now that I am seventy there is no need for me know the complete history of my Aboriginality. Curiosity is for the young.

I think Mumma had had a hard life. I know she nursed her mother who was very ill and died quite young.

When she was eighteen Mumma went to work in a brothel. The madam was Jewish and Mumma's knowledge of Yiddish helped her get the job. If a client only wanted 'a short time' (a quickie in today's parlance), the prostitute placed a towel on the counterpane of her bed. Mumma's job was to collect these 'short time towels' and wash them. She once told me that she liked working there and was treated very well by the madam and the girls. She said she wasn't treated like a freak because of her limp. It was while she was working there that she met my father. He was twenty-five years older than her and working in vaudeville. He was billed as 'The Original Coon Singer'.

The first born was my brother, Fred, in 1930. Then came Beverley, who I called Bev, in 1932 and then me. I was born in the Royal Women's Hospital, Carlton, on 25 December 1933, 1934 or 1935, depending on which of my papers you read. I was the third child born out of wedlock so in truth we could all claim the title 'little black bastard' that was bestowed upon me during my formative years. I was followed by Claudia and Francis. Fred was the first to be taken away by the Welfare at the age of ten to save him from 'a life and career of vice and crime'. This is what it says on his removal papers:

> Father street musician, poor home, drink and neglect. Mother Australian. Father shows colour line, boy beaten at school for

> dark appearance. Morton said his son could not go to school because he had no boots but when I questioned the boy he said his mother kept him home to look after the baby. I drew Mrs Morton's attention to the children's heads, which were verminous.

Freddie was taken to the Royal Park Welfare Depot for Children in the early afternoon of 7 September 1940 but later that night he escaped. Next morning began a day of great excitement for Bev and me. The police and Welfare came to our house looking for him but he was on the roof of the house opposite, hiding behind the chimney. One of the Welfare men spotted him and a policeman climbed up on the roof and Freddie took off with the policeman chasing him. Bev and me stood in the street and killed ourselves laughing as Freddie jumped from roof to roof whooping with cries of joy until they caught him.

He was sent to the Silesian Brothers in Sunbury, Victoria where he was well educated and looked after by the brothers. It was a few years before I saw him again. Mumma took me to visit him one Sunday. We were like strangers but we both pretended that we were happy to see each other. I never thought about him in a brotherly way because I was too young to have formed any kindred spirit with him. He was four years older than me and must have witnessed the full brunt of the terrible life we were being subjected to, which is why he never would talk about it when we were adults.

Bev was so much a part of my early life that my story is to a certain extent her story. We lived in Barkly Street, Carlton, described by the Welfare as, 'an old two storey house. The front room was clean and is used by the parents. The back room is used as a kitchen'.

I remember the kitchen was very dark; it had a black stove and an old wooden table which Mumma would stand me on so she could smear my legs with a paste made of treacle and sulphur to get rid of the scabies. It was under this table that my younger brother Francis was found 'in a pool of urine' by the Welfare when they took him away. I have no memories whatsoever of him as a baby.

When Bev and I returned to live in Melbourne in 1946, Mumma told me he'd been adopted by a wealthy family and that it would be too upsetting for him if I were to find him. Bev found him again after fifty years, living in country New South Wales. We spoke once or twice on the telephone when I lived in London. At the time of writing this book we still haven't met and in all honesty I don't think we ever will. I learnt the hard way that blood isn't thicker than water and too much of it has passed under our bridge.

The description of the house goes on: 'There are two rooms upstairs. One contained a stretcher bed with a filthy mattress. On the floor was a wire mattress with a dirty flock mattress and dirty pieces of blanket. These beds are used by the children.'

This room had a broken window and on cold wet nights Bev and I sat at the window and counted the yellow cabs that went by in the street below to stave off our hunger and the noise from the drunks. Often the police would come. One night they made my father stand on his hands in the street, a favourite trick of his when he was drunk. They threw pennies at him and called him names. I started crying; I felt sorry for him. I think this was the only time I ever felt anything for him and in those days I never felt anything for Mumma. My family was Bev. She was mother, father, brother and sister to me.

Another diversionary tactic of Bev's was to sit me on the bed, pick the fleas out of my hair and crack them between her thumbnails. During the day we played in the maze in the Exhibition Gardens nearby. The maze was a replica of an English maze. It was made of tall hedges and had a wooden lookout tower in the middle. The Royal Exhibition building that stands in the gardens was used in 1940 to billet hundreds, maybe thousands, of soldiers who were all preparing to defend king and country. The gardens smelt of urine. I think every tree was used as a toilet.

The endless days and nights of misery for Bev and me were only interrupted by occasional visits from the Welfare who always arrived unannounced. Then, for a few days after that, there would be food in the house and we would be washed. I was only five years old and too young to know or understand what was going on. Every December, Mumma would take me to the Salvation Army Citadel in Drummond Street. I would have my clothes changed and was given a toy for Xmas and photographed. Mumma would be given a bundle of clothing and food. After Christmas, a hand-coloured picture of me with yellow hair mounted on a card with a prayer would arrive in the post. But there was never any Christmas for us.

I have two distinct memories of those times and they are as vivid today as they were sixty years ago. We had a fruit tree in our back yard and I was determined to climb it. I scaled the tin fence, jumped onto a branch and started climbing. Bev came out into the yard and saw me up the tree. She grabbed my leg, I panicked and fell. On the way down I reached out for the fence and I landed on the ground minus the top of my little finger. Bev, not knowing the extent of my injury, put my finger under the tap and I yelled out in pain. Somebody came into the yard and saw what had happened. I was rushed to the Children's Hospital where my finger was stitched up and I was fussed over. The next week I fell out of the tree again and broke my arm.

It has taken several rewrites and much editing of this book for me to include the following story. When I was about three years old I was playing on an old vacant lot one morning, digging holes in the ground with my little bucket and spade when to my amazement I dug up a very tiny pinkish white person. It smiled at me and I put it back in the hole and covered up with dirt. Was it a doll? I have always believed that it was a real person. I often saw little people when I was very, very young.

I am a self-confessed and unashamed chocoholic and this is how and when my addiction began. Easter Sunday morning 1939, I came downstairs and all was quiet. The drunks were sleeping off a Saturday night binge. I went into the front room. Dad, Mumma, Aunty Chick, Aunty Flo and one or two others were out to it on the big double bed. I started looking around for the odd penny that might have fallen on the floor when out of the corner of my eye I saw a £1 note sticking out like a shining green star from underneath a pillow. Very carefully I slipped my hand under the pillow and eased the note out. I waited for a moment to make sure no one was awake, then I ran down the lane to the corner shop and bought Easter eggs for all the kids in the street. I got such a hiding when I came home covered in chocolate but it was worth it.

Uncle Josh lived next door with his mother. I don't think he drank. His house was a safe haven for me when the violence got out of hand and looked like it was heading my way or if I was hungry, which was often. Uncle Josh was kind but it wasn't always food that he put in my mouth. I thought this and his fondling of my genitals was how grown-up people showed you they cared about you.

Drunks, hunger, violence, filth, the stench of stale urine and vomit and the occasional day at St George's school was the norm and I had no reason to believe that other people lived differently. Then, one morning sometime in late winter 1941, something very strange happened. We were still living in Barkly Street. I woke up and the house was quiet and empty. Everyone except Bev and me had disappeared. Mumma and my father had abandoned us some months before and no one else was around. I don't know much about this episode in Mumma's life and I never wanted to ask her when I was older. The official document I have from the Carlton Courthouse merely says 'Whereabouts of mother unknown'. Bev told me that everyone had gone away and that from now on she would be looking after me. Uncle Josh seemed to have disappeared along with everyone else and I never saw him again. I deliberately blocked out all memory of him from that time on.

I had now lived or existed and survived nearly seven years of starvation, maltreatment and deprivation. That our parents had disappeared didn't bother me at all, I reckoned I was a lot better off with just Bev.

I was six and Bev was eight. A poem written by Bev earlier . . .

In the yard stood a tea chest
Deep and paper lined
I would place Noel inside
Cover him with rags
His 'blanket' body twined
Hush a bye 'little brother'
I will shield you from night's cold
The music indoors will quieten soon
Hush a bye little Noel
And I, your 'sister', 'mother'
Whose years count but seven
Will huddle beside you
In the yard, 'vigilant'
Our roof, God's stars in Heaven
Hush a bye, brother Noel

She assumed the role of little mother, a part she was to play many times in our childhood. For her it was part of a game but the inner knowlege she had of our situation was very real. Every day she would go out to the shops in Carlton and steal food for me. If the Welfare men came to the house to look for us she would put me in an old tea chest, cover me with dirty clothes and then go and hide herself.

Bev took me to school every day and we survived like this for several weeks. But eventually the nuns telephoned the Welfare Department. We must have stunk; I had lived in a filthy blue bunny suit for months and I was covered in lice, scabies, dried shit and bug bites. The nuns locked us in a shed in the yard and in the early evening we were taken by two men to the Royal Park Welfare Depot for Girls and Boys in Parkville.

The Depot consisted of two of the several buildings that made up the Victorian Welfare Department complex that stood beside the railway line at Royal Park. Built in 1874, its sole function was to receive young people who had been abandoned, were criminals or mentally ill. They were held there until places could be found for them in charity institutions, reformatories or foster homes. They would remain wards of the state until they were eighteen years old.

My official commitment document, Number 64714, states that I was taken there on 11 August 1941. The reason given was 'neglect'. A nurse led us to what seemed to me at the time a huge tiled bathroom. We were stripped and our heads were shaved. We were then placed in a very hot bath that smelt like it had sheep dip in it. Then we were lifted out and dried and our heads were wrapped in bandages that had been soaked in kerosene to kill any lice eggs that might still be alive. I have never forgotten the stinging sensation as the kerosene met my scalp. Bev and I were holding hands so tightly the matron had to force them apart. After this we were fed and I was put into a clean cot with clean blankets and given a toy penguin to sleep with. I assumed Bev was going to sleep in the next bed to me and I fell asleep feeling warm and secure.

Next morning, however, I became very distraught because for the first time in my life I had been separated from Bev. Where was she? I screamed and used every swear word I knew. 'Where's my fucking sister,' I yelled at one of the nurses. She gave me a sharp slap on the face and told me to stop crying and start behaving like a man. This was a big ask considering I was only six years old! Bev had been sent to the girls' Depot and I was going to the boys'. I saw her later that morning. We waved to each other through a wire fence. As time went by and she became more familiar with the routine of home life, she found ways of sneaking out of the girls' section at night and into the boys' dorm to make sure I was all right.

The Depot was not about remedial care or counselling. On the contrary we were constantly reminded that we were there because we were the dregs of society and no one wanted us. It was my job to help polish boots. The big boys, as they were called, would take their boots off on the verandah before going into the dining hall for breakfast. We little boys had to make sure they were cleaned and polished before the big boys had finished eating. Then we would go into the dining hall and have our breakfast of porridge.

The memories I have of that time are few and mostly about food. Wednesday was meat pie day. The pies were cooked in large tin baking dishes. On my first Wednesday there one of the boys told me not to eat the pie because cook had put cats and dogs in them. On Saturday morning we had to polish the floor of our dorm. The dorm had bars inside the windows, small iron beds and wooden floors. We would push the beds back against the wall, get down on our hands and knees and, like an army of ants, move across the room, polishing the floor with pure beeswax. One Saturday we found a boy hanging by the neck from the bars. Apparently he had hidden under his bed until we all left the dorm. From that day I have always thought of Death as someone I knew, a friend.

I distinctly remember the staff were extremely brutal with us and it was not unusual for all us little boys to cry ourselves to sleep in unison every night. But it wasn't all bad. There was a teacher there who was very kind to us. She was the exception to the rule. She had permission to take several of us to her house on Sunday for tea. The table in her front room was always laden with cakes and jellies. What we couldn't eat she let us take back to the Depot to share with our friends.

In October 1941, three months after arriving there, I was taken to the Fairfield Hospital. I had diphtheria. I was a carrier and had to have my tonsils out. They were badly infected. I also had post-nasal growths that had to be removed. I wonder how many other children have been traumatised by that same barbaric operation. No pre med, it was straight onto the operating table, staring up at a huge white light. The nurses and doctor, looking like creatures from another planet in their white masks and gowns, come towards you and a gauze mask is put over your face. Suddenly panic strikes as the chloroform is sprayed on the mask and you pass out. When I came to, I had a very sore throat and all I could eat was ice cream. Little reward, thought I, for enduring such pain. Now, seventy years later, I still have half of my tonsils, which they forgot to remove and which get infected regularly, and in 1988 I had to have an operation to remove the same post-nasal growths, which had regrown and multiplied.

I stayed in hospital for two weeks and was then returned to the Depot. On the way back to Royal Park, the nurse said, 'Matron has a big surprise for you today.' I was taken straight to matron's office. Bev was there in a new dress and looking very apprehensive. Matron came in followed by a man and without any further ado said, 'This is your new father.' Bev and me looked at each other and I know we both wanted to ask, 'What happened to our old father?' and, for that matter, our mother. Matron seemed to anticipate this question and she quickly said, 'Well now, I'm leaving you three here to get to know each other. Aren't you lucky children?'

I don't have much recollection about that first meeting except that our new father's name was Mr Challenger and that he told us he was taking Bev and me to his home in the bush where we would be happy and never have to worry about anything again. Bev and I stared at him in silence and total disbelief. I should never have been given to him. On my papers it states that I have 'above average intelligence' and the magistrate had recommended that I be sent to St Joseph's Home, Surrey Hills, Melbourne.

Three

Arthur Neville Challenger: I have great difficulty saying that name, even today, and when I look at the photograph of him on his police record, it's like looking at a stranger.

He applied to the Depot to adopt us and was interviewed by an inspector, a Mr K.L. Best on 3 September 1941. This is what the official report of that interview, dated two days later, said about him:

> Challenger, 79 Pitt St Waterloo, interviewed 3rd September. A widower. He is employed as Workshop Labourer at Eveleigh Railway Workshops. His wages are 4.18.0 pw. He seems a reliable type and states that his reason for wishing to take charge of the above children is because their father saved his mother's life some years ago. He has applied to the CWD Melbourne for adoption of the two children. Although he has applied to have the children adopted they will be living with

his mother who resides apart from her husband at Burren Junction where she is employed as Attendant in Charge of the NSW Government Railway Guest House. Her wages are 3.10.0 to 4.0.0 per month but Mr Neville Challenger will support the children. Her health is reported to be excellent. She is aged 58 and her religion is RC.

The following letters were released under the Freedom of Information Act. They are from the New South Wales Welfare Department.

RE ____ AND NOEL MORTON born ____ and 25.12.34
Named children were committed to the care of this department by the Carlton Children's Court on 11.8.41 as neglected. Father, having been convicted under Section 109 Children's Welfare Act 1928, neglected to provide adequate food and clothing for the children [and] is at present at Pentridge Gaol serving one month's imprisonment. He is described by the police to be of bad character. Occupation: Street singer. The mother is also stated to be of bad character and her present whereabouts unknown. The father has forwarded to the Department a letter from a friend, Mr Neville Challenger, 79 Pitt St, Waterloo, New South Wales, stating that his mother is willing to take charge of the children. Mr Morton has expressed himself in accord with the proposal. I'd be glad if you will allow an officer of your department to interview Mrs Challenger and report the circumstances and whether in your opinion the children could be safely discharged to her care.
Yours faithfully

NSW Welfare Dept. 13 October 1941
Mrs Challenger is a widow, 58 years of age, appears to be in splendid health and very active for her age. No children of

> her own are residing with her. Her home consists of five rooms with kitchen and large sleep out, and although not lavishly furnished, it is comfortable and satisfactory. Accommodation is available for the two children. Children would occupy a room each. She lives rent free as the house belongs to her, and she has been employed by the Railway Department for the past eighteen years. She informed that she is quite willing to take care of the children for the reason their father saved her life about four years ago by pulling her from the front of an approaching car. Public school and church are close to her home and from several enquiries made I am quite satisfied she is a reputable type of woman and there would be no risk whatever in placing the children in her care, but it would be impossible for her to care for these children on her present income and [she] would need to be assisted financially by her son.
>
> ____ , Inspector 76/10/41

We found out later that many people wanted to adopt us but 'the fickle finger of Fate' was pointed in another direction. My father wrote this letter to the Welfare Department from Pentridge Gaol on 6 August 1941.

> Dear sir or madam,
>
> I have been instructed to forward you this letter in reference to my two children ____ and Noel Christian Morton who are I believe in the Royal Park Welfare Depot for Children. Mr Arthur Neville Challenger and his mother are desirous of adopting both the children. I personally consider their offer a good and sincere one, and one by which the children's future would benefit.

On the bottom of an internal Welfare Department letter dated 28 August 1941 the following is handwritten:

> Father called this day and stated that he had been released from Pentridge Gaol this noon. He has no fixed place of abode and will probably [be] staying at Gordon House for the present time. He was advised of the present stage the application of Mr Challenger had reached and will keep in contact with the department (father is a coloured person).

There is no evidence in any of the official papers I have to substantiate the story about my father saving the life of Challenger's mother. It is simply not mentioned and I am still very suspicious of this highly dubious story. My father could have met Challenger anywhere given that he was, according to Mumma, bi-sexual, as well as addicted to cocaine.

We had been told by the matron that we would be leaving with our new father the following week and as the day approached I became filled with dread and fear. The way I coped was to remove myself from what was happening. When Shakespeare wrote, 'All the world's a stage and all the men and women in it merely players' he forgot to mention people like me. I wasn't a player, I was a member of the audience watching somebody else playing me on stage.

In 1987, my doctor in London sent me to see a therapist after I had had a severely traumatic experience. I was alone in my flat when two men tried to break in. The telephone was in the kitchen and I couldn't phone the police. I went into a completely catatonic state and sat up all night in the living room. Next day I called a friend who came round and he telephoned the police. I couldn't stay in the flat. In fact, I stayed with different friends for three months. I became anxious and depressed. My doctor, who was a very astute Lebanese woman, said my reaction to the event was unusual and added that she thought it had unlocked something in my mind. She recommended I see a therapist at Charing Cross Hospital. I remember tears were streaming down my face involuntarily as I walked towards the hospital.

After I had been with her for an hour the therapist said, 'Noel you are very articulate when you talk about yourself, but I'm no closer to understanding your problem. What we have to do is find out why you've left all your emotions outside the door.' After many visits I learnt that as a safety mechanism I had at a very early age developed a disassociation complex. I could in every sense step outside myself and observe what was happening to me. That kept all my emotional feelings intact. I, myself and me each had a different role to play in my survival. So leaving our parents behind didn't cause me any pain at all. I had already forgotten them.

First stop on the way to Burren was Sydney where we stayed for a few days. We were taken to meet the Williams family. I never knew if they were real uncles and aunties or just friends of Arthur Challenger's. They had a fish and chip shop in Elizabeth Street, Redfern. There was Mr Williams and Aunty Mary, Cousin Joan, who had long dark ringlets, played the piano and walked in her sleep, Cousin Normie, who was never around much and an older brother who was in the army and about to meet his fate in New Guinea. Two ferocious Alsatian dogs were in the back yard and later we met Aunty Daphne who lived around the corner.

Aunty Daphne disliked us on sight and over the next few years took great delight in beating me whenever I visited Sydney. As I was to discover over the next few years her other great delight was squeezing her pimples in front of the mirror. She had this face cleaning ritual that she would perform every Saturday night before she went out to the local dance. I would stand in the doorway of her bedroom and watch transfixed. She began by turning the wireless on and fiddling with the dial until she found the right station and, to the singing of The Andrew Sisters, she would begin.

First, she steamed her face with a hot flannel then, looking in the mirror, she squeezed the pimples. This was followed by another hot flannel and a thorough examination of the skin, pulling it in every direction. Finally, she would dry herself, apply cream and a very heavy make-up. Next, she painted her legs with 'leg tan' and while they were drying she would do her hair in the popular style of the day, piled high on top with 'bangs', as the Americans called them, in the front. This splendid creation was held together by a lot of strategically placed 'bobby pins' and her own secret recipe for hair lacquer, a mixture of sugar and water. While waiting for everything to dry and set she put on her white peep-toe slingbacks. She then placed a chiffon scarf over her hair and face, slipped her frock on, took the scarf off, clipped on large white floral earrings, did a couple of pirouettes in front of the mirror, turned to me and said, 'Isn't Aunty beautiful?' Then she picked up her handbag and gloves and swept out before I could answer.

A few days later we left Sydney on the overnight train from Central for Burren Junction.

Located 403 miles northwest of Sydney, Burren Junction was a tent town for itinerant railway workers in 1905 and the last main stop before Walgett. The name Burren is a Kamilaroi Aboriginal word meaning boomerang. We were met at the station next morning by Mr Challenger's mother. I was completely overwhelmed.

For six years I had lived in the city surrounded by drunks, had had a nightmarish time in the Royal Park Welfare Depot, travelled to Sydney by train and met the Williams. I had been terrified by Aunty Daphne and the dogs, now here I was standing on a railway station platform somewhere in Australia surrounded by more trees than I had ever seen, staring at a little grey-haired Grandma I didn't know and a man I already feared and hated. I clutched Bev's hand so hard it must have hurt her. If she was feeling as apprehensive and scared as I was she never let on to me.

We walked to our house which was about a half a mile down the railway track. It was a typical country house built on supports to let the air circulate and with a wide lattice-enclosed verandah sleepout on two sides. There were two beds on the verandah, a white-painted wrought-iron double bed, which was to be Bev's, and around the corner a single one for me. The kitchen was the largest room in the house; it had a long table and chairs and the biggest black stove I'd ever seen. I was given my first present that day—a brand new tomahawk—and told that it would be my job to chop the morning wood for the stove when I came home from school.

Mr Challenger then took me outside into the back yard and told me I had to call him Dad. He'd asked me to do this in Sydney but I had refused. This morning I could tell from the tone of his voice and the look in his eye that I was never going to win this battle so I pretended I was sorry for what happened in Sydney. I lowered my eyes and said, 'Sorry about Sydney, Dad.' I only ever called him Dad when I was speaking to him. I never referred to him as my father when I spoke to other people.

I spent the rest of the day exploring my new surroundings. There was a vegetable garden, an aviary with an assortment of bush birds and a pig pen with an enormous white sow. A few months later she gave birth to a litter as she walked around the yard. I remember I ran inside and yelled to Mrs Challenger, 'Grandma, Grandma, the old sow is shitting little pigs all over the yard!' I discovered a chicken coop and eggs, a few milking cows and an old horse named Billy that I learnt to ride on. Across the paddock were the abattoirs. I would go there after school and watch the men killing the sheep and cattle. I took an old billycan with me and they would give me the heart or liver to take home. A little further off was the Namoi River and the shearing sheds I ran away to a year later when my life became unbearable.

But that first morning I decided Burren Junction was better than Carlton. It had to be. Maybe it was the animals or the expansiveness of the bush but my first thought was that if anything went wrong here Bev and me could run away into the bush and no one would be able to find us. Before tea we were given a strict lesson in table manners and how to do the washing up. In due course we were allowed to listen to the serials on the wireless while we were doing it. My favourite was *The Search for the Golden Boomerang*.

I was happy when we were sent to bed. It had been a very confusing and perplexing day for me. I was not surprised when my new father got into my bed and started fondling me. Instinctively I knew that he would. Five years of sexual abuse followed. No wonder that I grew up believing this was normal and that sex equalled love and affection. After all, good old Uncle Josh had begun my sex education when I was four.

Next morning, I fed the chooks, had my breakfast and watched Bev suffer the torture of having her hair curled before we were taken to school. The headmaster was Mr Williams. All the kids in six grades shared the same classroom and they eyed us very suspiciously when we entered. How were we to know that our dad was considered the town weirdo? Many years later I was told that everyone in Burren except Bev and me knew he had a bad reputation and parents warned their children to stay away from him. We were allocated our seats and our first day of school began. We sang 'Advance Australia Fair' and 'God Save the King'. As it was wartime this was followed by a rousing rendition of 'Land of Hope and Glory' sung by Mr Williams. He made it quite clear by the end of the morning that we were all there under sufferance. At lunchtime I got into a fight with his son David, a pasty faced little show-off who called me a dirty Abo. There was no worse name he could have called me. I was eating a very hot pie and I slammed it in his face.

History, Geography, Spelling and Reading were shared subjects and we all studied these together. In no time I became the best reader in the school. Every morning we had a Geography lesson. Mr Williams would pull down a map of the world and read to us from a newspaper about the war in Europe. As he read, he would stick tiny flag pins in each country denoting allied advancement or retreat. We always applauded an allied victory.

Not long after we arrived Mr Williams left for greener pastures. He was replaced by Mr Clifton. He ruled the school with the strap, which he would wield at the slightest provocation.

Every day I dreaded going to school. Although the abuse at home was unbearable, going to school offered little or no relief. I was small for my age and very skinny which made me an easy target for the bigger boys so getting home from school was always hazardous. Whenever Bev was angry with me, she would taunt me by saying, 'Your lips are thicker than mine,' and if she was really angry she'd say, 'You look more Abo than I do.'

On Sports Day, the school was divided into two teams. Bev and I were never picked so Mr Clifton had to allocate us to one of the teams. Sometimes the kids would throw stones at us. One day a girl scratched Bev's back with a safety pin. In hindsight, Bev must have been having a terrible time but she never talked to me about it. I think she still looked upon herself as the 'little mother'.

I was only happy when I was doing things by myself. I read everything I could get my hands on. A travelling library came up on the train to Burren once a month. My favourite books were *Biggles* and adventure stories. When I was older I discovered John Buchan and then all the books on cricket by Neville Cardus.

(My passion for cricket, which I still have, began when I was at the Royal Far West Home.) I was already laying the foundations for my world of make believe. I looked forward every afternoon to chopping the morning wood. In my macabre imagination every blow of my little tomahawk landed in the crotch of Arthur Challenger and I enjoyed watching his bloody genitals fall to the ground.

Our first Christmas in Burren was as disappointing in its own way as every Christmas had been in Carlton. There, I learnt never to expect anything. Here, at first I was so happy when I was given a two shilling piece as a birthday present and a balsa wood model aeroplane kit for Christmas. My happiness soon vanished. I had to give the money to Grandma and I discovered that it would have taken a degree in aeronautical engineering for anyone to be able to construct the plane. I was so angry I smashed it up. I was given a beating and sent to bed without supper.

Arthur Challenger was a very sick man. The ongoing sexual abuse was just part of it and frankly it was only at these times that he was gentle with me. Out of bed he was extremely sadistic and would punish me for any petty misdemeanour. At the end of the school year, there was a fancy dress party for the kids in the local hall. Bev went as a Land Army nurse. Challenger made me a complete set of evening tails, including shirt and top hat, out of old sugar bags and called it 'The Austerity Suit'. It was torture to wear. I was hot and I itched like crazy and broke out in a rash. First prize in the girls' section was won by a pretty little blonde named Myra. She went as a pale pink powder puff. I won first prize in the boys' section and received a box of chocolates. Chocolates in wartime was some prize and I couldn't wait to get home so Bev and I could eat them.

When we got home, Challenger took the box of chocolates away from me and locked them in his cupboard and told us that he was saving them for a special occasion. He had done this earlier in the year with a football that I had won for reading. I was desolate and told myself that at the first available opportunity I would pick the lock and eat one of the chocolates. Several weeks later when he was away I did exactly that, but I was very careful to rearrange them to hide my theft. I had totally forgotten the chocolates until one Sunday morning he called me and Bev into the house, opened the cupboard and with great ceremony told me this was a special occasion. He handed me the box and offered me a chocolate. I took it and bit into it. Suddenly my mouth was on fire. He had discovered my theft. He must have counted the chocolates and to teach me a lesson he had carefully removed the bottom of each chocolate, scooped out the centre and replaced it with crushed red chillies. Bev and I were made to eat them all. We took it in turns to lie under the tap of the water tank with our mouths open. The water only made the stinging worse.

On another occasion, I was having my Sunday night bath when I looked up and saw two large tarantula spiders on the wall. I yelled and Challenger came into the bathroom to see what I was yelling about. I was rigid with fear and pointing at the spiders. He told me that they were harmless and only ate flies. To prove his point he took one off the wall and held it out to me in the palm of his hand and made me touch it.

As I sit here writing this it's still very hard for me to understand how I survived living with that madman. I was only eight years old. Every day I would tell myself that this wasn't happening to me and sometimes I would fantasise about killing him. Bev and me planned many different escapes but in reality we knew we had nowhere to escape to and so it became a game for us to go into the paddock and plan another one.

Challenger was a train drover; the sheep from surrounding areas were loaded on to a train in Burren for transport to Sydney and it was his job to make sure they arrived there in a fit condition for the city abattoir. He seemed to be away a lot during the spring and summer. The trip took several days and three times a year I went with him. At the back of the train was a small compartment for the drover. Once the train pulled out of Burren station his personality would change completely. He became very jovial and would start fondling and caressing me. Eventually he would take all my clothes off and indulge in his favourite pastime. This would occur several times on the way to Sydney. Once there though, he would revert to the strict disciplinarian.

We always stayed at Aunty Daphne's house. She lashed out at me all the time and I hated her as much as I did Challenger. The Williams family, on the other hand, were very kind to me and always gave me a battered saveloy to eat when I went to see them at the fish shop. Cousin Joan taught me to play 'Chopsticks' on the piano.

The unloading of the sheep and the turnaround took several weeks so I had to go to school. I was enrolled at Our Lady of Mt Carmel Catholic school in Elizabeth Street just up the hill from the fish shop. I can't begin to describe how different this was to school in Burren. The nuns fussed over me and made me feel welcome. They called me their little friend from the bush and it didn't take them long to find out that I could read better than most ten-year-olds. Every morning, Sister asked me to read the catechism out loud. I would stand in front of the class and intone, 'Who made the world?' and the other kids would answer, 'God made the world.' I discovered a feeling of pride at that school. I also discovered religion. Even though I had attended the 'Bubs' at St Georges in Carlton I was too young to really understand religion and I didn't trust nuns because they were the ones who sent Bev and me first to Royal Park and then Burren. Here I learnt to trust the nuns and, more importantly, I learned that the baby Jesus was born on my birthday and that he could perform miracles. Morning, noon and night I prayed, and making my first communion was like being summoned for a meeting in

Heaven. It also meant I got my first suit. It was navy blue and came from the second-hand shop in Redfern.

Bev and me did go to church in Burren. It was a small white-painted weatherboard building and shared by all the denominations in the district. Our Catholic service came around every three weeks but Grandma thought it would be good for us to go to all the services. I told the priest this in my first confession at Our Lady of Mt Carmel because I knew it was a mortal sin to go into a Protestant church, or so I thought at the time.

One Monday morning, Sister asked the class if anyone knew a song. Feeling full of confidence I put my hand up and said, 'I can sing "Old MacDonald had a Farm", Sister.' She stood me on the table and I sang it for the class, complete with animal noises and impersonations. It was my first performance. I was such a success that Sister split the class into groups of different animals and I sang it again and this time the kids made the appropriate animal sounds and actions. From then on whenever I came down from Burren the first thing I was asked to do when I arrived at the school was to sing 'Old MacDonald'.

The following year I was old enough to go to the Christian Brothers. No one knew what class to put me in. My reading and writing skills were good enough for the senior class but Maths kept me in a lower one. I was now nine years old and my education was a complete mess.

Returning to Burren was always a nightmare train ride for me. It was the days of the 'rattler' and we travelled second class. The compartment was usually full and everyone was friendly. As soon as the lights went out, Challenger would sit me on his lap, put a blanket over me, take down my pants and penetrate me, all the while chatting to the other passengers. Only terror kept me from telling everyone in the carriage what he was doing to me. I often thought of throwing off the blanket and yelling, 'Hey everybody, look at my father fucking me!' Not long after one of these trips I ran away to the shearing sheds. I hid out for nearly a week, stealing food from the kitchen, but I knew I couldn't hide indefinitely and I didn't know where else to run to, so I returned home and suffered a terrible beating. I decided that one day I would kill Arthur Challenger when I got older.

Sometimes in the school holidays Cousin Joan, another young girl named June and Cousin Normie would come and visit us. Challenger must have been deliriously happy surrounded by his little harem. I don't know if he was abusing them; Bev has since told me she thought he was. That was the year he told us that our real father had died. I remember walking slowly like a tightrope walker along the railway line to school telling myself that people cry when someone they know dies. But I couldn't cry because I didn't feel anything.

At the beginning of 1944 I developed a stammer. I was afraid to talk for fear of saying the wrong thing, so when I started getting a lot of pain in my right knee, I didn't say anything to anyone about it. Besides, Bev and me weren't allowed to be sick. The pain got so bad I could hardly walk; I waited until Challenger was away and then I told Grandma. I didn't stutter when I was talking to her. Once a month a special carriage from the Far West Scheme came on the train from Sydney to Burren. It was shunted off to a siding and stayed there for a few days. It was a library and health care centre combined with an emergency medical service. In June 1945 Grandma took me to have my knee examined by Doctor Haneman. When he saw it he told her that he would arrange for me to see a specialist in Sydney and stay at the Royal Far West Children's Home in Manly.

A month later a letter arrived addressed to Grandma telling her that the arrangements had been made. There was also a letter to Arthur Challenger asking him to fill in the enclosed documents and take them and me to the Burren Junction station on the evening of August 7th. I was to be accompanied to Sydney by

Mrs Roughley. She was a kind woman and I felt no apprehension or fear at all about going to Sydney with her. I would have gone anywhere with anyone just to get away from Arthur Challenger. My only misgiving was leaving Bev behind; I wanted her to come with me but I knew that was impossible. I didn't know how long I was going away for but I knew I wanted it to be for ever and I wanted Bev to be with me. She reassured me that she would be all right and that she would come to Sydney and visit me.

Mrs Roughley thanked Challenger for my papers, which included my ration coupons for meat, butter, sugar and clothing, and asked me to say goodbye to him before we got on the train. I don't remember much about the farewell but I do remember that was the last time I ever saw him.

Four

Going to Sydney was nothing new for me but getting on the Manly ferry was. I could hardly contain my excitement as the ferry bounced over the waves and Mrs Roughley gave me an ice-cream. I was so happy to be going to the Far West Home. At last I had left Arthur Challenger and life in Burren Junction behind me. They say God moves in mysterious ways. In my case he certainly did. For eight years, He'd shown me hell. Now, on 8 August 1945 as the ferry made its way across the harbour He was about to show me a little bit of heaven.

The Far West Children's Health Scheme was founded in 1924 by the Reverend Stanley Drummond, a Methodist missionary minister. It was his dream to be able to bring children of poor families from the remote far western regions of New South Wales, who had never seen the ocean, for a summer holiday at a camp on Manly beach. He was also very concerned at the numbers of crippled children who came from these areas. The summer camps were successful for ten years and with the help of public donations and volunteers the Far West Home in Wentworth Street, Manly, was officially opened in 1935. Nine years later the school was established. The NSW Railways gave huge discounts to the scheme and the Home is still run mainly on charity.

Mrs Roughley and I got off the ferry at the Manly wharf. On this side of the harbour there was a long swimming pool, an amusement pier with a huge ferris wheel, merry-go-round, slippery dip and a razzle dazzle. We walked up the Corso past the picture theatres and shops full of sweets, ice-creams, fruit and all sorts of nice things to eat. There were people everywhere, mainly servicemen having a good time with their girlfriends. Everyone was happy because the war in Europe had finally ended. I could smell the sea and hear it roaring and the gulls screeching in the distance. By the time we reached the Home I was so excited I thought I was going to wet myself.

We stood outside the front door, which was made of glass, and I could see down the long wide passage into the dining room, which was filled with kids all chattering away and eating their lunch. Mrs Roughley rang the doorbell and a nurse came and welcomed us in. She introduced herself as Nurse Mac. She had a brief conversation with Mrs Roughley, took my papers from her and told me to thank her for looking after me on the train and say goodbye.

I was taken to meet Matron Hill in her office. She smiled at me and said, 'Well, young man, we'll have you fixed up in no time.' Next on the list of introductions was Nurse Clarke; she was second in command to Matron and everyone was just a little bit afraid of her. It was more her manner than her actions. She was quite tall and very straight backed. She had a bright red face and never smiled. When she strode down the corridor or through the wards in her starched white uniform and veil she looked like one of the big yachts sailing on the harbour.

She eyed me up and down and said, 'I hope you're going to be one of the good boys.'

'Yes, nurse,' I replied meekly.

Nurse Mac then took me to the boys' locker room and, pointing, said, 'This is your locker, Noel.'

My locker, my very own locker! I wanted to hug her, I was so happy. She opened it for me and there inside were new pyjamas, a dressing gown, a pair of slippers and a toothbrush. We all used the same combs; there were four of them soaking in a mixture of Dettol and water in a tumbler. On the opposite wall above the washbasins was a row of face towels.

Adjoining the locker room and bathroom was the boys' ward. Nurse Mac took me by the hand and led me to a bed with my name on it and then she said the magic words, 'If you're really a good boy, Noel, you'll be allowed to sleep on the verandah when Jackie goes home.'

Right then and there I decided to be the model of perfection. It would have been impossible for me not to have been, here where everyone was friendly. Nurse Mac and I walked back down the hall to the dining room, she sat me down at one of the tables and then left. I was asked all the usual questions by the kids: 'Where ya from?' 'My name's Jimmy, I'm from Walgett.' 'What's your name?' 'I'm from Milparinka. What's the matter with ya? You an Abo?' I was offered a peanut butter sandwich and it was instant friendship all round. It didn't bother me that the kids called me an Abo. Somehow everything was different here.

The word 'Aboriginal' was never officially used at the Home. It was as though it didn't exist, though there were four or five Aboriginal children there when I arrived. In the *Far West* magazine the Home published we were referred to as having 'dark complexions'.

After lunch I had to go to bed; I stayed there until I had had all the usual tests and vaccinations. A week later I saw the specialist in Macquarie Street and I was diagnosed with a somewhat confusing ailment of the right knee. The exact diagnosis was '*a separation of the tongue shaped epiphysis for the tuberosity of the right fibia*' then almost as an after thought, the '*condition was probably of traumatic origin rather than Osgood Schlatters disease*'. To remedy this, my leg would need to be encased in a felt-lined back knee splint that went from my ankle to my upper thigh.

I arrived at the Home needing new boots, which Grandma eventually bought, and sent to me without Arthur Challenger knowing. I think she was as scared of him as I was. It has always been a matter of debate between Bev and I as to whether she knew what her son was doing to us.

This morning my brain packed up and I couldn't find my way through the maze of memories. The only thing to do was to try to get all my original files from the Far West Home and the Department of Welfare. This was easier said than done but after a lot of official toing and froing I had the thirty-year restriction on my records lifted.

They were found in the Mitchell Library in Sydney and forwarded to the Royal Far West Home.

So, sixty years later, I took the ferry across the harbour to Manly to collect my files from the Home. It was a very emotional experience to see the small loom I used to weave scarves on for therapy and the little chairs from the dining room.

I had decided not to read the files until I got home but curiosity got the better of me and by the time the bus reached Potts Point I was thoroughly depressed. All the old fears and uncertainties I had about myself momentarily returned. I discovered that Arthur Challenger had lied about my age on all the official admittance forms to fiddle the child allowance. He referred to me as his adopted son and said that Mumma was deceased. What was a most extraordinary revelation to me was that the feelings of hate and loathing I had for him for sixty years were no longer there and now all I felt was pity. The love I always had for Grandma hadn't changed and just to see her handwriting brought back all the memories of her kindness to me.

This is some of the correspondence between her and Matron Hill between August 1945 and April 1946:

> Dear Mrs Hill,
> I am very pleased to hear Noel is happy and being a good boy. I miss him very much. Will you please let me know if my son has sent him a pair of boots as the shoes he has will not last him very long. I am sending Noel some chocolate. We don't have any chewing gum at present. I will send all the clothes he needs.

> Dear Mrs Hill,
> I have your letter to hand. I am pleased Noel is getting on so well. I will get Noel a pair of boots up here and send them on today's train. Please let me know if he needs anything else.

> Dear Mrs Challenger [*'Grandma' . . . to us.*],
> [*Noel is*] keeping well and still having his treatment. There is nothing else he needs now that he has his new boots. Noel is a good boy and no trouble at the Home. He sends you his love and a letter.
> E. E. Hill, Matron

After I had been in bed for a week I was allowed to get up and attend the small school at the back of the Home. I met Miss Phipps, the teacher. She was a largish woman with red hair, lots of make-up and she always wore masses of beads and sparkling jewellery. She spoke to us as if she were singing and everything we did was in her own words 'simply Divoone darling'.

Now this school was not like any other school in Australia. For one thing, you could come and go, depending on your treatment or therapy, and Miss Phipps was certainly like no other teacher. Every afternoon after she had read us a chapter from *Winnie the Pooh* out would come her record collection. She had a passion for musical comedy. There was a gramophone near her desk and we were all allowed to take turns to wind it up. Once ready she would put on a record, usually the 'Totem Tom Tom' from the 1936 musical *Rose Marie* and perform it for us. We would copy her actions and make Indian sounds to accompany the words. I think we were the only eight-year-old kids in the world who could sing along to excerpts from *Maid of the Mountains, The Chocolate Soldier, Rose Marie* and *The Desert Song*. I was in seventh heaven and Miss Phipps was an angel.

Our day started soon after breakfast and before school began. We listened to 'Kindergarten of the Air' on the ABC. Every Friday afternoon we took part in the rhythm and movement classes that were conducted by Heather Gell. We finished school at three o'clock and were taken down to the beach directly opposite the Home for our afternoon swim.

> Dear Mrs Challenger,
> Noel is now able to get up and walk with his splint. He is quite happy and contented at the Home. The children who are able to get around are looking forward to having some swimming. The people down here are so good to them. 3 times a week they are given ice-cream. Noel sends his love to all.
> E. Hill, Matron

Swimming, sunshine and physical exercise were part of the treatment for children who were recovering from infantile paralysis or any other form of physical ailment. The Home was run more or less on the lines of Sister Kenny's method. Sister Kenny was an Australian nursing sister who became distressed when she saw the number of children with limbs that had withered away from lack of exercise when they were in plaster. Her method was no plaster, lots of physical exercise during the day for muscle building and splints at night to correct the bone structure and growth. The exercises weren't structured as such nor were they in any way a chore to do.

We swam twice a day for most of the year. I was caught in the rip one morning and had to be rescued. That summer there were several shark fatalities along the Manly shoreline. I grew up with a fear of swimming in the ocean, which I still have. The only small blot on my good behaviour record was that although I always wrote to Grandma I never mentioned Arthur Challenger. He wrote to Matron and drew her attention to this fact.

1945

Dear Sister,

You will excuse me writing, but not having had an answer to my last two letters I wrote to Noel has me a little worried.

Yours, Challenger

Dear Mr Challenger,

I am very sorry to know that you had not received a letter from Noel. We do encourage the children to write to their parents, we have told him to write one to you to include in this envelope. Noel saw the specialist and is to continue wearing his splints for another 3 months.

E. Hill, Matron

When we returned to the Home after our swim we had a shower, got into our pyjamas and dressing gowns and stood in a line for Nurse who inquired about our bowel movements. We had to answer simply yes or no, meaning you had or hadn't had a bowel movement that day. If you answered no, you got a dose of cascara before lights out. Tea consisted of cereal and a piece of fruit. Then it was into the ward and splint time.

I had to wear my full splint for eight months. I was only allowed to take it off to go swimming and for our rhythm and movement exercises. Once a week after tea, when we were all strapped into our splints, Mr Churchill would arrive with his film equipment and show us silent films of Charlie Chaplin and Jackie Coogan. He projected them onto the ceiling of our ward. In the winter he took the boys to the Manly oval to watch the rugby and in the summer to the cricket.

Mr Churchill was a volunteer at the Home for more than twenty years. The Home had many supporters and we were always being entertained by local amateur dance groups. They also raised money for the Home. The staff were very kind and one nurse in particular, my Nurse Mac, got great joy out of taking me and another boy to the pictures on a Saturday afternoon. Her boyfriend was an apprentice jockey named George Moore, who became one of Australia's most famous jockeys. The occupational therapist was also kind to me. She was an amazing woman: she had no arms below the elbows and yet she could knit using extra long needles. We could make belts out of macrame, do weaving or model figures in barbola clay. I made a complete set of pirate glove puppets, which I saw displayed in a showcase when I visited the Home again in 1968. I became a particular favourite of hers and she once took me for a trip on the river to Parramatta where we gathered blackberries that she made into jam.

Two months after arriving at the Home, I was rewarded for having been a good boy by being allowed to sleep outside. There were three beds on the verandah. On my right was Vere who was a little older than me and had acute osteomyelitis of the hip. It smelt like rotting meat when he had his dressings changed. The hole in his hip bone had to be plugged every day with green ointment and cottonwool. On my left was Billy. I had never seen anyone who was a total spastic before: he was so frail that his bedclothes were supported by a wire frame. He couldn't talk but he was very alert. He had a stamp collection in an album and I would sit on the side of his bed and turn the pages and talk to him about the different stamps and where they came from. I could tell from the look in his eyes that he understood every word I said. Some days he would be allowed to get up. Nurse Clarke would dress him and strap him into his wheelchair. This took a long time because every movable joint in his body had to be secured, from his ankles to his head. I would push him through the ward and down the hall into the yard. The kids were great: they all called out to him and talked to him as though there was nothing wrong with him at all.

When I returned to Australia in 1968 to restage my London choreography for a production of *The Boy Friend* in Sydney, I was taken to the Far West Home for some publicity shots with a very old Matron Hill and I learnt from her that Nurse Clarke had adopted Billy and had given up nursing so she could take care of him.

Sleeping outside had its own rewards. My career as an actor and con man began on that verandah. Next door to the Home was a small amusement park and nightly there would be a stream of servicemen and young women walking to and fro. I would sit up in bed with my splinted leg resting on top of the blankets for all to see. Everybody spoke to us as they walked by but the crazy Yankees, as we called them, were the most vocal. 'Hiya, kid!' 'Geeze, look at that poor kid.' 'What happened to ya leg, kid?' 'Y'all like ice-cream?' and so on. Then they would go to the park

The Royal Bohee Brothers at the height of their fame, in London in the1880s.

My father *(right)* with his organ, on the streets of Carlton in the late 1930s.
The man on the left was probably a cocaine dealer.

SECOND SCHEDULE. D.J. 016

BIRTHS in the District of MELBOURNE, in Victoria, Registered by ARTHUR FEGAN.

1 No.	016
Child—	
2 When and where born	25th December, 1934. Women's Hospital, Carlton, City of Melbourne, County of Bourke. U.R. 21 Palmerston Street, Carlton, City of Melbourne.
3 Name, and whether present or not	Noel, not present
4 Sex	Male
Parents— FATHER— 5 (1) Name and Surname, and occupation of the father .. (2) Age and (3) Birthplace	
6 (1) When and where married .. (2) Previous issue— Living and Deceased	
MOTHER— 7 (1) Name and maiden surname of the mother .. .. (2) Age .. .. .. and (3) Birthplace	Winifred Ann TOVEY 26 years Carlton, Victoria
Informant— 8 Signature, description, and residence of Informant	C. McBall [signature] Authorized Agent, Women's Hospital, Carlton
Witnesses— 9 (1) Accoucheur .. .. (2) Nurse by whom certified .. and (3) Names of occupiers or other witnesses	Dr. Charlton Sister Barkes
Registrar— 10 When Registered, and where ..	3rd. January, 1935. Melbourne.
11 Signature of Registrar	A. Fegan [signature]
12 Name, if added after registration of birth	

X.373/9.34.—6738. 016

I hereby certify that this is a true copy of an Entry in a Register kept in the State of Victoria, in the Commonwealth of Australia

Registrar

REGISTRY OF BIRTHS DEATHS AND MARRIAGES

MELBOURNE

My birth certificate.

Loving Birthday Greetings!
BLOOD AND FIRE
Little son so dear, you have lived a year!
Mother looks with joy on her birthday boy!
That you grow in grace, as the moments race
And in wisdom too, is our prayer for you.

Aged 2.

The Salvation Army organised photos of 'needy' children — and the contrast of my everyday life with these photos was indeed stark…

Loving Birthday Greetings!
BLOOD AND FIRE
Oh, the days fly fast! you are two at last,
Little Sunbeam lad with your smile so glad,
And our hopes are high for your "bye-and-bye,"
So we greet this day in a gladsome way.

Aged 3.

Loving Birthday Greetings!
BLOOD AND FIRE
It is good to grow, little son you know
And we note with joy you are now a Boy.
May your heart be given to that Friend in Heaven
Who was young like you and had birthdays too.

Aged 4.

Pd 15/9/41

RH/ER.

r. Heritage E. 23rd August, 41

The Secretary,
Child Welfare Department,
Box 18a, G.P.O.,
SYDNEY, N.S.W.

Dear Sir,

re [redacted] & NOEL MORTON, born [redacted] and 25.12.34 respectively.

The abovenamed children were committed to the care of this Department by the Carlton Children's Court on 11.8.41 as neglected. Father having been convicted under Section 109 of Children's Welfare Act 1928, neglect to provide adequate food and clothing for the children, and is at present at the Pentridge Gaol, serving a sentence of one month's imprisonment. He is described by the police to be of bad character, and occupation a street singer. The mother is also stated to be of bad character and her present whereabouts are unknown.

The father has forwarded to the Department a letter from a friend, Mr. Neville Challenger, 79 Pitt Street, Waterloo, New South Wales, stating that his mother is willing to take charge of the children. Mr. Morton has expressed himself in accord with the proposal.

I shall be glad if you will allow an officer of your Department to interview Mrs. Challenger and report on the circumstances and whether in your opinion the children could be safely discharged to her care.

Yours faithfully,

67413

Secretary.

The Challenger experience begins…

6 AUG 1941 5. 8. 41 Fredk Morton 24

(Form 94

1. Prisoners may write a letter on arrival to their friends, and one other every month.
2. They must confine themselves strictly to their own domestic or private matters.
3. They are not to write closer than the ruled lines nor across.
4. Any matter which may appear objectionable will be expunged, or the letter may be withheld, as provided by the regulations.
5. Prisoners are allowed to receive one letter every month from one person only, but no printed matter
6. Communications from different persons in one envelope will be treated as separate letters.
7. Prisoners must not refer to petitions or matters respecting their convictions
8. At Christmas time first convicted prisoners may receive two extra letters two photographs and two cards, other prisoners one extra letter, one photograph and one card.
9. No visits will be allowed on Saturdays, Sundays or Holidays.

Postage Stamps will not be received on behalf of Prisoners.

H. M. Gaol, Pentridge, N.13

Gov. Aug 6th 1941

Dear Sir, or Madam

I have been instructed by Mr Ackeroyd to forward you the enclosed letter. It is in reference to my two children, [redacted], and Noel Christian Morton, who are, I believe, in the care of the Children's Welfare Home, Royal Park.

A Mr Neville Challenger, of 79 Pitt St, Waterloo, Sydney, and his mother, are desirous of adopting both of the children, and, subject to your approval, I will readily consent to sign any papers that would make them theirs by legal adoption. I personally consider their offer a good, and sincere one, and one by which the child's future welfare would be greatly benefitted.

But that, however, is for you to judge

As you will observe by the above regulations, I am permitted to write one letter only. So I will ask you to be good enough to communicate with Mr Challenger, acquainting him with my earnest desire for him to have the custody of my children. Should you find Mr Challenger's credentials satisfactory, you could, perhaps commence the necessary formalites for the adoption of the children. I will be in town about the 1st of Sept., and will call upon you to conclude anything in reference to the matter herein referred to.

Will you kindly return my letter, when you have finished with it

I am
yrs respectfully

Fredk. Jas Morton
No. 411. C. Division
Pentridge Penal Establisment
Melbourne

My father agreeing to us going into Challenger's care.

THIRD SCHEDULE. S.C. 1671

DEATHS in the District of MELBOURNE, in Victoria, Registered by SAMUEL HENRY EDGERTON HOLLOW.

1 No.	Nº 1671
Description—	
2 (1) When and where died ...	18th February, 1943, Royal Melbourne Hospital, Melbourne, City of Melbourne, County of Bourke.
(2) Usual Place of Residence ...	Unknown.
3 Name and Surname ...	Fredrick James MORTON,
Occupation	Labourer.
4 Sex and age	Male, 54 years.
5 (1) Cause of death	Broncho-pneumonia - days,
(2) Duration of last illness ...	Right sided fibrous pleurisy and pericarditis - days,
(3) Legally qualified medical practitioner by whom certified ... and	Carcinoma of oesophagus with perforation - months. Dr. R. Fleming,
(4) When he last saw deceased ...	18th February, 1943.
6 Name and surname of father and mother (maiden name, if known), with occupation	Unknown, Unknown, Unknown.
7 Signature, description, and residence of informant ...	[signature] Authorized Agent, Royal Melbourne Hospital, Melbourne.
8 (1) Signature of Registrar ...	[signature]
(2) Date ... ... and	22nd February, 1943,
(3) Where registered	Melbourne.
If burial registered—	
9 When and where buried ...	19th February, 1943, Fawkner Cemetery,
Undertaker by whom certified ...	C.E. Armstrong.
10 Name and religion of Minister, or names of witnesses of burial ...	M. Lander, R. May.
11 Where born, and how long in the Australian States, stating which	England, 38 years in Victoria.
If deceased was married—	
12 (1) Where ... ... and	Unknown,
(2) At what age ... .. and	Unknown,
(3) To whom	Unknown,
(4) Conjugal Condition at Date of Death	Married.
13 Issue in order of birth, the names and ages	Unknown.

W.282/7.41.—8000. Nº 1671

I hereby certify that this is a true copy of an Entry in a Register kept in the State of Victoria, in the Commonwealth of Australia

Registrar

REGISTRY OF BIRTHS DEATHS AND MARRIAGES

MELBOURNE

5783(F4)

My father's death certificate.

NG/ER. 67413

r. Garnet 64 6th September, 45

The Director,
Child Welfare Department,
Box 18a G.P.O.,
SYDNEY, N.S.W.

Dear Sir,

With reference to your letters of 9/10/41 (41/9604) and 2/6/43 (42/8590) regarding the placement of [redacted] and Noel Morton with Mr. A. N. F. Challenger formerly of 79 Pitt Street, Waterloo, but now of Railway Parade, Burren Junction,

I desire to inform you that Mr. Challenger called at this office on 3/9/45 to enquire as to the procedure involved to obtain legal adoption by him of [redacted] and Noel. He was advised that as these children are now no longer wards of this Department, adoption was now a matter between himself, the mother and your Department, though I did [redacted] point out to him the doubt as to his acceptability as an applicant owing to the fact that he was a widower with no suitable domestic establishment. He informed me that the father of the children died some months ago, and indicated his intention of endeavouring to locate the mother of the children in Melbourne to discuss with her the matter of consent. I did not, of course, communicate to him the unsatisfactory nature of the report of the Burren Junction Police, copy of which was forwarded to you on 28/9/42.

Yours faithfully,

Secretary.

Part of officialdom knew that all was not as it seemed in Burren Junction.

and return with ice-creams and hot dogs, which we shared with the other kids.

Dear Mrs Challenger,
Noel has quite settled down and is very happy and a very good boy. What wonderful news we have received this week. It is hard to realise the war is over and our boys will soon be returning home. The children are enjoying lovely days now and will be able to spend time on the beach.
Yours, E. E. Hill, Matron

On the other side of the hallway was the girls' ward. There were also three beds on their verandah. The boys used to tease me about one of the girls. Her name was Phyllis. Most nights I would climb out of my splint, sneak past the glass front door and sit on the end of her bed. I always gave her a very innocent kiss goodnight on the cheek. Our meetings would have gone unnoticed but then she and the other girls went down with scarlet fever and when we were all examined it was discovered that I was the carrier. I probably had the disease when I had arrived but, being a carrier, it never affected me. However, I lost my bed on the verandah when I was sent to the isolation ward. By this time I knew my stay at the Home was coming to an end: my knee had responded to treatment and I didn't need to wear my splint as much. Luckily, I wouldn't require callipers or special boots even though my right leg was fractionally shorter than my left leg and I had a niggling little bit of soreness under my kneecap.

Dear Mrs Challenger,
Noel was seen by the specialist last Friday and he advises that Noel can gradually discard his splint but he is to continue with his other treatment. We do hope that Noel will soon be able to return home.
E. Hill, Matron

A month later she wrote:

> Dear Mrs Challenger,
> Noel is going without his splint practically all the time now and we feel sure that the next time he is seen by the doctor he will be allowed to go home.
> E. Hill, Matron

I was preparing myself mentally for my return to Burren. What I wasn't prepared for was Matron Hill's apparent change of attitude towards me. Nurse Mac sent me to her office one morning before school and the first thing she said to me was, 'Something terrible has happened in Burren and we don't know where to send you.' This was followed by: 'Now, what is your real surname, Noel?'

I said, 'Challenger, Matron.'

She was very angry, but not with me, as I found out sixty years later. She said, 'I have a letter here from a Mrs Morton in Melbourne who says *she's* your mother and wants me to send you back to her.'

I had completely forgotten the name Morton and I hadn't heard anything about Mumma since before we were taken to Royal Park.

I was completely panic-stricken. I had to make a choice. I didn't want to go back to Burren and Arthur Challenger but I did want to see Bev. As well, I realised that being abused by him was certainly a lot better than being abused and starved by the drunks in Melbourne. However, when it came down to it, it was a traumatic decision to take, whichever option I chose. In the end I just stood there and screamed, 'My name's Challenger and I want to go back to Burren Junction.'

I don't know how long it took them to calm me down but finally Nurse Mac put me to bed and gave me a mug of cocoa.

I had no idea what was going on at the time. These are the letters that were received by a very distressed Matron Hill between March and April 1946. The first letter she received was from Grandma who was now living in Narrabri.

> Dear Mrs Hill
> I was so pleased to hear from Noel and to hear that he is much better. I have been very ill and only came out of Hospital on Sunday. Mrs Morton is coming to Narrabri to see the children and may take ______ back with her to Melbourne. She does not say anything about Noel but if he wants to go I will not stop him. If he wants to stop with me he can. I will be very pleased to have him with me as I will be alone. We will be down about Friday so will go over to Manly. I am going to Melbourne in about 3 weeks time so if he would like to go to Melbourne I can take him with me then. Thank you for your goodness to Noel.
> I am yours sincerely, Mrs M. Challenger

On 26 March 1946 Matron sent the following telegram to Mrs Challenger:

> HAVE YOU RECEIVED THE WIRE I SENT YOU YESTERDAY INFORMING YOU THAT NOEL WILL BE ARRIVING IN NARRABRI NEXT MONDAY STOP WE WOULD LIKE TO MAKE SURE YOU ARE THERE TO MEET HIM STOP

The following day she received two letters, one from a Mrs Ryan:

> Dear Mrs Hill,
> Arthur Challenger is in gaol charged with rape of the Morton girl also known as Challenger, Noel's sister. The case will be

heard before judge and jury hear [sic] next Tuesday the second of April and Noel's mother will be over from Melbourne and she is taking both children back with her. Mrs Challenger left here the day of the hearing and I have not heard from her since. The police are making enquiries so could Noel stay [*at the Home presumably*] until his mother picks him up on Wednesday on her way back to Melbourne as there is no one here to take charge of him and she is only a working woman and a widow. I am an old age pensioner so you understand how things are for me.
Yours, Mrs Ryan

The other was written from the Narrabri Gaol:

I am sorry to have to write to you under such circumstances, but it is necessary for me to have Noel here in Narrabri on the morning of April Second 1946. If no one calls to collect him by Sunday afternoon could you have him put on the NorthWest Mail on Monday afternoon. You can let me know the fare or any other amount that may be owing to you. I thank you for all you have done for him during the eight months he has been at the Far West Home. If you need him back I will see that he returns. I will make arrangements and have him met by someone at the Narrabri Station. He is to come to Narrabri only. Please wire me when he is on the train or you can wire Mr Swanston (Acting Gaoler) direct or telephone Narrabri.
Once again, I am yours faithfully, Arthur N. Challenger

That same afternoon she received this telegram from Bev:

MRS CHALLENGER NOT AT HOME STOP LETTER FOLLOWING STOP

On 30 March Grandma sent a telegram to Matron:

SEND NOEL TOMORROW WITHOUT FAIL STOP MAY CHALLENGER

The irony of this episode in my life is that no one read the last letter from Matron Hill, part of which said: 'The specialist has advised that Noel be allowed to go home for six months then be returned to us for X-rays and further treatment.'

I never was returned for further treatment and when I had my knee examined by a specialist in London in the sixties he told me that I should never have been a dancer. He advised me to end my career or become a cripple. I had lived with pain in my right knee for most of my life. The only time I didn't feel it was when I was skating or dancing. I had now achieved the one thing that I had worked so hard for and I didn't like the idea of giving up dancing. I ignored the specialist advice for several more years until the pain became so acute I had to stop.

Matron called me into her office and told me that I was going to Narrabri the next day. That evening Nurse Mac helped me pack my few things into an old battered suitcase and on 31 March 1946 she took me to Central railway station. I was leaving the only place I had known any happiness or had made any friends. I cried when I was given over to the station master who in turn gave me to the train guard who found me a seat and said he would come back and see me once the train got under way. I must have fallen asleep because the next thing I remember was being woken up by the guard and taken off the train at Narrabri on the morning of April 1st. April Fools Day.

Grandma was standing on the platform by herself. I thought she was crying because she was happy to see me but, in that uncanny way that small children have, I sensed something was wrong so I remained silent and let her do the talking. She told me that there had been some trouble while I was in the Far West

Home and that we would not be going back to Burren. She was crying most of the time and I couldn't understand her.

When we reached the house where we were staying she turned to me and said, 'You and your sister have to go back to Melbourne to live with your mother.' I asked her why. She said I was too young to understand. Now the floodgates opened and we were both crying. I was bewildered. I knew something bad had happened to Bev, otherwise she would have been there to meet me. I repeatedly asked Grandma where she was and all she kept saying was, 'You'll see her tomorrow.' As well as being worried about Bev, I was filled with fear and loathing at the thought of us going to live with the drunks and violence in Melbourne again.

I was not taken to the trial on 2 April. I must have been considered too young to give evidence. When Grandma arrived back from the courtroom that night, she said it was all over. I didn't know what she was talking about. After tea, she stitched five two shilling pieces into the lining of a new jacket she had bought me for my return to Melbourne. I told her I would use them to buy a train ticket and come back to live with her. Next morning she took me to the station.

Bev was there waiting for me. She was wearing a brightly coloured dress and looked much older than she did before I went to the Far West Home. I didn't understand what was happening to us but I felt safe with Bev there. She and Grandma just stared at each other in silence. No one from the Welfare Department came to take us on the 1000 mile journey from Narrabri to Melbourne. They had deserted us. So had Mumma; she never came to Narrabri as she was supposed to. I have several letters from Mumma to the Welfare Department saying she would come to Narrabri and collect us. I also have a letter from Grandma to the Department saying I could stay with her if I wanted to and another offering to take me to Melbourne. In the interim period

Grandma became very ill and was admitted to hospital. She was discharged in time to collect me from the train.

The journey took nearly two days and we were hungry most of the time. We had no food or money and once again I was Bev's responsibility. We were silent most of the time, lost in our thoughts of the past and what lay ahead for us in Melbourne. A man sitting opposite us gave us some fruit. I think Bev was angry with me for not spending the money I had in my jacket but I told her it was for a train ticket. We had to change trains in Sydney and again in Albury. We went to the wrong platform and nearly missed our connection. My recollection of the trip is very fuzzy. By the time we arrived in Melbourne we had both changed. Our childhood and our belief in humanity had been left behind in Burren Junction.

The special memories I have kept of the Burren years are yabbying with my mate Jimmy at the bore drains that snaked their way through the bush. There was an artesian bore about a mile from our house and I learnt to swim in the hot water that gushed forth from the belly of the earth below. We loved to go swimming in the evening, particularly during the winter months. It is now a tourist attraction. Jimmy left half his scrotum behind on a barbed wire fence the day we had a race to school.

We had lived in Burren during one of the worst droughts in history. Trains with water tanks would come from somewhere down the track and fill our rain tanks with muddy river water. Bushfires ravaged the whole of New South Wales. I remember once on the way back to Burren after a stay in Sydney seeing both sides of the Hawkesbury River ablaze as the train jerked its way slowly across the bridge.

I have never forgotten the day I watched my mate Jacky Trehannis die. We were coming back from an auction at the Harris boarding house and our flattop truck was packed with furniture. Jacky was swinging from the back when he lost his grip and fell off. I raced back to help him up but he was already turning blue. He had broken his neck.

Then there was the morning I discovered my pet emu chick dead on the verandah. I cried my eyes out. I had found the chick out in the paddock after its mother had been killed by dogs. I brought the chick home and put it in a box on the verandah. I asked Grandma what emus ate and she said anything, even old tins and nails. That night I gave it a special treat: I emptied a small tin of tacks into its box. Next morning, I found it dead on its back with the tacks sticking out of its neck and body.

Grandma Challenger was never unkind to me. Even though in the future Mumma and I became close friends I could never love her the same way I had Grandma. Everyone in Burren remembers her with great affection. If I came home from school wet and covered in mud when Challenger was away, she would give me a hot bath and put me into her big bed with a mug of steaming hot cocoa. Once she took me to Walgett for the weekend and a man in the hotel dining room gave me a shilling for being so well mannered. I can still taste the puftaloons she always cooked for Bev and me as a special treat. Puftaloons date from early colonial days. They are a scone, deep fried in fat and sprinkled with sugar or split open and spread with golden syrup and eaten hot.

But my favourite memory of all is the particular quiet and smell of an approaching storm on a late summer afternoon and rabbits as far as the eye could see popping up out of their burrows after the sudden downpour.

A friend drove me back there in the early nineties to lay some ghosts. When we reached Wee Waa it was early morning and we stopped for breakfast. We were served by a woman a bit younger than me who wanted to know where we were heading. I told her that we were going to look at the school I went to in Burren when I was a young feller. She said she had gone to the same school and asked me my name. I told her that my sister and I were adopted when we lived there and our surname was Challenger. She looked at me for some time and slowly her eyes filled with tears and she ran inside. She had remembered me and the scandal that followed Challenger's arrest. Bev had had a similar experience when she and her husband went out there for a visit ten years earlier.

When I was in the Far West Home in 1945, Arthur Challenger went to the Welfare Department in Sydney and told them he wanted to legally adopt Bev, me and our younger brother Francis. I have no idea how Challenger knew about Francis, who would have been about seven at that time. He was just a few months old when the Welfare took him away. He remained a ward of the state until he was eighteen. In that time he had been shunted between seven different institutions.

Perhaps Challenger thought his position as a paedophile would be more secure if he legally owned us. In this he was unlucky.

> Regarding the placement of ____ and Noel Morton with Mr A.N.F. Challenger formerly of 79 Pitt St Waterloo, but now of Railway Parade, Burren Junction, I desire to inform you that Mr Challenger called at this office on 3/9/45 to enquire as to the procedure involved to obtain legal adoption by him of ____ and Noel. He was advised that as these children are no longer wards of this department, adoption was now a matter between himself, the mother and your Department, though I did point out to him the doubt as to his acceptability as an applicant owing to the fact that he was a widower with no suitable domestic establishment. He informed that the father had died some months ago, and indicated his intentions of endeavouring to locate the mother of the children in Melbourne to discuss with her the matter of consent. **I did not of course, communicate to him the unsatisfactory nature of the**

Burren Junction Police report, a copy of which was forwarded to you on 28/9/42.

Letter from Welfare Department of New South Wales

I discovered that in 1938 he'd been charged by the police seven times for crimes ranging from horse stealing to various others forms of stealing and fraud and had served more than two years in gaol.

What really angers me now is that the Welfare departments of both States, knowing that Arthur Challenger had a police record in 1942, did nothing to remove us from his care. In fact, we should never have been given to him in the first place.

Had the Welfare acted in our best interest we could have been spared four more years of physical, sexual and mental abuse. Luckily for Francis, he was saved from being my replacement.

It was many years before Bev spoke to me about what had happened to her in Burren. She told a little friend of hers at school what Arthur Challenger was doing to her at home. The girl told her father who was the town policeman. He went down to our house, arrested Challenger and took him to the gaol in Narrabri. Bev was also taken to Narrabri to be medically examined in the hospital. While she was there, Challenger escaped from the gaol by using a spoon to pick the lock on his cell. He made his way to the hospital, scaled the drainpipe to Bev's room and told her to tell the police that it was a cousin from Sydney who raped her. Just as he was about to physically attack her, two policemen came into her room and apprehended him.

Before the court in Narrabri, he was charged with 'carnal knowledge of a girl under the age of sixteen'. The mandatory sentence for this was ten years but he was allowed to plead to the minor offence of 'transgressing a trust' and was sent to prison for two years' hard labour with recommendation that he serve his sentence on a farm. The following was printed in the *North Western Courier* on 4 April 1946:

> *Evidence was given that the accused had been the sole support of the girl, who had been adopted by accused's mother. His Honour remarked he had obviously transgressed a trust which should have been his first consideration in life; only the fact she was not in trouble, and was obviously willing, deterred him from imposing a longer sentence.*

Most or all of the official documents relating to the trial have either been lost or destroyed. It is obvious from the summing up that the Burren Junction police report on Arthur Challenger was not entered as evidence at his trial. The sexual abuse started when Bev was eight and I was six. Because she didn't say anything about what must have been an exceptionally traumatic five years for her it was assumed by His Honour that she was 'obviously willing'.

Arthur Challenger was an evil person who affected everyone around him. He died on 3 March 1971 at Mascot, New South Wales of natural causes. His sister, Mattiwilda, hanged herself. The policeman who arrested him that day in Burren Junction committed suicide with a gun some years after the trial and Bev and I were so severely damaged by him that it was impossible for us to lead a normal life.

In Burren Bev and I had both been living our own lives of hell and unfortunately neither of us could, would or did talk to each other about what he was doing to us. I had become quite hardened to Challenger's frequent sexual abuse and odd behaviour. In fact, I totally accepted it as my lot in life. Long silences developed between Bev and me and gradually we drifted apart. On the train, the last thing of any consequence that she said to me was just before we arrived in Melbourne: 'You don't know what he did to me', she said rather quietly.

I was too embarrassed to tell her what he'd done to *me*. Some childhood memories are too painful to share and we were never close again.

I don't know what happened to Grandma after we left Narrabri. I hope she finally found peace in the Dreamtime.

Five

At Spencer Street station Mumma was standing on the platform. I looked at her; at first I wasn't sure that it was her. She was sober and neatly dressed. There was no kissing or hugging. Mumma must have felt guilty because the only word she said was 'hello'. I was very wary of the whole situation. I had stopped trusting her and people in general a long time ago. We went from the station to Aunty Myrtle's house. There were a lot of people there and I didn't know who I was related to.

My younger sister Claudia was there. She was eight years old and she didn't know who we were. I haven't seen her since. My niece, Greta, spoke to her in the mid-1990s and she said that she did not want to be involved with the remnants of our family and I respect her wishes. I can't even begin to imagine the terrible pain she must have suffered when she eventually discovered the circumstances of her birth. She was born one night at Aunty Myrtle's when Mumma was drunk. A few days later Mumma took off, leaving her behind. She grew up believing Aunty Myrtle was her mother and it wasn't until she was an adult that she learnt the truth.

Aunty Myrtle was a big woman with a face the colour that comes from years of boozing and a mop of fuzzy black hair. She had been an old girlfriend of my father's. She and Mumma worked in Sideshow Alley at the Royal Agricultural Show when they were young. I believe Aunty Myrtle was fired out of a cannon. She was obsessive about Claudia and so afraid that she would be taken away, she never let her go to school.

In the early evening, we were taken to our new home in Mark Street, North Melbourne, which was very different to the trendy North Melbourne of today. Melrose, Canning, Alfred, Dryburgh and Mark Streets were lined with cottages. Melrose Street had a greengrocer, butcher's shop, milk bar, fish and chip shop, dry cleaners, a paper shop and a corner shop where everything was put on tick until pay day.

Our house, number one, was the first house in the street. It was on the down slope of a hill that started in Melrose Street and flattened out at Buncle Street. The lower part and right side of the house had subsided and we always walked on an angle down the hall. When it rained the lower part of the house was like an indoor swimming pool. It must have been quite a residence when it was first built: a single storey, double-fronted white weatherboard cottage with four bedrooms. It also had a large living room with an old ice box and the remains of a once respectable dining room setting, a kitchen that had worn-out lino on the floor, a rickety wooden table and chairs, a gas meter and a picture on the wall of the queen mother and the young princesses. The kitchenette had an open fireplace and a gas stove. There was a decrepit bathroom with no hot water and no shower, only an old rusted tin bath. If I wanted to have a bath I had to fill a kerosene tin with water and heat it on the open fire in the kitchenette.

The house had been condemned for many years but that didn't stop seven people and sometimes more living in it. Old Jim, the landlord, slept in one front room, Mumma and Uncle Les in the other. Old Alice, another pensioner, had the bedroom off the once grand dining room, Bev had the back room with a window that had lost all its glass a long time ago and I had the sleepout. It had the same old worn out lino as the kitchen on the floor, timber walls that had buckled out with the damp and a window that had a broken wooden shutter. When the bills weren't paid, there would be no electricity or gas. I was scared of the dark and I would sit outside on the kerb all night under the street light until dawn.

It didn't take long for Mumma to bust after Bev and me came back to Melbourne. The first Friday night, she staggered in drunk after work slobbering all over me and saying, 'I'm sorry, Noely boy, I'm sorry.' Every bad memory I had of Carlton came rushing back to me. I missed Grandma Challenger, but I had long ago spent the ten shillings she had given me and I had no idea how to find her. If this was the way my life was going to be from now on I thought I would be better off dead. All the years I was in Burren Junction when things were really bad I only wanted to kill Arthur Challenger, never myself.

Uncle Les was Mumma's de facto. Technically speaking, he was our stepfather and Bev and me nicknamed him Steppy. He and Mumma met when Bev and me lived in Burren. They eventually got married twenty years later. He was a big man, well over six feet tall, and very gentle by nature. But that changed when he was drunk. Then he became violent and anything and everything in his path would be wrecked. Mumma told me that when she first met him he drank methylated spirits. He drove a horse and cart during the day and liked to play two-up in the lane behind the pub after work. Some Friday nights he lost all his pay, which was a good excuse to bust and come home drunk. On Saturdays, I would take his two-shilling bets down to the SP bookie who also sold sly grog. On one occasion I read the betting slip and decided that the horse Uncle Les had bet on was going to lose so I tore the slip up and pocketed the two bob. Bev and me went to the pictures in Newmarket. Unfortunately, the horse won and I got a hiding I've never forgotten.

Old Jim had lived in the house before it subsided. He looked like a character out of *Dad and Dave* with his big grey beard. He died soon after our arrival. I was half asleep in the back room one night when I heard a noise like someone gargling. Next morning when I woke up I found him dead on the floor. I went and woke Mumma up and said very casually, 'Mumma, Old Jim's dead on the kitchen floor.' Within five minutes, the house was in a turmoil. Mumma went out to call an ambulance and have 'just one drink' to calm her nerves. Naturally, this led to a major bust. Everyone was frantic except me. This was the third time I had seen Death at work. First at the Royal Park Welfare Depot, then the day Jackie was killed in Burren and now this.

Not long after Old Jim died Fred Trout came to stay. I hated him on sight. He was very small, very dark and looked like a ferret. He always referred to Bev and me as 'those little black bastards'. I put him on my 'hit list', together with the names of all the other people I promised myself I would pay back one day. Revenge is a strong motivating force for survival and it kept me going for many years.

Old Alice lived in the front room. She was a total enigma: I didn't know who she was or where she came from. To a young feller like me she was an extraordinary character. She was old, had wispy grey hair, walked with a limp and her dentures clicked when she talked. She gave a new meaning to the word eccentric. She didn't trust electricity and every night she would get into bed, put a candlestick with a lit candle in it on her chest and place her book behind it and read. She had a hoard of pennies underneath her mattress that I would raid every now and then. What was most unusual about her was she didn't drink and when everyone in the house was absolutely drunk and totally incoherent she would talk to them as though they were sober. I once heard her say to Mumma, who was using the most foul language, 'Oh Winnie, you *are* funny.' I never once heard her swear. I really liked her and I know she cared about Bev and me.

One of the few pleasures Mumma had in life was getting her special shoe back from Mr Weston the shoemaker. It had to be built up on one side to compensate for her shorter leg. Mr Weston had been born with a club foot and had his own boot built up. Mumma had been crippled by polio in the days when the only known treatment was to put the leg and foot in plaster. Consequently her leg withered and her foot remained the same size. She walked reasonably well once her shoe had been repaired but more often than not she couldn't afford to have it done.

Mumma's best friend and drinking partner was Mrs Molloy. She lived with her husband, Mick, and their son, Ray, in a grey brick house in Buncle Street. The house was dark and dirty and always stank of wine and urine. Ray was about the best-looking boy in North Melbourne. He was a sharp dresser and I don't know how he managed to distance himself from his terrible home life but he did. He was Bev's boyfriend for a while. Living opposite the Molloys were the Halls. Mrs Hall suffered from an emotional illness, not that anyone knew about it in those days; we all thought she was mad. She would stand on her verandah and yell abuse at the top of her voice to whoever was in the street.

I quickly settled into life in Mark Street. I introduced myself to the local gang: Chooka, Wally, Bluey, Duddy, Charlie, Sparrow and Clarrie. In the summer we played cricket using the street light as a wicket or went to the baths and watched Clarrie bounce.

In the evenings we sat on the grass in the park and smoked forbidden cigarettes and talked about sex and girls. They didn't know that on the subject of sex I was already an expert and I didn't intend to tell them. They were all in love with a girl named Joan who lived in my street. As for me, I only had eyes for her cousin, Betty. I never once told the gang about Arthur Challenger or my life in Burren. I knew instinctively that it would have spelt disaster for our friendship. When anyone asked me where I came from, I'd say the bush. They assumed I was Aboriginal and that was that. They accepted my family just as we accepted Mrs Hall. They never came into my house but I was always welcome in theirs. If Clarrie wanted me, he would stand at the front gate and call out, 'Hey, Noely boy.' He knew I hated that name but from him it was an affectionate sign of his friendship. I clung onto that little gang when all about me was falling apart at home.

In the 40s and 50s, schools in Australia were denominational. I was the only member of my gang who was a Catholic so I had to go to St Michael's, a secondary school run by the Sisters of Mercy. The school faced Royal Park on Flemington Road. At the outbreak of the war the park was turned into an army camp for British, American and Indian troops. They were housed in Nissen huts and access was forbidden to the general public, especially children. The plantations on Flemington Road and Dryburgh Street had trenches dug in them and at night searchlights pierced the sky. When the war ended the Nissen huts remained to house the thousands of New Australians who arrived daily from Europe, and the area became known as Camp Pell.

The boys at St Michael's ostracised me from day one. I knew most of them and they all knew about my family and how I lived. They took great delight beating me up and calling me names. Every one of them beginning with the word black: black bastard, black cunt, black shit and so on. Even in that working class environment I was at the bottom of the ladder. Every time one of them said the word black it was like they were adding another brick to the wall I was building around myself. Soon I wouldn't hear their words or feel their blows. They also abused me sexually. An older boy who thought nothing of punching the shit out of me during the day would make me go into the park after school and have sex with him. He told me that he liked me and didn't want to hit me but he had to because of the other boys. He later became an officer in the police force.

I was sure Sister Mary Isidore hated me. One morning she was verbally laying into me in class for not paying my school money, which was a shilling. I stood up and said, 'I don't have to take this from you. I'm going home.' I turned around to walk out of the room and she brought me to the floor with a flying tackle. She was also the football coach! Sister Bernadette was very kind and always gave me a piece of cake whenever it was my turn to go to the nunnery on Saturday morning to work in the garden.

I was having misgivings about my absolute belief in the Church and God. There were certain incidents in which I thought He could have intervened. I saw one of my mates get killed when his bike careered down the hill and into an oncoming tram, decapitating him. God was never around when I needed Him. I had certainly said enough prayers over the years to warrant some help and I started to think that the price of redemption was too high to pay.

I wanted to fit in and be accepted by the others. I really tried. I joined the school band. I got a newspaper round in the mornings and earned enough money to buy a fife (a small brass flute) and learnt to play the 'Wearing of the Green'. One day the fife disappeared from my desk and so did I. I'd had enough. Next morning, instead of going up the hill to St Michael's, I went down the hill to the Boundary Road State School and sat in class with one of my mates. I stayed there most of the day before the teacher noticed me. It was my own fault. She wrote a sentence on the blackboard and asked the class if anyone could read it. Like a flash and wanting to show off my exceptional reading skills I did just that. The teacher looked at me in amazement and said, 'Who are *you*?' 'Noel Morton, miss,' I replied. The kids howled with laughter as I was led off to the headmaster who didn't understand me at all when I told him I wanted to go to his school because I was no longer a Catholic. I was given a lecture and sent back to St Michael's.

Returning to any school seemed pointless to me; I'd turned twelve the previous Christmas, it was now March and in less than two years I would be fourteen and able to leave school anyway. Mumma's drinking bouts were becoming more frequent and longer and no one in the house knew whether I was at school or not, or cared. This was survival time. I could already cook rice and tapioca, make pancakes out of flour and water and there was always a jam tin filled with delicious dripping to fry stale bread in on the shelf above the old gas stove. I did my own washing in an old copper in the back yard and ironed my clothes with a flat iron. I was meticulously clean, almost to the point of obsession. I think it began when I was old enough to understand the phrase 'dirty little black bastard', which everyone called me. In the winter when it was cold I would go down to Spencer Street railway station and for threepence I could have a hot shower. The station was the terminal for Melbourne's country and interstate trains. In the summer, I went to the North Melbourne baths. I was never broke either: I always had a few bob tucked away. I collected empty bottles and sold them to the rag-and-bone man. I saved all the old newspapers and sold them to the Greek at the fish and chip shop for sixpence and I had my newspaper job in the city. All in all, I was well equipped to take care of myself. I never went to school again, much to my regret in later years.

I became what is known today as a street kid; my days were spent roaming the city. I learnt all the tricks of the trade of a petty criminal. I could pick the pocket of whoever I was sitting next to at the pictures and stealing from Coles and Woolworths in Bourke Street became a daily exercise. My mates and I had a competition to see who could get the most stuff. Our booty was mostly lollies, small toys and other useless junk. After all, we were just kids. I quickly became an expert at avoiding store detectives, the police and the truant officer. Within a few weeks there wasn't a locked door in Melbourne that I couldn't open. I could get in the back way to every picture theatre in the city and I would spend the bitterly cold days in winter watching the same film over and over again. My imagination ran wild: I was Alan Ladd, Veronica Lake, Clark Gable, Bette Davis, John Wayne and all the other stars. I learnt whole chunks of the dialogue and later I'd amuse my mates with impressions. This early movie mania informed all my later work in the theatre.

Even though street kids appear to associate in gangs, they are by nature loners and suspicious of everyone. Sometimes, though, they have one special friend, as I did. His name was Tommy. He was deaf so we invented a language to communicate with each other. Every night during winter we went to Flinders Street station and bought a baked rabbit for a shilling from one of the shops on the concourse. The Venetian-style station, built in 1905, with its Don't Spit signs printed on the tiles that lined the inside walls, was the hub of Melbourne.

'HeyNoelymeetyaundertheclockssarvo' roughly translated meant, 'I'll meet you under the long row of clocks at the entrance to the station this afternoon.' The clocks told the arrival and departure times of the suburban trains. Everyone met under the clocks. The most colourful time to be there was at dusk in winter. Crowds of servicemen meeting their girlfriends, over made-up prostitutes in tight skirts and high heels being moved on by the police who were always there, couples kissing in shadowy corners, office workers rushing to get their trains home, the mingling sound of voices, street noise and the reflection of the coloured traffic lights on the wet pavement made it seem a bewitching place to be.

Tommy and I slept in hallways of city buildings and sometimes I would break into an empty warehouse by the river in South Melbourne and we would sleep there. We went everywhere together and took care of each other. If there was an argument with anyone or if he needed anything from a shop or, more importantly, if the police stopped us and asked us questions I was his voice. For his part, if I got into a fight, he was my fists. He was a couple of years older than me and very strong. During the long summer months we stayed out of the city and hung around Luna Park and St Kilda beach. We discovered a lot about life together, Tommy and me. We shared everything we had. We drifted aimlessly from one day to the next stealing enough food or money to keep us going and always trying to avoid trouble.

One hot evening we were on the beach and Tommy went to get something to eat. I waited there all night and when he didn't return I went into the city. I searched all our usual haunts and secret places but I couldn't find him. I was very upset and for the first time in a long while I felt lost and lonely again. A few days later I heard from one of my other mates that Tommy had been picked up by the police and taken away. I never saw him again. After that I never had another special friend again. I never knew anything about him. One of the rules of the street was 'don't ask me any questions'. That was life on the streets.

From the day I met Tommy I wanted to learn sign language. When I returned to Australia in 1990 one of the first things I did was enrol for lessons at the Deaf Institute. I made quite a few friends in the deaf community and I did some work with a group of young deaf people who wanted to be actors. I studied Auslan, the Australian language of the deaf and in 1999 I was invited to give the keynote opening address at the International World Congress for the Deaf in Brisbane. My speech was titled 'Survival in a Minority Community'. Tommy would have liked that.

After I lost Tommy, I reluctantly returned home to Mark Street. Nothing much had changed there. If Mumma was sober she would ask me where I had been and accepted whatever answer I gave her. I didn't bother with the Mark Street gang anymore either but I always made sure I found Clarrie. I never told him what I was doing. I didn't have to: we were mates.

Without telling Mumma, I left Mark Street again and slept rough. There was one particular building I knew at the Paris end of Collins Street in the city, so called because it was a wide, tree-lined boulevard with fine shops and boutiques. This place, which Tommy and I had found, had a long hallway and a settee and I decided that this would be my new home. I knew all the flotsam and jetsam of the Melbourne gutters. Whores, petty crims, con men, artists and actors, some of whom are now famous. I was friends with the female impersonators who worked as prostitutes on St Kilda Road. They all had exotic names: Amber St Claire was a tall haughty redhead, the Jungle Queen was an Islander. She always wore white. She was thrown into the Yarra River one wet Friday night by two drunken sailors who got a handful of cock and balls when they groped her. My favourite was Boadicea, a small, rather ugly Pommie 'girl' with frizzy blonde hair and a broad Liverpool accent.

I also knew all those other social misfits like myself who lived from day to day and who were trying to come to grips with the rapidly changing city. There was Claire who was slightly dotty and had a huge hairy Russian lover who paid her to beat him like a schoolboy. She always shared her earnings by taking us for a meal at the self service café in Woolworths. Another woman,

Mary, had been a nurse and developed an addiction to ether, which could be bought over the counter at any chemist shop. She would put it on cottonwool and suck it. We were in Gibby's Coffee Lounge one afternoon and she passed out; I ran around the corner to the chemist and he told me to make her drink lots of milk. The manageress called an ambulance and Mary was taken to the hospital. There were many, many others.

The war had ended two years before and even though petrol had come off rationing there were still things that were difficult to get, like cigarettes and nylon stockings. Many people were making their fortunes out of a thriving black market, sly grog, SP bookmaking and illegal abortions.

I discovered that there were some well-to-do men in Melbourne who were willing to pay me for what others had been taking for nothing all these years. There was an interstate newspaper editor, a well-known bookmaker, a chocolate manufacturer and others I have now forgotten. My favourite was a merchant sailor named Tom who picked me up one night in Collins Street. He told me stories about Jakarta and the Indies. Whenever he came to town, he hung around the Raffles Coffee Lounge until I showed up. Then he took a room at the Victoria Palace in Little Collins Street and I would sneak in past the desk clerk. Before he left Melbourne he always gave me a lecture about the life I was leading, some money and told me to keep out of trouble.

Another was Jim, a classic paedophile. He opened up a bank account in my name, put £5 in it and gave me my first cheque book. He liked to watch while I had sex with another street kid. It was all a game to me and a means to an end, which was using whatever it took to make my life the way I wanted it to be. I drew the £5 out of the bank and bought Mumma a tea set with a grey floral design on it and threw the cheque book away. I always went to see Mumma except when she had busted.

By the age of thirteen, I had forced myself to become, physically and emotionally, a robot. It was Rohan Scott-Rowan who became the rent boy and man about town, not me. I had successfully put the 'real me', whoever that was, into a very strong box and placed it in the left luggage department of my subconscious. I was inured to the act of sex; my obvious good looks, exotically coloured body and total lack of morals were my entree to some of the best addresses in Melbourne. Only by not thinking about what I was doing could I possibly survive. The alternative would have been suicide. The mortality rate among street kids has always been high and only they know why. When all the laughing and bragging about the number of tricks you've turned and what you're going to do when you've met your millionaire disappear, you're left standing at the end of the tunnel thinking there is no way out, and that's when a fatal decision can be made.

One Friday morning after a wretched night's debauchery I went to St Francis' church in Elizabeth Street. I don't know why I did it but I went into the confessional. As I poured out all my sins to the priest I started crying and not long after that my faith in God returned. I went to church a lot, still hoping that He would perform the ultimate miracle and get me out of Hell. I had already accepted that the Devil was sitting by his big fire waiting for my arrival one day. I got great comfort from just sitting in the church and saying some prayers. Sometimes I would be so wracked with feelings of guilt because of the number of mortal sins I had committed that I tried to imagine what it was like to be celibate like Father Joseph. In my most desperate moments I would pray that my penis would shrivel up and disappear while I was asleep. I thought that without a penis people would have to like me for some other reason.

And yet, through all this, I always believed I was entitled to and destined for better things. I had to be, why else was God testing me? I had an innate sense of my survival and I believed God had a hand in it.

Life wasn't completely grim. On Saturday afternoons I would give myself a treat. I would go to the box office of the Regent Theatre in Collins Street, feeling very grown up, and buy a seat in the lounge for the evening performance. These were the best seats in the theatre and just the setting for me to live out my Rohan Scott-Rowan fantasy. The seats were so soft that I had to sit on the edge to see the film. The Regent Theatre is a splendid confection of architecture with a wide stairway from the box office to the foyer. The interior is very ornate with marble statues, chandeliers and soft carpets. The main film was preceded by a recital on the Wurlitzer organ that rose like a flower in bloom from the orchestra pit.

Everyone in Melbourne dressed up to go to pictures on Saturday night. It was their big night out. Men wore suits and snap-brimmed Akubra hats and their wives or girlfriends wore The New Look that Dior had created in Paris. The long flowing skirts that reached down to the ankle were seen as the antidote to the austerity of the war years.

My night out started at Spencer Street station. I had a shower, checked my fingernails, sponged my trousers and polished my boots. Then I caught the tram up Collins Street to the St James Milk Bar on the corner of Regent Walk. I liked to watch the young men and women in uniforms and white hats frantically making milk shakes and elaborate ice-cream sundaes for the Saturday night crowd. The cashier sat in a box above the counter and kept an eye on all the action. I always had the same thing: waffles with ice-cream and maple syrup and a chocolate frosted. The milk bar was on my list of places where I wanted to work when I was grown up. Eventually I did but it was only a short stay. I got the sack for sneak eating when I should have been working.

On Sunday nights at the Savoy Theatre in Russell Street there was a vaudeville show and talent quest. During the week the theatre showed continental films. Entry was by donation, because on Sunday they couldn't charge admission. It was one of my favourite haunts, particularly in the winter. I saw two famous male impersonators there: Nellie Small, who was black, said many years later that the only way for her to survive in this world was to dress like a man, and Nellie Kolle, who wore a top hat and tails and sang 'Burlington Bertie'.

I'd been plucking up the courage for weeks to enter the talent quest. I was already convinced that one day I would be Rohan Scott-Rowan, film star. On Saturday morning, I stole the sheet music of the hit song 'Coming in on a Wing and a Prayer' from Allan's music shop and practised the words in the back yard all day Sunday. That night, when the compere asked the audience for volunteers for the talent quest, I practically ran up on to the stage. I'd spruced myself up for the big event; I'd had a haircut, polished my shoes and I was wearing my first pair of long trousers. At only thirteen years old I was the youngest entrant they'd ever had. I was very nervous as I handed my music to the pianist so I closed my eyes for a minute, took a deep breath and swung into the song with actions. I came second and won ten shillings.

In 1947 I was living at Mark Street again, still planning to leave there one day and still continuing to live my nefarious street and nightlife. I lied to Mumma and everyone else about going to school. In fact, I wagged it for the rest of that year and all of the next.

Meandering around the city one night I walked past the Tivoli Theatre in Bourke Street. Its billboard advertised their new vaudeville revue *Forbidden City*. I didn't know what vaudeville was but I liked the title of the show. Undaunted, I went to the box office and bought a ticket, climbed the stairs to the 'Gods' and saw my first live stage show. It was magical and funny with dancers, jugglers and comedians. It was that night that I decided to become a vaudeville performer. I saw many shows there. It was one shilling and tenpence to sit in the Gods and a penny to get home on the tram.

In 1948, I saw *Starry Nights*, which was staged by English director Joan Davis. The name meant nothing to me at the time but thirteen years later she gave me my first job in England as a singer/dancer in a vaudeville revue at the Palace Theatre Manchester called *Show Time*. Top of the bill was comedian Tommy Cooper and bottom of the bill was a new young musical act, the Springfields. Dusty eventually left the act, went solo and became a huge international star.

We celebrated Christmas 1947 in the usual way. Mumma went to the Victoria market a few days before Christmas Eve and bought food and presents and then she and Uncle Les had a few festive drinks at the Laurel Hotel. On the way home they stopped off at Mrs Molloy's house and by Christmas Day the food had rotted. Mumma staggered into the kitchen Christmas morning and wished me happy birthday, gave me an envelope with a card and £2 and said, 'Sorry, Noely boy.' This was her way of apologising for another drunken Christmas.

On the St Kilda Road side of Princes Bridge where the Arts Centre and South Bank complex now stands was the YMCA, Wirth's Olympia with its big circus tent, the Trocadero Ballroom and a roller skating rink. Further down City Road was the Glaciarium ice rink, better known to us simply as 'the Glaci'. The first time I went there I was thirteen. Clarrie and I drifted over the bridge one Friday night, looking for something different to do. I became totally obsessed with skating the moment I put the blades on. I fell over and gashed my leg open but that didn't deter me from wanting to become a skater.

I started going to the Glaci almost every night of the week. Mumma often gave me the money and one Friday she came home with a pair of skates for me. They had brown boots and were very old fashioned. She said that they were a present from Mrs

Parker, the owner of the toy factory where she worked. Next time I went skating I enrolled for lessons at the morning session with Peggy Langrige. They cost me seven and sixpence for a quarter of an hour and I only had enough money to pay for the first two lessons. I would arrive at the Glaci at 9 am, put my skates on and mark out my practice patch with three large circles. Tracing figures was both hypnotic and meditative.

The different components in my life were becoming increasingly hard to juggle. I was living on the streets, avoiding the police—difficult to do, the city area of Melbourne being so small—and I was still wagging it from school and avoiding the truant officer, who was calling regularly at Mark Street. I was stealing to pay for my lessons and for new clothes and a pair of good skates to complete the scenario I had chosen for Rohan Scott-Rowan, skater.

I became friendly with a group of boys who were members of the Glaci Club and very snobbish about it. Most of them were older than me and had been to private schools. Their families could afford to pay for two or three lessons a week for them. I wasn't asked too closely about my family or home life and when I was, I lied. I told them I lived out of Melbourne and only came to the city for my skating lessons. Luckily, I had a good speaking voice, impeccable manners and I was already an accomplished actor and liar. I bought a second-hand pair of 'Four Aces' blades from one of the boys. They were considered by the experts to be the best and I paid him £12 for them, which was a bargain. I knew the boys' interest in me was more than skating but I had learnt long ago how to feign innocence.

I was now mixing socially with a different class of people and hearing words I didn't understand like 'plebeian' and 'unsophisticated'. I wanted to be just like them so I bought an Oxford dictionary that I kept in my skate bag. It became compulsive reading for me and in no time I had memorised quite a few useful words.

By the end of the year I was a very good skater and became a member of that very select group who had their own locker room. I thought I had finally found a place where this version of myself could survive but my new friends were asking me difficult questions. Charlie was not the only one whose sexual advances I had turned down and my lies were no longer convincing. They eventually found out about my street life, and there was an incident at the rink in which I was implicated. To pay for my lessons, I stole purses or wallets out of the pockets of jackets that patrons left on the seats. Someone must have seen me and that night when I went into the locker room the manager was there standing next to my locker. In his hand were several empty purses. I became 'persona non grata' at the rink and my skating career was put on hold. Luckily, the manager didn't report me to the police.

Christmas Day 1948 came and went as most other Christmas days had done before with one big difference. This was the year I turned fourteen, which meant no more school and no more threats of being sent to a reform home. After the Christmas holidays, I got a job at the Willow tin factory directly opposite our house. My boss was a little man called Darkie who taught me how to solder handles with a gas-fired soldering iron onto tin buckets that came whizzing by me on a conveyor belt. Timing was all important and my first day ended with my hands covered in spot burns from the soldering iron. I felt really grown up and showed off my burns to Clarrie.

I worked from 7.30 am till 3.30 pm and was paid an adult's wage of £13 a week—a fortune to me and a lot more than I made from selling newspapers. I gave Mumma £3 a week and the rest went on clothes, soaps, colognes, hair oil and going into the city for a night out on Friday. First stop for Clarrie and me was the

Downyflake Doughnut Parlour in Swanston Street. It was next door to the Princes Bridge Hotel, or Young & Jackson's as it is better known. The hotel is famous for the 1875 painting of *Chloe*, a nude by Jules le Fĕbvre, that hangs in the saloon bar. Downyflake had imported the very latest automatic doughnut machine from America and we would stand there mesmerised as we watched it make our doughnuts. We sprinkled them with sugar and swallowed them down with a hot chocolate malted milk while we spent the next half hour or so flirting with the girls before we went square dancing which was all the rage in the early fifties.

I was growing up fast, not that I'd ever been young really. However, my capacity for questioning myself and my life was expanding in ways I didn't understand. I began to change without even noticing it. Out of sheer curiosity, boredom and loneliness, I started spending some of those winter Sundays in the museum and art gallery. I'd always liked to draw and I had a box of watercolours. Being scared of the dark I would sometimes sit up all night drawing. Most of those early sketches were of horses or landscapes with roads disappearing into the distance. I particularly liked the landscape paintings of Tom Roberts and Longstaff's painting of Burke and Wills. I would sit in front of it for hours; I could share their feelings because I also knew about loneliness and despair.

By the end of April it looked like 1948 was going to be a good year. Mumma had been sober since Christmas and was really trying to keep 'on the straight and narrow', as she called it. Meat and clothing were no longer rationed. I could even buy Mumma cigarettes, which were still very difficult to get in the late forties, from one or two of my old street mates. I got a great kick out of seeing her face light up when I pulled a packet of Turfs out of my pocket.

Life at Mark Street was totally different when Mumma wasn't drinking. She cooked all my favourite meals, tripe and onions being at the top of my list, and she gave me money to go to the pictures if I was broke. I respected her when she chastised me for not going to work and promised her and myself that I would not do it again. Sometimes when she gave me advice about my life in general, I thought, why can't it always be like this? She never talked about the old days. That was a closed subject and we had a tacit agreement that we would only talk about what I was going to do when I was older. She knew I wanted to be an entertainer and said it was in my blood. Bev and me took every advantage of Mumma's sober periods and we often gave play readings for her and Uncle Les. Drunk or sober, Mumma was generous to a fault. She always made a big pot of stew to feed the drunks and methos who lived in the lane that was also a cul de sac at the back of our house.

Even the character of the old house changed when Mumma was sober. We laughed about the rain coming in and Mumma made jokes about me buying us a big house when I was rich and famous. Lapsed Catholic or not, I still said my prayers and prayed every night that Mumma would stay sober. These were, emotionally speaking, the most bizarre and incomprehensible years for me. Living in Carlton, I had accepted that it was normal for everyone to get drunk every day and mete out the abuse that Bev and me had received. At least we knew what to expect. Now I was living with people who only got drunk occasionally. Not knowing when this would happen made me extremely nervous and distrustful and I could never fully enjoy Mumma's loving, sober periods.

We were slowly becoming friends. I no longer blamed her for everything that had happened to Bev and me in Burren. I hadn't figured out yet who was to blame but I knew instinctively that it wasn't all Mumma's fault. I got her to come with me to the pictures one Saturday night. This became a regular outing for both of us. On sober Sunday nights after tea I would sit on the end of her bed in the front room and we would listen to the

Maples amateur hour on the wireless. One Sunday night I heard Joy Grisold sing 'My Ain Folk'. Little did I know then that six years later I would be working with her at the Princess Theatre.

I saw my first opera that year. I was mooching around the city in Spring Street and I stopped outside the Princess Theatre to shelter from the rain. I had no idea what opera was but I was cold so I bought a ticket in the Gods. There, at least I would be warm for a couple of hours. From the first bars of the overture of *Rigoletto* I was entranced; the whole performance was a very beautiful experience and for three hours I was transported from my life of drudgery to one of joy.

The following year I asked Mumma if I could take her to see her first opera. *La Boheme* was playing at the Princess. I explained to her that we would have go to the theatre early because it wouldn't be easy for her to climb all the stairs with her crook leg. She said that she could manage the stairs and that she was looking forward to it. I bought two tickets in the 'Gods' and she bought herself a new dress from Paynes Bon Marche in Bourke Street for the occasion. She cried a lot during the first act and at interval I bought her a box of her favourite licorice allsorts. After the performance we walked down to Elizabeth Street and caught the tram home. This was the first time in fifteen years that I had been truly happy.

From that night on whenever Mumma busted and called me her 'Noely boy' I let her put her arms around me and didn't push her away as I had always done before. I still hated all the other drunks calling me 'Noely boy' and telling me I was the image of my father and asking me to sing for them. McWilliams red label port was like the nectar of the gods to Mumma, Uncle Les and their cronies. The smell of it on the breath of Mrs Molloy as she lurched toward me saying, 'Gimme a kiss, Noely boy', made me physically ill and I made a vow that I would never ever drink port.

However, in 1962 I was forced to break that vow. I was in a musical at the Ashcroft Theatre, Croydon, called *State of Emergency* starring Millicent Martin and Kevin Scott. My dancing partner was a young girl named Camilla Powell. I was invited to her 'coming out dance' at her parents' house in Kent. The dinner that preceded the dance was a very grand affair at the end of which the ladies retired to the drawing room and the butler brought out the host's best Havana cigars and vintage port. This was my introduction to the aristocracy. I watched very apprehensively as each guest poured his own port before passing the decanter on. As it got closer to me, I became terrified and thought that I would vomit all over the assembled guests. I knew I couldn't say that I didn't like port in this company so when the decanter reached me I took a deep breath, poured the required amount into my glass and waited for his lordship to propose the toast. Finally, as I raised my glass, I could no longer hold my breath and I inhaled the aroma of its contents. To my surprise I didn't vomit. It smelt nothing like McWilliams red label rotgut.

Mumma usually only spoke to me about my father when she was drunk and that was to tell me over and over again that if I had his brains and talent I could 'make something of myself'. Then, one night, for the first time, she spoke to me about him when she was sober. On the way home from the theatre she told me a very funny story about something he did during the Depression. Wirths Circus was performing in Melbourne. My father being in vaudeville in those days was given two tickets to attend a special performance that was being held to raise money for the Children's Hospital. One of the highlights of the show was a £5 prize to any member of the audience who could stay sitting on a bucking horse for ten seconds. One after another, various members of the audience tried and were thrown off within a few seconds. My father stood up; he was immaculately dressed and when he reached the centre of the ring he handed the ringmaster his pearl-grey derby hat and mounted the horse. To everyone's delight he stayed on it for more than the required ten seconds. Mumma said all she could think about was what she was going to buy with the £5 but my father, always the showman according to Mumma, refused the prize and in a sweeping gesture and to great applause he donated it to the Children's Hospital. That gesture reminds me so much of the younger me.

It was not long after that night out that Mumma became very ill and had to go into hospital for an operation on her stomach. She was there for about a week and two days before she was to come home Bev started cleaning the house. She scrubbed it from top to bottom and boiled the sheets in the copper in the back yard. Meanwhile, Uncle Les busted. We didn't see him from Friday until the Sunday Mumma was due home when he came in drunk with his mate. They went into the front bedroom that Bev had cleaned. My memory of what happened next is a bit fuzzy, but I think he pissed in the chamber pot and emptied it on the floor. Bev was so upset she went to the corner shop and telephoned the police who came and took them away. Then she and I cleaned the house again. Mumma came home in a taxi. She was very weak and went straight to bed. She was in pain and as the afternoon wore on the pain became more intense. I've never forgotten her cries. Bev went out and rang for an ambulance and Mumma was rushed back to the hospital. When they opened her up again they found a piece of draining tube that someone had forgotten to take out after the operation.

I lasted about six months at the Willow tin factory. Mumma and Uncle Les busted and I stayed away from work for days at a time; in the end it became too embarrassing for me to go back there. Life at Mark Street had returned to normal. I had a succession of factory jobs in the following months but they all ended in the same way. I was either sacked for being late or I left. I decided I couldn't handle the monotony of conveyor belts and the factory mentality. I also hated the nicknames I was given. I was usually called Choc or Nig or a poof just because I spoke well. Most of the time I felt like I was swimming in one direction while everyone I knew was swimming in another.

I asked myself why I should care about my life if no one else did. I became very depressed. I hated everyone, including myself, and I started sleeping all day and wandering the streets at night. All my feelings manifested themselves in manic temper and a strong desire to self-destruct. The slightest racist remark or accusation would set me off.

Fred Trout felt the full force of my temper the morning he called me a 'fucking black bludger'. I was sitting in the back yard reading my dictionary when he said it. I flew into a blinding rage; I ran into my bedroom, grabbed all my things—clothes, books and anything else I could lay my hands on—and took them into the back yard and set fire to them. This was the pattern of my temper. Inflicting physical pain on myself was somehow cathartic. I was crying hysterically as I ran out of the house yelling, 'I'll show youse, I'll show youse!' I returned to the streets; at least I knew who I was with that mob, all things being equal. I never slept rough again though: I knew any number of men who wanted to feed and bed me.

Ron and Neil were two of Melbourne's more infamous homosexuals. I was thirteen years old when Ron picked me up on Princes Bridge selling newspapers. They gave me their old clothes and wanted to look after me but there was always a price to pay. They were both in the rag trade. Over the next decade they scandalised Melbourne with their wild behaviour and sex orgies. They lived their lives with utter contempt for the Establishment.

I don't know what it was about me in those days that elicited sympathy from certain people; I've been told that it was my total ingenuousness. For all my street cunning and behaviour, I was still an innocent. The lessons in good manners I had paid so highly for in Burren Junction, coupled with the unique speaking voice Miss Cullen had given me and my dark, animal-like demeanour, contributed to people's curiosity about me. No one could figure me out. Little did they know that I was having the same problem. Many did try to help me but I was always suspicious of these offers. I had learnt the hard way that help often meant I had to give myself in return.

Part Two

The Epitome of a Bohemian

Six

I slipped deeper and deeper into my world of make-believe. I wanted to change my life but I didn't know how to do it. I had been warned several times by the police to get off the streets. Then I got a job selling newspapers for Collins Book Depot. They owned three shops in the city: the one where I worked on the corner of Spencer and Collins Streets, another in Elizabeth Street and one in the Australia Arcade. I not only sold the newspapers, I also read them; I knew everything that was happening in the world. Furthermore, I spent a lot of time going to the small picture theatres that only showed newsreels, documentaries and cartoons. I was arming myself for the day when I would get out of Melbourne and Australia. Rohan Scott-Rowan would be able to hold an informed conversation with anyone anywhere in the world.

I got on very well with the manageress of the shop. I think she was one of the owners. She would often talk to me about my future and told me that I couldn't go on selling newspapers all my life. One evening after I'd been there about three months she asked me if I would like a full-time job in the Elizabeth Street shop. I thanked her and asked when I could start. The following Monday morning at 9 am, she replied. She told me that I would have to wear a jacket and tie and asked me if this would be a problem. I told her that Mumma would help me get the necessary clothes.

Once again, I returned home to Mark Street and Mumma. I told her about the job and asked for her help. She had a budget account at Paynes Bon Marche into which she paid a little money each week. On Saturday morning we went into the city and I got a new shirt, tie, trousers, jacket and a pair of black boots. Mumma and me made a day of it; we had lunch at a café and went to the pictures.

It was raining on Sunday so I stayed home all day. I was nervous and apprehensive about my new job and spent most of the afternoon going through my dictionary memorising some new words I thought I might need—words like edition, publisher, radical. I decided that I was not going to lie about myself. This would be my opportunity to get my life back on track and enable me to face the world truthfully. Thankfully, I wasn't tested. Everyone had been told about me by my friend; she had given specific instructions that I was not to be asked any questions about my home life.

Monday morning I arrived at the shop quite early. Already my new boots were hurting but I ignored them as I waited outside the front door. The first person to arrive was Miss Alberti; she was absolutely charming and remained so all the years I knew her. I last saw her in the 80s. She was not Australian by birth and had a dark olive complexion and spoke with a slight melodic accent. She opened the shop and one by one the other members of the staff arrived. Everything about the shop and staff was formal, something I wasn't used to, and I felt very much on trial that first morning. I knew instinctively that this was the job for me and I also knew there was a lot to be learnt by watching these people. My chores were simple—helping Miss Roth to empty the windows and prepare them for a new display. Miss Roth was a poster artist. She taught me about mixing colours and added considerably to my knowledge of painting.

Every morning I had to take new books to the Australia Arcade shop for Mrs Payne, the manageress. She has always held a spot very near the top of my list of all the extraordinary people I have known. She was rather tall with silver blue hair, smartly dressed, an acquired proper accent and a terrible snob. In conversation she would always refer to 'My good friend Mrs Hope-Wallace' (I think she was Melbourne socialite) 'said or did . . .' and so on. I longed to see Mrs Hope-Wallace, but I never did. If Mrs Payne needed to go to the bathroom, she would put on her hat and gloves and walk out of the Arcade and up the front steps of the Hotel Australia looking like one of their most treasured guests who'd come down to Melbourne for the Cup.

The Hotel Australia, with its long arcade of shops, was built in 1939. It was very popular with American soldiers during the war. It had a multi-level lobby, an upstairs bar, a ladies lounge and the Vienna Room, which was the favoured restaurant of Melbourne society and boasted a fine continental menu and orchestra.

What I enjoyed most about Mrs Payne was watching her selling technique. She would stand behind the counter poised like a spider waiting for someone to enter her web. She watched the browsers who came into the shop at lunchtime and, as if by instinct, she would strike one with the following words, 'Ah, I see you've picked up Marghanita Laski's new book. It's *so* moving; she's my favourite writer.' She would then go into her spiel about the author, name some of her other works, give a brief description of the book and what the critics had said about it, find something about the customer to flatter and hand the book to Paddy Smiley or Betty Pounder (a dancer and in-between shows when I first met her) to wrap up for the unsuspecting buyer who had only come into the shop to while away a little spare time. Mrs Payne's parting words to the customer were always, '*Do* come in again and let me know how much you enjoyed it!' After I'd been there a while and witnessed this remarkable feat of selling many times, I asked her if she had read all the books in the shop. 'Good heavens, no!' she replied. Then she said, 'I'm going to let you into my little secret, Noel.' She told me that all she did was read the flyleaf of each new book when it came in and memorise the important facts about the author and the plot.

Miss Curtis took me under her wing that very first morning. Her real name was Frances, but she called herself Franchesca, or Chesca to her close friends. She was short with dark straight hair, strong facial features and a rather brusque British manner. She was a few years older than me and, like me, she had created her own fantasy world. Sensing that I was a fellow traveller in the world of sexual ambiguity, she asked me to have a coffee with her at the morning break. She smoked black Sobranie cigarettes and used the word darling a lot. Without pausing for breath, she told me that she was a lesbian and that one day she would be a famous writer and really we should think about going to Paris and live on the Left Bank where everyone was an existentialist. I pretended I understood every word she was saying but as soon as the break was over I rushed upstairs to look up the words lesbian and existentialist in my dictionary, which I now carried everywhere with me.

I was shocked by what I read. I had no idea that homosexuals existed. I knew there were poofs—after all, I'd been having sex with men and boys all my life. I thought that was part of growing up but it didn't stop me from thinking that one day I would get married and have a family. It never occurred to me that men or women could feel the same way about each other as I had felt about Betty Pollock. Maybe that was the way I had felt about my best mate Clarrie all these years . . . I didn't quite grasp the meaning of the word existentialist. The concept of freedom fascinated me but it took another forty years for me to fully understand it. Freedom to live my life the the way I wanted, freedom of choice sexually and politically, and freedom from the restraints of Irish Catholicism and the knowledge that I could not have altered my course of destiny. I was born to be what I am today—free.

Chesca gave me a list of books to read including *La Porte Etroite* by Sartre and *The City and the Pillar* by Gore Vidal. In 1998, when The Honourable Bob Carr, Premier and Arts Minister for New South Wales, introduced me to Gore at a literary dinner I told him how I'd put a brown paper cover on a copy of his book and he very wittily replied, 'My dear, that's how I wrote it'.

For the first time in my life I got up early to go to work. Every day brought a new experience and a new word with it just for me. My Paynes Bon Marche outfit changed considerably. In the weeks ahead, I bought a pair of 'nigger-brown' corduroy trousers that I boiled in the copper in the back yard until they faded. I found a checked vyella shirt, somebody else's old school tie and a second-hand Harris tweed jacket at the Vic market. I borrowed the money from Chesca to buy a pair of essential Clarks desert boots and in time I added an oversize white turtleneck sweater and a beige duffle coat to my wardrobe. I tried out some new words on Chesca. I told her that I now looked the epitome of a bohemian. She agreed.

Somewhere in Melbourne there is a portrait of me in this outfit by Mary Talbot. Mary was an artist who specialised in very delicate pen and watercolour wash portraits. I don't know if it was the fashion of the day but she had a mane of bright red hair piled high on top of her head. Her face was extraordinary; in fact, on anyone without her personality it would have been described as ugly. Because of her eccentric dress sense and behaviour people referred to her as Mad Mary. She lived in the cellar of a Victorian house in Tasma Terrace. I was convinced that it was an extension of the crypt of St Patrick's Cathedral, which was nearby. It had granite walls, dirt floors and was always cold and damp but Mary warmed it up with music and her laughter. I spent a lot of time there listening to records of Billie Holiday and watching her paint. Every Friday night was party night at Mad Mary's.

I went everywhere with Chesca; I met the elite of the coffee lounge set. We would go to Raffles, a basement coffee lounge in the Block Arcade. It was there that I saw my first live existentialist. Her name was Val Myers. She had long flaming red hair, lots of eye make-up and was doing a very meaningful Central European expressionist dance in between the tables. All her friends were talking very loudly and making strange orgasmic sounds. Chesca turned to me and, breathing heavily, said, 'Isn't she *wonderful*? She really understands.' I was desperate to ask what it was she understood but I just nodded and said, 'Yes, wonderful.' Eventually, Mrs Palmer, who was the manageress and a very tolerant woman, had to ask Val not to dance on the table.

A year later, she sailed to Europe and if one could believe everything one read in *Pix* and *People* in those days, she soon became the darling of St Germain des Près and the Latin Quarter in Paris. She returned to Australia a few years ago. I saw her just recently having a coffee in a Melbourne arcade. Her hair was still flaming red, her skin alabaster white and her eyes were circled with black make-up. For a moment we stared at each other and I said to the young friend who was with me 'That's Val Myers!' and my friend said, 'Who's Val Myers?'.

One of the assembled crowd of Val's admirers whom I met

that evening at Raffles was a young girl named Zoe Caldwell. She was studying at the university and was a member of the Union Theatre. She had a very individual, slightly husky speaking voice. I saw her perform many times. She played one of the Women of Corinth in the 1955/56 production of *Medea* at the Comedy Theatre starring the legendary Judith Anderson. She has since played the title role in *Medea* herself on Broadway and added another Tony to the impressive collection of awards she has received both for acting and directing.

On Sunday nights Chesca and I would go to Cinders at the Paris end of Collins Street. Cinders Coffee Lounge had a regular clientele of Melbourne's bohemian intellectuals and dancers from the Borovansky Ballet. Cinders herself was another Melbourne eccentric. She always looked and dressed as if she were going to a ball. Her long black evening dress had seen better days and if you looked down at her feet you saw she was wearing old slippers instead of evening shoes. I had just read *Great Expectations* and I told Chesca that I thought she looked like Miss Havisham. Cinders was the original balletomane. On opening nights of the ballet, she would put a sign in her window: GONE TO THE BALLET. OPEN AFTER THE PERFORMANCE. To complete her outfit she would add a string of pearls and an old fur stole. The menu was very limited and never changed; we always had slightly burnt raisin toast and terrible coffee out of cracked cups for 1/6d and felt very sophisticated.

It was at Cinders that I was befriended by a dour, rather earnest Harold Stewart, a poet and oriental scholar who had only recently returned to Melbourne from Kyoto. I appealed to his sense of the exotic. He invited me to his flat for tea and talked to me about Japan. I know he was more interested in my body than my mind. I remember I thought him very eccentric at the time. He wore a kimono in his flat and burnt incense. In 1944, he and another poet, James McAuley, had perpetrated Australia's most famous literary hoax. Together they wrote sixteen poems under the fictitious name of Ern Malley. They also invented Ethel, Ern's sister. She wrote a letter to Max Harris, co-editor of the experimental literary magazine, *Angry Penguins*, telling him she had found two poems amongst her brother Ern's papers after he died from Graves disease in 1943. She asked Max to give her an opinion of Ern's work. He was so excited, he devoted the 1944 autumn edition of *Angry Penguins* to the recently discovered work of the poet Ern Malley with a glowing introduction he wrote himself. The poems, titled 'The Darkening Ecliptic', were deemed to be obscene and Harris was later prosecuted by the South Australian court. Harold died in Japan many years later.

During the winter, I went to a series of classical concerts at the Town Hall. Not that I paid to get in. I would make enquiries and find out what time the first break was. Then I would sit in Gibbys Coffee Lounge and drink coffee until it was time to cross Swanston Street and mingle with the paying audience in the foyer. At the end of the intermission I waited until almost everyone was inside and seated. Then I would go in and find myself a seat and watch the second half of the concert. I saw Walter Gieseking, Solomon, Menuhin and many other great musicians before I was sixteen and I have always remembered the exquisite singing of Mattiwilda Dobbs, the black American soprano.

Under the tutelage of Chesca, my education was boundless. I was a walking six foot sponge. I soaked up everything and everyone I came in contact with. In this free and easy atmosphere, surrounded by people who accepted me for who I was, I totally accepted my sexuality. Whatever it was it now didn't seem at all strange to me.

This book is as good a place as any to try and explain it. I didn't grow up having crushes on other boys, nor did I think I was that different to them. I had my first sexual experience with a little girl in Burren when I was nine years old. Grandma

Challenger found us at it in my cubby house. I remember she didn't say anything at all. Uncle Josh and Arthur Challenger had both made me an expert in male sexuality. I was more traumatised by all the physical abuse I had received than I was by any sexual abuse. At this stage of my life I indentified with all the new friends I was making. They were sophisticated, arty and very witty and I knew I wanted to be just like them. I still didn't think of myself as being totally homosexual. That came later.

I was still living at Mark Street and Mumma and Uncle Les continued to periodically bust. Having been encouraged to read Sartre by Chesca, I decided in my own naive existentialist way that this was the choice they had freely made in order to live their lives and who was I to question them. When it came to looking at my own life, I knew it wasn't perfect and I resented anyone who questioned me about it. 'Chacun à son goût', ('Everyone has his taste', or 'each to their own') a recently acquired French saying, became my new catchphrase.

I had another close female friend at that time. Her name was Rachel or Ray in our circle and, like Chesca, she had an enormous influence on me. She loved the theatre and we talked about it all the time. She was one of my staunchest supporters and encouraged me to become an actor. She did a lot of writing and was extremely left wing politically. As tall as me and Jewish, her handsome face was framed by thick luscious black hair. Whenever I was broke and out of work I would stay at her place. She would cook me lamb and eggplant stew and sometimes when it was cold I used to climb into the end of her bed. One evening her aunt arrived unannounced and saw the both of us, one at each end of Ray's bed, reading. She never spoke to me again. Many years later, Ray told me that Auntie thought we were having an affair. Eventually, being a good Jewish daughter, Ray got married, to a poet I knew. I went to the wedding. It was strictly kosher and her family was now happy that Rachel had settled down.

Talking of weddings, Bev married a truck driver from Sydney when she was sixteen. It was a whirlwind affair. They hadn't known each other for very long. I think she saw it as her way out of the life she was living and an escape from Mark Street and the past. Like me, she wanted to be in showbiz. She had wanted to be a showgirl at the Tivoli. She auditioned for the producer and lied about her age—she was only fifteen at the time. She had real talent and it was only her puppy fat that prevented her getting the job. Somewhere along the way she got caught up in the parties and backstage life and her career didn't eventuate.

My elder brother Fred was overseas looking for work and his life. He had left the Silesian Brothers when he was in his teens. He stayed at Mark Street for a while but we didn't get on. He had closed the door on his past and our past and there was no common ground on which we could communicate. He hated my way of life. When he returned to Australia in the fifties, he spent some time working for ABC Radio and enrolled at Melbourne University. He got an Arts degree, majoring in Dutch. He later married Ann, his long time girlfriend, at a church in Royal Parade, Parkville. Mumma and I went to the wedding. We sat on one side of the church and Ann's family and friends sat on the other side. They were not entirely happy with their daughter marrying someone who they thought was outside their class. Later, at the reception, which was held in a smart restaurant in Toorak Road, Mumma refused to have a drink. She didn't want to embarrass Freddie by getting drunk. He was her favourite and remained so until she died. Freddie loved Mumma in his own way. Later, when she was in a nursing home, he would visit her and, after a rather stiff 'hello', they would sit silently in her room, both locked in thoughts of the relationship they never had. After his son Damian was born the family moved to Europe. Fred had a successful career working as an attaché for the Australian Embassy in Holland and France. He came back to Australia in the mid 1970s and worked for a while as a radio and news editor for the Immigration Department in Canberra. In the 80s, he produced films about Aboriginal issues for the Aboriginal Affairs Department. He died in 1995 and in 1997 the University of Melbourne, where he had lectured, named a communications award in his memory.

Chesca loved the ballet. Her cousin, Jenny Liddel, was a beautiful dancer of considerable talent, who never fulfilled her early promise. Jenny was responsible for me getting my first job as a professional dancer in 1954.

I met Chesca for a coffee before work one morning and she told me she had a surprise for me. She was taking me to see a student performance of *Les Sylphides* at the National Theatre that evening after work. It was my first classical ballet. I was totally enthralled. The music, set and costumes stirred something deep within my psyche. It seemed to me that I was watching my real world. Then, almost as if she were reading my mind, Chesca nudged me and said, '*You* could do that,' and I knew I could. I also knew that this could be my way out. Out of Melbourne or even out of Australia and into a new life.

After the performance we went to Val's Coffee Lounge for supper. Val's was *the* place to go after Raffles and Cinders closed down. It was in Swanston Street on the first floor above the Renee Rose frock shop, a famous Melbourne camp icon. For those of you not old enough to remember, the word 'gay' wasn't used when I was young; the word was 'camp'. Just about everything that was out of the ordinary or anti-Establishment was camp. It described the totality of a homosexual way of life much better than gay. Camp meant out of the closet, outrageous, funny and often sad.

I had a friend who worked for a large company. He was small, dumpy and not very bright but always jolly. He desperately wanted to be accepted by the smart camp crowd. He started giving large expensive parties and in no time he was on everyone's A-list. No one cared where he got the money to pay for his extravagances and when he was arrested for embezzling, he killed himself rather than face being ostracised by the very people he had stolen the money for. I overheard the following conversation a week later. 'Darling, did you know jolly fat Ursula? She died last week. I went to his funeral. My dear, it was so camp.'

The plaster models in the window of Renee Rose were definitely camp. They had been there since the thirties, and each one had a hand-painted sign to go with its frock. There was 'Mother of the Bride', 'Happy Holiday' and everyone's annual favourite, 'Melbourne Cup Day'. Facing you as you entered the coffee lounge was a portrait of Val painted by Veni Stephens. It could have been the model for *The Portrait of Dorian Grey.* Val was a very handsome, androgynous blonde lesbian. She looked like an effete young man wearing grey flannel trousers, white open-necked shirt and a red waistcoat.

There was a definite pecking order as to where you sat in Val's. If you were known to Val and part of the 'in crowd' then you were allowed to sit at a long table in the rear of the lounge. Chesca and I liked to sit near the small baby grand piano in the corner. The pianist was a very large lesbian named Toni who played our requests.

Over crumpets and coffee, I discussed my forthcoming career as a ballet dancer with Chesca. First, we decided, I would have to kit myself out. I'd have to get a pair of tights. I had no idea how or where to buy tights and what shop would stock tights for a six-foot-tall man? We would have to improvise. Next day at lunchtime we went to Paynes Bon Marche and I bought a pair of long white underpants for 12/6d and a packet of black Dolly Dye for a penny. After work I rushed home, found a needle and cotton and stitched up the crotch of the underpants. I mixed the dye in the copper and, when it started to boil, I put the pants in and stirred them around. After half an hour, I lifted them out and rinsed them under the cold water tap and then hung them out to dry. My first pair of tights. I kept them for nearly thirty years as a reminder of that day. Chesca found the address of the National Ballet School and the times of the classes for me. There was an evening class for beginners and on the following Monday at 5.30 pm I climbed the stairs to the third floor above the Kings Theatre in Little Collins Street to attend my first ballet class. The teacher was Miss Jean Alexander. I must have looked a bit of an oddity to the other students in my homemade tights and bare feet but that didn't bother me. I was there for one reason only. When class finished, Miss Alexander asked one of the boys to introduce me to the mystery of the jock strap, or support as it is known in ballet terms. He told me what it was for and where to buy one and that I should purchase a pair of ballet shoes.

The dancing boys reacted to me in the same way the skating boys had done at the Glaci. Without intending or even knowing it, my very existence challenged every male I came in contact with, especially if they themselves were homosexual. What did I know about 'closets'? Take me or leave me, was my attitude. I know I appeared very standoffish to them, but it was far from the truth. The more insecure or threatened I felt, the more arrogant I became.

The girls were different. I still have a very good friend who I stood behind at the barre that first class. She and I were in *The Music Man* together at the Princess Theatre in 1960. I loved ballet lessons. The music and movement released something in me that was akin to what I felt when I skated, only more so. When I danced it was in my world and nobody else was there. It was as though I had been dancing for a thousand years or more. I could feel it in my bones. Without knowing it, I was connecting with my culture through dance—not that I was aware of it at that time.

As a result of my ice skating, I had no difficulty with jumps or turns. Many things about dancing came easily to me, so much so that instead of working hard at class I became a 'show off' and thumbed my nose at all the boys. Miss Alexander and I clashed and the more the boys gave me a hard time the more I showed off. I didn't last too long at the National School.

When I was fifteen years old I met Brian Finemore. It was at the art gallery, during an exhibition of the French avant-garde. I think this was the first exhibition of foreign art to be held in Melbourne after the war. I was sitting on the floor, looking at one of the exhibits, a piece of brown paper that had the number forty-four painted on it. The blue paint had run and it looked to me like it had been painted in a kindergarten. I was trying to figure out why this particular painting was called art and I wasn't aware of anyone standing next to me until I heard a voice say, 'Well, what do you make of that then, eh?' I looked up and saw a tall elegant man, immaculately dressed in a dark suit and wearing a polka dot bow tie standing next to me. It was Brian and that is how I always remember him. I said I didn't like it and that it wasn't art to me, not like my favourite painting of Burke and Wills. He said he often saw me in the gallery and asked if I was a student. I can't remember what I replied and then he said that if I had lunch with him, he would explain the French avant-garde to me.

He took me to a restaurant called Number One Swanston Street, which was on the top floor of Young & Jackson's Hotel. He was obviously well known by the staff who sat us at a table near the window. Over lunch Brian talked to me about art and the avant-garde; he told me that the number forty-four represented the end of the war in Europe. That made sense to me but most of the conversation was way over my head. I did remember quite a few words to look up in my dictionary though. Brian drank copious amounts of wine and when we said goodbye on the corner of Swanston Street I watched him weave his way down Flinders Street. He lived at the Spencer Street end of the city.

And so it came about that whenever Brian saw me at the gallery or in the street, he would take me to lunch at Number One and continue my instruction in art. His speciality was Australian art. He never pried into my life or asked me embarrassing questions and, even more important to me, he never 'put the hard word on me' or made improper suggestions. He was a lonely man who was genuinely kind to me. I was his sounding board. In time I learnt that he had an acid wit that he used to good effect to annihilate the reputation of well-known Melbournians. The more he drank, the more he insisted that everyone and everything in Melbourne was, 'Trash, darling boy. Save your pennies and get out of Australia,' he would say to me.

I bought some cheap Van Gogh prints that I pinned on my bedroom wall at Mark Street. They lasted until the next time it rained. I also bought a bow tie and added the words 'trash' and 'trashy' to my vocabulary. Brian was my first role model and for the thirty years or so that I lived in Europe I always wore a bow tie when I wore a suit. In 1959, he was made curator of Australian Art at the National Gallery of Victoria and I had one last lunch with him in 1960 before I sailed for Europe. His life ended tragically when he was brutally murdered in his apartment in 1975, a crime that is still unsolved.

But back to ballet. The first time I went to the Borovansky Ballet Studio, I was taken there by John O'Toole. Every evening after work, he and his friend Gwenda would walk past me when I sold newspapers on the corner of Collins and Elizabeth streets when I was twelve. John always gave me threepence for the paper and I made a penny tip. It wasn't until he spoke to me one night when I was at the theatre with Chesca two years later that we got to know each other. He was six years older than me and very conservative. He told me that I reminded him of the boy who changed into a wolf in a short story by Saki. His best friend was taking ballet classes with Madame Borovansky and John thought it would be good for me to study with her. He came to class with me, mainly to make sure I went and to keep an eye on me, and Chesca also came for a while.

Madame Boro, as she was affectionately called, came from an aristocratic Russian family who fled the country just before the revolution. Being too tall for a career as a dancer, she became a teacher and married Edouard Borovansky, founder of the Borovansky Ballet Company. When I look back at all the teachers I had in my long career, I would have to say that when it came to teaching style there was no one better than Madam Boro. She had a soft spot for me and often gave me extra classes for nothing. I now wish I had worked harder in class for her. I had no problems with the boys at Boro's either; maybe I had changed.

I fell madly in love with a boy for the first time in my life at ballet class. It was a very strange emotion for me to experience. I'd had crushes on different girls and probably my mate Clarrie before but I didn't have wild erotic dreams about them. All the dreams I ever had about sex were nightmares. He was the same age as me and we would always walk part of the way home together after class, surreptitiously hold hands and talk about life, ambitions and ballet. When we reached the Royal Melbourne Hospital, we went our separate ways. He caught the tram to Coburg and I floated home to Mark Street. He became a well-known dancer and the last time we met was at the Royal Opera House in London in the 80s. By that time I was a West End choreographer and he had risen from principal dancer in a famous ballet company to become a highly renowned teacher. We had both come a long way since the days we held hands at Madame Boro's.

Another student at Boro's was Ivor Freeman, a very tall, excessively camp English migrant from Manchester. He thought he looked like the bust of the ancient Egyptian Queen Nefertiti in the British Museum and he always held his head in profile to show off this remarkable likeness. Being so totally outrageous and so obviously homosexual, no one wanted to be seen in public with him except me. We were living in the era of blackmail, poof bashing and intimidation. We became very close friends. When the Borovansky Ballet Company was performing at Her Majesty's Theatre, Ivor and I were extras. After our first appearance in *Petroushka* and *Scheherazade*, we were told off by the stage manager, Colleen Gough, for wearing too much make-up and overacting. We had a lot of fun and also got the opportunity to see the best dancers in Australia close up. He worked during the day as a 'seamstress', as he put it. He was a terrible dancer but somehow managed to get into the chorus of *Kiss Me Kate* at Her Majesty's in 1952. He barely made it to the opening night before the chorus boys ganged up on him and he was sacked.

John O'Toole thought I was very flighty and irresponsible, which I was. He developed a 'crush' on me and decided that he could change me. He introduced me to his friends Gwenda and Tita and Anthony. Anthony and Tita lived with their parents in a grand house in Caulfield with real silver candlesticks on the sideboard. Going there for tea was always an occasion for me. They were English, slightly eccentric and so well bred that it never occurred to them to treat me in any way other than as an equal. Gwenda didn't like me at all and couldn't understand why John wanted to take me everywhere with them. His family owned a hotel in Albert Park and sometimes in the summer we would sit on the balcony with his friend Peter Hogg at the pianola and sing Gilbert and Sullivan.

John was grooming me and a lot of my future success I owed to that grooming. He loved the theatre and took me to all the shows I couldn't afford and the ones he thought I should see if I was going to be serious about my career. I saw Sonia Dresdel in *Message for Margaret* at the Kings Theatre and Robert Morley in *Edward My Son* at the Comedy. John also took me to the best restaurants for dinner, the Latin, the Ritz and Marios. The Society in Bourke Street was my favourite. I saw my first foreign film with John, Cocteau's surrealist masterpiece *La Belle et la Bête*. Next day, I bought a copy of *Teach Yourself French* and began learning the language. I felt very comfortable with John and most of his friends. It didn't bother me that they knew nothing about me.

Chesca and I went to all the amateur theatre productions. Sometimes we went twice a week if we could afford it. At last my fantasy had become my reality. I joined various theatre groups. There was a plethora of amateur companies in Melbourne when I was young. Every suburb had one, some were better than others and no one questioned me about myself. For better or worse I had now become Rohan Scott-Rowan, Bohemian Melbournian.

My first stage appearance was in *Sunshine and Rain* at the Cathedral Hall in East Melbourne in 1949. The show had been written and directed by a rather dubious entrepreneur named Rick Marshall. His boyfriend, Sonny, who I later danced with at the Tivoli, did the choreography. In the cast were Frank Gatliff and Bunney Brooke. Frank was a professional actor performing mostly on radio. Bunney worked during the day as a tram conductor. She was having a very public affair with a girl I knew. A year before, she had been having an affair with a boy from Ceylon, which somewhat alarmed her mother. When Bunney's aunt found out that she was now having an affair with a girl, she telephoned her mother and said, 'Dorothy's having an affair with a lesbian.' Her mother replied, 'Good God! What colour are they?'

I was a conundrum to these people. No one knew who I was or where I came from. I was living in a world that I had created for myself that was safe and impenetrable. I had an answer for every question. They certainly couldn't understand my passion for sport, which was 'too Australian and plebbie' for them. I went to the Davis Cup, was a fanatical football supporter and I loved cricket.

In 1950, John O'Toole went to England for six months. When he returned I led him a merry dance. I behaved like a beautiful butterfly, easy to see but difficult to net. I introduced him to a lot of people he would not have met under ordinary circumstances and I took him to parties that he suffered only because of me.

Ivor held Friday night soirees at his flat in St Kilda. Everyone who went there had to perform something. He served cheap Wynvale sauterne, which was sold in glass half gallon flagons, and read poetry or gave impersonations of famous female stars. I didn't drink seriously until I was in my early twenties. I often pretended to though, just to fit in. Ivor always wore a red and gold brocaded dressing gown to hold court and quoted Gertrude Stein a lot. If ever there was a country that he should not have emigrated to it was Australia. I don't know how he withstood the insults he suffered every day. Whenever I was broke he would take me to the Old Vienna Café in Russell Street for schnitzel and a glass of non-alcoholic cider. Mumma loved him. Drunk or sober he treated her like a lady. He often came over on Sunday afternoon for tea and Mumma would fuss around and make scones and cakes. She was a good cook and Ivor enjoyed her food. In return, he would do her hair.

I was still working at Collins Book Depot, but only just. For some time, I'd been having a battle of wills with one of the senior salesmen. He had a very grand, superior and patronising manner, particularly with me. I was no longer the shy little boy who joined the staff a year or so earlier but he still treated me with contempt. One morning after we'd had a quarrel, I went downstairs and scrawled the words 'Mr O'Neill is a poof' in large black letters on the wall of the men's bathroom, which was in the basement of the block and used by every male in the building. At closing time that day I was called into Mr Dickens' office. I was the obvious culprit and he asked me to explain my actions. I couldn't do so adequately enough to prevent my dismissal. I was sad to leave the friends I had made working there.

My next job was serving the counter lunches at Young & Jackson's Hotel. It was not as interesting as the Book Depot but I got to eat for free as well as earning some money.

John, Gwenda, Tita and Anthony enjoyed dressing up and going to first nights at the theatre. John often asked me to go with them. Our big night out started with dinner at the Windsor Hotel, the show and then supper afterwards. I didn't own evening clothes, not that anyone would have known; I hired my tuxedo from a costume hire shop in Swanston Street, had a shower and changed at the railway station. I put the clothes I was wearing in a locker at the left luggage counter. John recently told me that he assumed I lived a similar life to everyone else and could not understand why I never invited anyone home. It never occurred to me at the time. They would not have understood what my home life was like and, besides, I was very proud of my make-believe life. As I got to know them better I no longer enjoyed playing games but I thought it was too late. I had no alternative, I felt, but to keep up the pretence or I would lose their friendship. If I had only know then that it wasn't necessary. However, it all turned out well because seventy years later we're all still friends.

I had several jobs in a very short space of time. I was a filing clerk at the Land Titles Office in Queen Street for a few weeks, then I got a job selling the latest electric rotisserie ovens at the Homes exhibition. But I couldn't settle anywhere. Wherever I worked I was subjected to jokes about 'boongs' or 'niggers'. Not surprisingly, I was extremely insecure and convinced that no one liked me. I always had been unconfident but I covered it up with an outward show of arrogance. The only time I felt remotely secure and to a certain extent real was when I was dancing. I was also pathologically shy. I would never get on a tram if it was full and I was the only person at the stop and I hated walking into crowded rooms. I thought everyone was looking at me, judging me. It was at these times that I felt black. The only place I was free was on the streets. There, I didn't have to lie about who I was or where I came from. I knew my worth and why I was liked there.

Seven

At the beginning of 1951, I was out of work again and hanging around the Australia Hotel. Most of my mates from my earlier street days were either in gaol or had graduated to harder, more lucrative crime. I stopped mixing with them when I started working. Now I was tempted to see some of them again. I had become so involved in my world of make-believe that I wanted to touch base with what I thought was my reality. I didn't particularly want to go back to hustling but needs must as the old saying goes. Now I was seventeen and a lot wiser. Several old friends were glad to welcome me back. The half hour before closing time between 5.30 and 6 pm in all hotels was called the 'six o'clock swill' and in that half hour everyone swilled down as much alcohol as they could. This very odd ritual came about in 1917 when as part of the temperance movement 6 pm was proclaimed closing time for bars. The proclamation was finally lifted in February 1966.

Like all big cities, Melbourne had a subculture that existed only after dark. Illegal gambling clubs abounded in Carlton and St Kilda. The red light area was Little Londsdale Street in the city. Homosexuals went searching for 'trade' along St Kilda Road and other well known beats. At the junction of Fitzroy Street and Beaconsfield Parade opposite St Kilda beach was a cream stucco pseudo Spanish-style public toilet. It was nicknamed the Spanish Mission and was a favouite pick-up place. It was also dangerous because it was well known to the Vice Squad.

After the bars at the Australia Hotel closed, everyone I knew hung about outside on the pavement in Collins Street waiting to hear if there was anything happening anywhere later. The lesbians, who had nothing to fear from the law, wore masculine clothes and Elvis Presley hair dos. They had very Butch names like Terri, Pedro, Rikky, Toni and Billie. The men, with the exception of one or two who deliberately flouted themselves in a camp way, were mostly straight-suited. There was always a party somewhere. They were usually wild drunken affairs, everyone giving vent to their repressed desires. Addresses were given out in whispers. Drag parties were the big thing in the fifties. Dressing up in women's clothes was very daring and the ultimate gesture in defiance against the police.

Although 'drag' and 'drag queen' were in the vocabulary then, they had quite a different meaning in those days. Today, drag queens are, for the most part, caricatures of women, whereas in the forties and fifties they were true female impersonators. They claimed to be professional entertainers and as such were persona non grata with the camp crowd at the Hotel Australia. They mostly lived on the fringes of Melbourne's crime scene, some working as prostitutes with pimps, while others worked as hostesses in illegal baccarat clubs. Some had regular jobs and lived completely as women. One 'girl' I knew hired Kelvin Hall for her wedding to a sailor. It was to be the full ceremony, complete with bogus minister, parents, six bridesmaids, as many matrons of honour and a hundred guests. It ended in a drunken brawl with the police arriving. On the front page of the *Truth* newspaper the following weekend was the headline 'WEDDING OF THE PAINTED DOLL' and a photograph of the 'girls' doing high kicks. The photographer had been one of the guests.

I was invited to a party at Max du Barry's flat in Albert Park. Max was a well-known female impersonator. By the time I arrived at the party, everyone was well charged and having a good time. Max had mixed a bennie cocktail, in all probability the first designer party drug to be used in Melbourne. Benzedrine inhalers were sold without prescription at the chemist and were used to unblock the nose, relieve the symptoms of a cold and make you 'feel good' as the ad said. Max would buy several, take the solid blocks out of their containers and melt them down in hot water. As the water cooled, the paraffin floated to the top, leaving the benzedrine, a very strong amphetamine, in the water. This was mixed with cherry brandy and called a 'bennie cocktail'. I once stayed awake for three days on it but the comedown I had was so terrible I never touched it again. I don't remember heroin, cocaine or grass being around then.

The guests at the party were drag queens and their boyfriends, a couple of standover men, several prostitutes and their tricks, a few soldiers who were on their way to Korea and Max's mother who looked more like a drag queen than he did. Max was dressed in a black crinoline and was singing an aria from *La Traviata* when the police arrived. A few of the crowd managed to scramble out of the window into the back yard and get away.

At seventeen I was the youngest person in the room, but I told the two detectives who questioned me that I was eighteen because I didn't want to go up before a juvenile court. That would have meant being sent to a reform school for consorting with criminals, or vagrancy. I didn't know it then, but I was being set

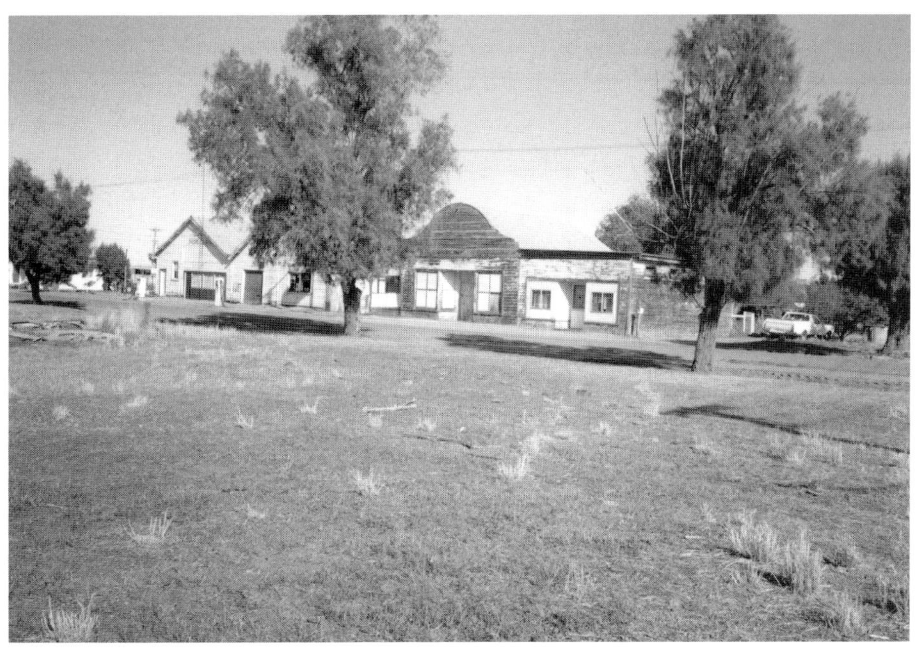

Burren Junction today — its appearance hasn't changed greatly.

As a young patient (head down, second from left) while at the Royal Far West Children's Home in 1946.

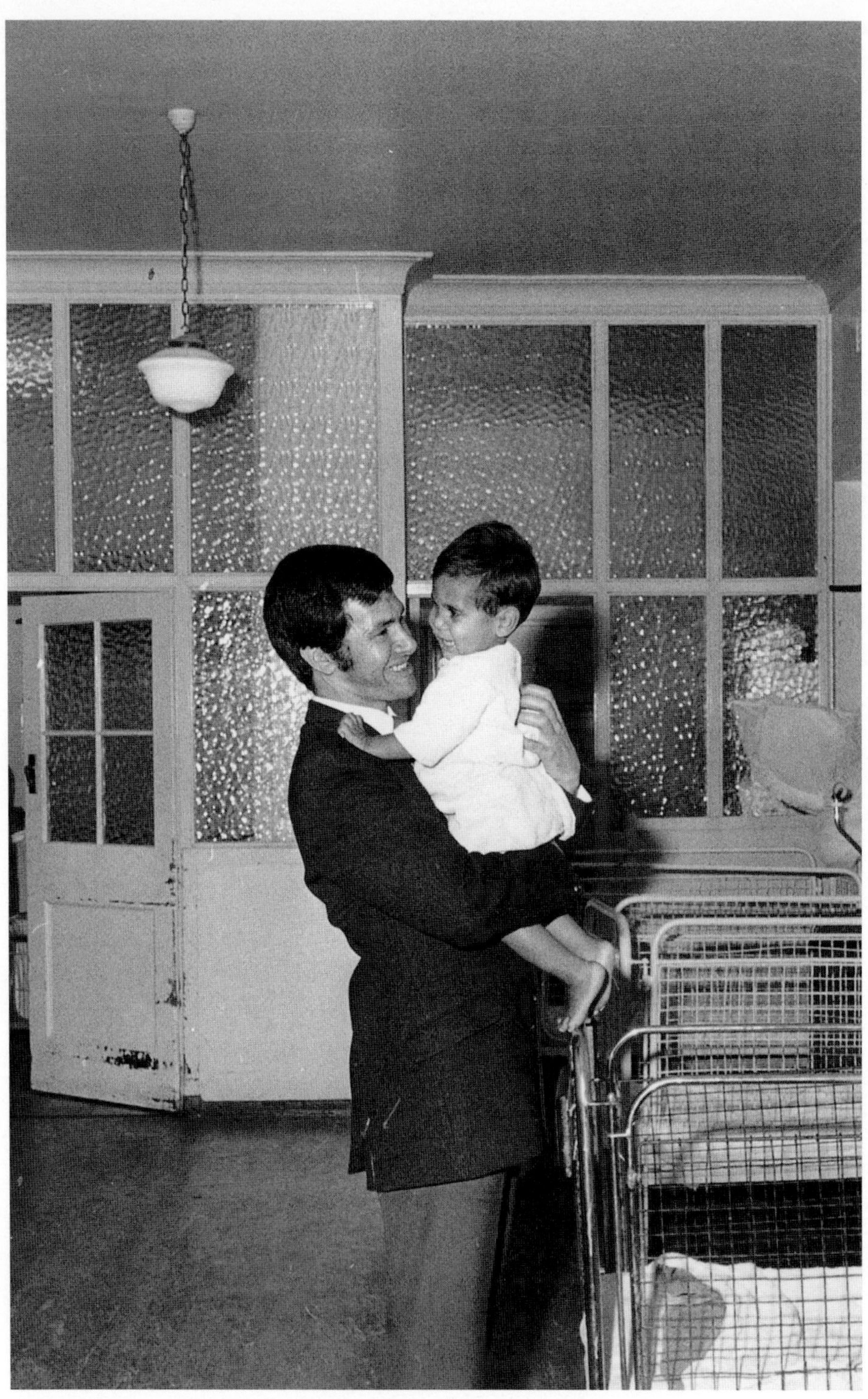

Paying a return visit to the Home in 1968.

Yes, if you're "circled" in the above picture (and others elsewhere in this issue) taken at Saturday's games, just call at our office, 4th Floor, The Herald, on Friday, between 11-12.30 or 2.30-4 p.m. with your Wednesday Globe, be identified, and you'll win £1. Each week a Globe cameraman will take pictures to be circled in our Wednesday edition. And don't forget, copies of all photos on this page can be bought from the Photo Sales Department, which also is on the 4th Floor, The Herald Office.

As a keen footy fan in the late 1940s (from the Melbourne *Sporting Globe*).

Ready to take on the world — taken in 1954 in Adelaide, during the season of *Paint Your Wagon*.

In Melbourne in 1955.

With Fay Parsons *(left)* and Mary Hardy, Collins Street, Melbourne, in 1954.

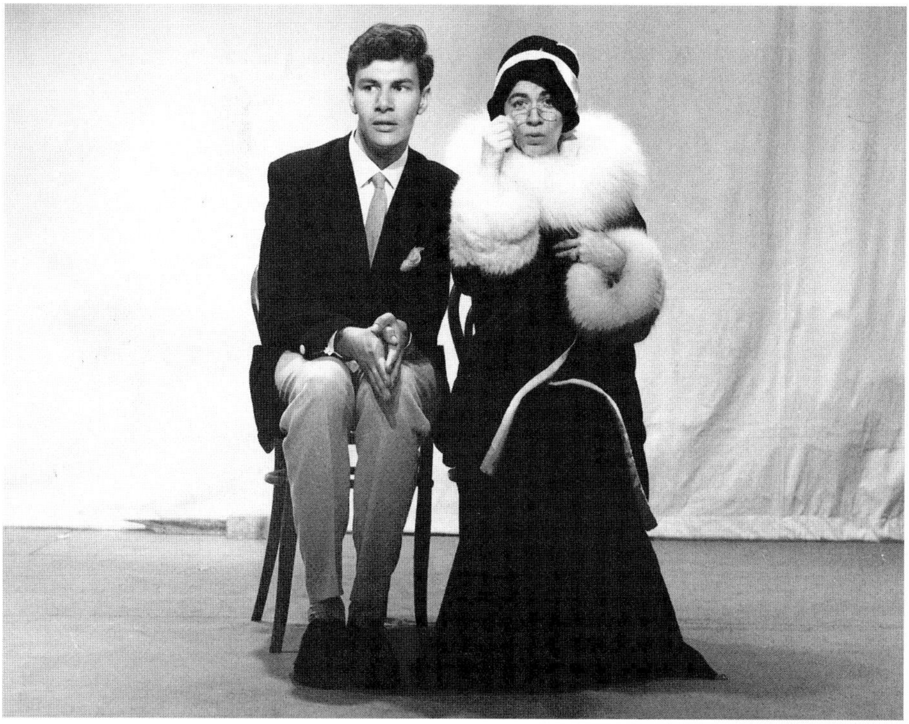

With Mary Hardy in 1956, at the Arts Theatre, Melbourne.

Left to right: Margaret Horsely, Mary Hardy, John Muirhead, Beris Sullivan and me during *The First Arlen Revue*.

With Mario Vecchi, in *Aladdin*, 1958.

With Bunney Brooke in 1958, during *The Member of the Wedding*, National Theatre, Melbourne.

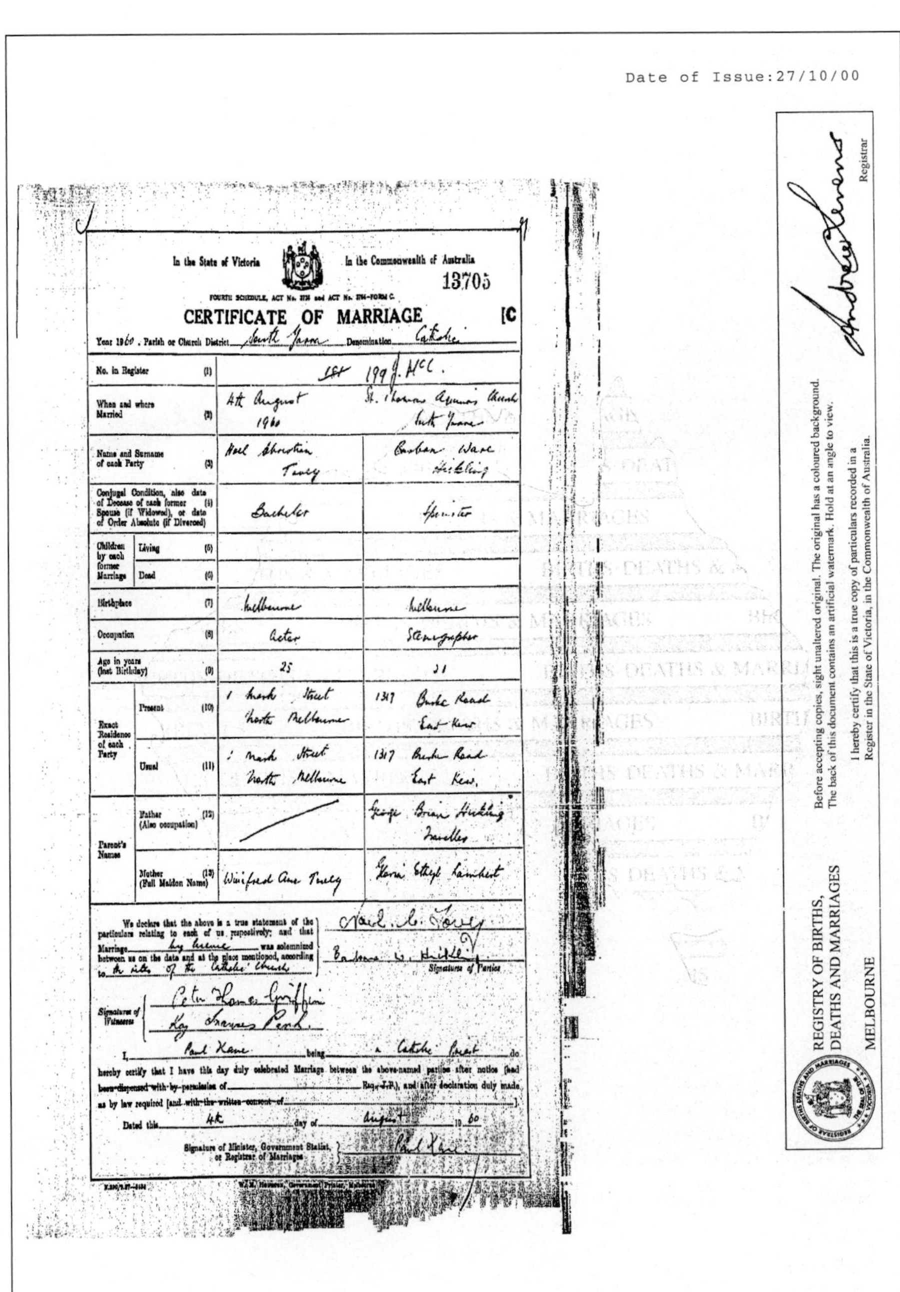

Date of Issue:27/10/00

In the State of Victoria — In the Commonwealth of Australia

13705

FOURTH SCHEDULE, ACT No. 3726 and ACT No. 3744—FORM C.

CERTIFICATE OF MARRIAGE

[C

Year 1960. Parish or Church District South Yarra Denomination Catholic

No. in Register (1)		199	
When and where Married (2)	4th August 1960	St. Thomas Aquinas Church South Yarra	
Name and Surname of each Party (3)	Noel Christian Tovey	Barbara Ware Hickling	
Conjugal Condition, also date of Decease of each former Spouse (if Widowed), or date of Order Absolute (if Divorced) (4)	Bachelor	Spinster	
Children by each former Marriage — Living (5)			
Children by each former Marriage — Dead (6)			
Birthplace (7)	Melbourne	Melbourne	
Occupation (8)	Actor	Stenographer	
Age in years (last Birthday) (9)	25	21	
Exact Residence of each Party — Present (10)	1 Mark Street North Melbourne	1317 Burke Road East Kew	
Exact Residence of each Party — Usual (11)	1 Mark Street North Melbourne	1317 Burke Road East Kew.	
Parent's Names — Father (Also occupation) (12)	—	George Brian Hickling Traveller	
Parent's Names — Mother (Full Maiden Name) (13)	Winifred Ann Tovey	Gloria Ethyl Lambert	

We declare that the above is a true statement of the particulars relating to each of us respectively; and that Marriage by licence was solemnized between us on the date and at the place mentioned, according to the rites of the Catholic Church

Noel C. Tovey

Barbara W. Hickling

Signatures of Parties

Signatures of Witnesses: Peter Hume Griffin; Kay Frances Perch

I, Paul Kane being a Catholic Priest do hereby certify that I have this day duly celebrated Marriage between the above-named parties after notice (had been dispensed with by permission of ________ Esq., J.P.), and after declaration duly made as by law required [and with the written consent of ________].

Dated this 4th day of August 19 60

Signature of Minister, Government Statist, or Registrar of Marriages: Paul Kane

Before accepting copies, sight unaltered original. The original has a coloured background. The back of this document contains an artificial watermark. Hold at an angle to view.

I hereby certify that this is a true copy of particulars recorded in a Register in the State of Victoria, in the Commonwealth of Australia.

Registrar

REGISTRY OF BIRTHS, DEATHS AND MARRIAGES
MELBOURNE

My marriage certificate…

up as the fall guy to trap Max. I was taken to the local police station and one of the detectives, knowing that roughhouse tactics wouldn't work with me, assumed the 'best mate' role and took me into the toilet. While he was urinating, he asked me questions about my life on the streets and talked a lot about 'poofs taking advantage of boys like you'. He asked me if I'd ever had sex with a man, attempting to make the question sound innocent saying that all boys played around when they were young. Even he had, he 'confided'. I told him that I had had sex with men and he said that if I signed a confession admitting to having had sex with Max I could go home and Max would be fined 'a couple of quid'. He dictated most of the confession to me and used words that I didn't understand. This was one time I really needed my dictionary but I didn't have it with me. Instinctively I knew he was trying to get me to incriminate myself but I couldn't lie my way out of there so I signed.

The confession was part truth and part invention. I had no idea of the gravity of the situation or the charge; I was very naive. I knew having sex with men was against the law but I didn't understand why it was a crime. I certainly would not have involved Max had I known.

I had stayed many times at Max's flat. He and his mother were very kind to me and Max took particular care to make sure I wasn't involved in anything heavy. Two other guests were also arrested at the party: Max Price, known in the trade as Mildred Pierce, was a very likeable drag queen who looked more like a truck driver than her Hollywood namesake, and a handsome young boy named James. He had admitted to having had sex with Max on a previous occasion. Millie was fined for wearing women's clothes and let go. James was committed for a hearing in the magistrates' court.

Instead of being allowed to go home, I was put in a cell until the next morning. Mumma came down and bailed me out. When we got home she asked me if I'd done what I'd been charged with. Then I told her about Uncle Josh, Challenger and all the other men. She burst out crying and all she could say was, 'Those bastards, those bastards!' I hadn't told her before because I didn't want to talk about it. I thought sex was dirty and I still don't like talking about it, which is why I'm having difficulty writing a lot of this down.

Two detectives came to see Mumma and told her that they weren't interested in putting me away. They said that if I pleaded guilty I would get off with a warning or at the worst be put on a good behaviour bond. Mumma reported what they had said. When I asked her what I should do she said, 'It's up to you.' I decided no way was I going to do what they wanted.

At the first hearing, I stood in the dock and when the judge said, 'Noel Morton, you have been charged with the abominable crime of buggery. How do you plead?' to everyone's surprise except Mumma's I said very loudly, 'Not guilty!' Max and I were committed for trial by jury and I was sent to the remand section at Pentridge Gaol pending payment of my bail, which had been set at £100. James pleaded guilty and was remanded for sentence.

I was terrified about going to Pentridge. My fears were well founded. I learnt the hard way from a prison guard that young homosexual offenders were expected to deliver, even in gaol. I was given the equivalent of what today is called legal aid and the lawyer made it very clear that normally he would not take this sort of case because he hated poofs. I told him I was innocent and that I could defend myself if he didn't want to. The first of several damning articles about Max, James and me appeared in the *Truth* newspaper the following Saturday with the headline 'NORTH MELBOURNE DANCER ON SERIOUS CHARGE'.

Meanwhile, John O'Toole had moved into a house in Oakleigh with his friend Lex. In the seventies Lex became one of Europe's leading interior designers. Also living in the house was a mutual friend of theirs, Hans Spier. Hans and his aristocratic Dutch family had survived three years of being prisoners under the Japanese occupation in Java. He was very gentle and caring.

It took Mumma several days to raise the money to get me out of Pentridge. Eventually, she went to see John O'Toole at the office where he worked and asked him for help. The only person who John could borrow that much from without being embarrassed was Hans. He put the money up without question. I was extremely relieved as there was a long period of time between that initial hearing and the trial.

Max was very well known to the police. During the break in our trial, he went to the Arts Ball in drag and sold kisses at £1 each for charity. The Arts Ball was the culmination of the Arts Festival every year. It was so popular that people spent from one year to the next planning their costume. It was the only night of the year when the police turned a blind eye to the number of drag queens walking around the streets looking for a cab. The governor of Victoria, not knowing Max was a man, bought a kiss and posed for photographs with him. This led to a witch hunt for Max. I went as Puss in Boots and Ivor went as Greta Garbo. He wore an old tweed suit, heavy lisle stockings, brogues and large felt hat. To be in character, he sat by himself for most of the night and refused to talk to anyone.

I moved into John's house at Oakleigh. I knew that the two detectives who arrested me were angry with me for pleading not guilty. I kept away from the old haunts in the city as much as possible because, after the first article appeared in *Truth,* the friends I had made at ballet class shunned me in the street. Mumma couldn't afford to look after me and I certainly couldn't apply for support so I got a job in a factory under another name. I saved enough money to buy a salt and pepper tweed suit. I wanted to look respectable in court.

Every morning, John and I scanned the law lists in the *Sun* newspaper to see if my trial was listed. Just when I was beginning to think that everyone had forgotten about me, we saw the notice for the date of the trial. Mumma took me to the courthouse in William Street and we sat in the hall and waited until cur names were called. We selected a jury and the trial began. The detectives gave their evidence and read out my confession; I told the court that I was innocent and that I had been asked to write the confession by the detective and that I didn't understand the words. The trial lasted several days and at the end of each day I was allowed to go home to Mark Street (although I actually went to John's house); bail was continuous.

On the last day of the trial Max arrived bennied up and in drag. He was so high he didn't know where he was. He said he wanted to prove he was a female entertainer and at one point started to sing. Up till that moment, I thought I had acquitted myself very well and believed I would get off lightly. Max and I were both found guilty and, considering I was on the more serious charge of the two of us, I was surprised when the jury recommended me for mercy. The headline in the *Truth* that week, 5 July 1952, was 'BALL BELLE MAKES A COURT CURTSY'. 'For one of those belles who rubbed shoulders at the Arts Ball with the Governor and his lady last month and who rubbed shoulders with Noel Christian Morton in the dock at General Sessions the other day, it's all a matter of dress,' said the article.

I was sent to Pentridge to await sentencing. James had been sentenced some weeks earlier to a year in gaol. The maximum sentence could have been fifteen years. In his final address to the court, the judge said he 'did not think Morton was much harm to the community except that he might initiate others into his cult'. I spent nearly three weeks in Pentridge. The talk from the boys in the yard was all bragging and bullshit, with every one of them trying to outdo the other. I learnt how to 'hot wire' a car and about dope for the first time. I knew I was a curiosity to them because of my charge. None of these boys thought it wrong to have sex with a man. They all lived so far outside of the square that their lives were constantly at risk; they had all turned tricks at some time or another or had been sexually abused when they were young. To them, sex was money, food or a bed, not a crime. Other homosexuals had been gaoled from time to time, mostly for masquerading as women and working as prostitutes or 'loitering with intent'. Inside, they were called 'Cats' and well taken care of by long term prisoners.

The day-to-day routine inside was always dangerous and menacing. After sleeping—or in my case not sleeping—on the floor of my claustrophobic cell I had a wash from the tap above the toilet and waited to be taken outside to the exercise yard with other boys. This was a release for me from the demons that haunted me during the night and on more than one occasion led me to seriously consider suicide.

I was in the exercise yard on my last Friday in Pentridge with a group of boys all about my age. It was raining and we were huddled under a corrugated tin shelter, which was also the latrine, eating our lunch and staring in silence and disbelief at a boy who had climbed up onto the wall. He had been brought in that morning and his face was badly bruised and swollen. He looked as though he'd been beaten up. He was crawling toward the spikes. The guard in the lookout turret fired a warning shot over his head; the boy kept crawling and the next shot fired by the guard hit him in the upper thigh. Blood spurted out of it like a fountain and splashed down onto the yard below. Several of the boys threw up before a guard took us back inside to our cells.

I told John O'Toole about my experiences inside, and in his diary for 1952 he wrote: 'Noel came out of Pentridge full of stories of what went on behind those bars; they seemed far too fantastic to be true.'

On the day I arrived at the courthouse to be sentenced, I

looked around for Mumma but she wasn't there; she had finally busted. I couldn't blame her with all she had put up with on my account. She and Uncle Les were drunk when the detectives went to see them to discuss my impending release. They told the judge that I didn't have a proper home to return to. Fortunately for me, Bev was in Melbourne and she came to court looking like a million dollars. She was twenty years old and strikingly beautiful. When the judge asked who would be responsible for me and my good behaviour bond, Bev stood up and said she would. I was bonded into her custody for two years. I had only seen Bev intermittently over the previous two or three years. We were both living our separate lives but she kept in regular touch with Mark Street. Mumma had told her about my trial and asked her to go to the courthouse.

Max was sentenced to a year in Pentridge Gaol. Three months later, he appealed his sentence. He was very articulate and amusing in his defence. On the subject of owning a pair of rubber falsies, he said, 'If I am to be suspected and prejudiced by possession of them then so should every female impersonator in the same position, including the whole company that played a long season here two years ago.' He was referring to the famous Kiwis, an all-male revue from New Zealand. When questioned about his drag name, Heather Page, he turned to the jury and said, 'One can't masquerade as a woman under the name of Charlie Brown. Wearing a dress is the same for me as a labourer wearing a pair of overalls to work or a diver wearing a rubber suit.' His appeal was quashed. The *Truth* newspaper was now particularly and unfairly cruel to Max. Under the headline 'BALL BELLE BOWLED' the reporter wrote, 'Maximilian Eugene Nigel du Barry, Belle of the National Theatre Arts Ball, by achieving a new trial only added two months to his one year sentence'.

My name had been dropped from the last articles that appeared in August 1952. My first thought when I left the courthouse was, what do I do now? I wanted to leave Melbourne and the trial behind me but I had no idea how I was going to achieve this. I had no job and no money. After the articles in the *Truth*, the only two people who would talk to me were Clarrie and Ivor. All my other friends dropped me. Even though he had raised the bail, I didn't see much of John O'Toole when I got out of Pentridge; our friendship had waned considerably. This was my fault as I was too embarrassed to see him. I couldn't go to dance class or get a job. I was now a known criminal and even my street friends could be arrested or at least questioned for 'consorting' with me, which was against the law.

Max and the rest of us were forced to live as we did because of our sexuality and our non-acceptance by the rigid society of the day. In my case, it was also my colour and upbringing. We deliberately challenged those laws and people who tried to deny us the right to exist. I knew several men who killed themselves because of the fear of coming out or the guilt they were made to feel every Sunday morning at mass. Some who did come out suicided when the weight of their excesses became too much for them to live with and they were left with nowhere else to go. It's ironic when I think about it. Eventually I would have been forgiven by everyone if I had murdered Max but no one could forgive me for having sex with him. This made me think about all the other men I knew in Melbourne who couldn't openly declare their sexuality. The trial and *Truth* newspaper had publicly defined mine. Even if I had wanted to run away—and I did many times in the next few months—I couldn't and nor could they. There was nowhere to run to and so they lived with the fear that one day someone would find out about them too. This was Australia, outpost of Catholic Ireland, land of the digger, good mates and fair dinkum Aussies. I knew from my days on the street that it was also the land of fair dinkum married bisexual men and where every closet not only had a skeleton in it but probably a 'poof' as well. It was definitely a country of double standards. In 1946, for example, the stars of a Tivoli revue had been six of the top female impersonators from Finnochio's Night Club in San Francisco. The name of the club is Italian slang for 'fairy'. And the most successful show in Australia after the war was the all-male revue from New Zealand, The Kiwis.

The trial had its repercussions. Mumma was abused by our next-door neighbour for having a son like me; she must have been incredibly strong because she kept off the booze and went to work every day. I was pretty miserable most of the time. My old Mark Street mates, with the exception of Clarrie, steered well away from me whenever they saw me. I was beaten up a couple of times, and one Saturday night on my way home from the pictures in Newmarket I was raped by some boys I knew. A week later I noticed a white discharge coming from my penis. I knew what it was: my first dose of the clap. I was too embarrassed to go to the clinic so I bought a bottle of Dettol and dabbed my penis with it but the discharge got worse. I had no alternative but to go to a doctor. I lied when I was asked who I'd had sex with. I told the doctor I got drunk at a party and couldn't remember. He gave me a penicillin injection and some pills, and it soon cleared up. But there was no injection or pills that could cure my mental condition. That I had failed myself as a person and brought shame to Mumma caused me great pain and the sadness that accompanies the contemplation of suicide engulfed my whole body.

Just when my self-esteem was at its lowest a letter arrived for me. It had a government stamp on it. I thought it would be something to do with my good behaviour bond but when I read it I was filled with excitement: it was my call up papers for National Service. Disappointment followed as suddenly as the excitement had arrived. Question number one on the form asked if the applicant had a police record. I was pretty down by the time Mumma came home from work. I gave her the letter to read and told her that I really wanted to do National Service. She agreed that it would be good for me to go away. After she read the letter she told me to stop crying and said, 'No one needs to know about Noel Morton, or the trial. Fill in the papers using the surname on your birth certificate.' That was the day I found out that we were all illegitimate. Bev knew but she never told me. I had grown up assuming that my surname was Morton because that was my father's name.

How ironic that being a 'little black bastard' was now going to save me. I went to the Registrar's Office and got a copy of my birth certificate and there it was: 'Name: Noel Christian Tovey. Date of birth: 25–12–1934. Mumma told me that I was actually born in 1933 and registered in 1934. Once again she had come to my rescue. I felt an upsurge of arrogance and defiance as I sat down at the kitchen table and reinvented myself. I filled in the papers answering all the basic questions with a lie: (1) I had no record of criminal charges against me, (2) I left school in the eighth grade, (3) I had no known health defects. Where it asked for choice of service, first, second and third, I put Air Force in all three spaces. I posted the papers off to the department and anxiously waited for a reply.

Several weeks later I was called for an IQ test that I passed very well. This was followed by an interview. The officer conducting the interview asked me why I had been so adamant about joining the Air Force. He explained that the number of boys chosen was very low compared to the Army and Navy. I then played my trump card. I replied, 'Tradition, sir.' I remembered Grandma Challenger telling me that her nephew was a famous fighter pilot. One of the other officers asked me to explain and I gave one of my best performances. I stood up and with all the ease I could muster said, 'My adopted uncle was Bluey Truscott, fighter pilot and football player, sir. He played for the Demons.' The officer stepped forward and shook my hand, called me son, and told me that I would be hearing from them.

What I'd told them was true. Grandma Challenger's maiden name was Truscott and her nephew was Squadron Leader Keith W. Truscott DFC and Bar. Like all Australians with red hair, he was nicknamed Bluey. Many articles have been written about Bluey's phenomenal sporting prowess. He played VFL football for Melbourne. He was equally noted for his flying skills particularly in Europe and later in the battle against the Japanese invaders at Milne Bay in Papua during the war in the Pacific in August 1942. He died when the Kittyhawk aeroplane he was flying accidentally crashed into the sea on 28 March 1943 somewhere on the north coast of Australia. The obituaries hailed him as one of Australia's greatest fighter pilots and a fine sportsman.

Noel Tovey was born that evening. It was my coming out. Having passed the first test with my new name, I felt confident that I could find some sort of work that would keep me interested and away from the streets until my National Service began the next year. I didn't want to be seen around the city during the daytime. I figured that if I disappeared for a while people would accept me and my new name much more easily when I returned.

I got a job at the *Argus* newspaper as a galley boy. The hours were from four o'clock in the afternoon until the paper was 'put to bed', which was usually quite late. I had to pick up the galleys from the compositors and take them to the proofreaders. When they were checked, I took them back to the compositors who corrected any mistakes and reset the type. I enjoyed the work and learnt a lot there and I had no trouble being one of the blokes.

I saw a lot of Max's younger brother during this time. He thought I needed looking after so he collected me when I finished work and drove me home. He knew that I had been very upset when Max went to prison and assured me that Max didn't blame me. He said he knew he'd been set up by the police. I never saw Max again and my friendship with his brother ended the night he told me he loved me and tried to seduce me in his garage. He was supposed to be the straight member of the family.

For a long time after the trial I was thought of as easy pickings. I received a lot of letters with dubious offers of help. I never replied to any of them. John O'Toole kept this one in his diary

> 1/6/52 Would you care to write to me? I feel sure we would be able to arrange an appointment and discuss things in common, etc. to our mutual advantage. I could see you one afternoon as I work night work. I read the newspaper report several weeks ago in *Truth*. Bad luck but I hope you came out of it alright. PS Give me your p/o address and I will write to you.

I made contact with John again. I knew I couldn't hide away forever from the people who I knew genuinely cared about me, particularly John. I told him I was sorry and embarrassed that I had repaid his kindness by involving him in a situation that was so out of kilter with his own life. He and Hans invited me to go with them on a university Riding Club weekend at Raneleagh, an estate on the Mornington Peninsula. The weekend had been organised by the charismatic Woodsy-Lloyd, the president of the Students Union. I spent most of it with a girl whose name I have completely forgotten. I was trying to prove something to myself, maybe that I was still capable of a heterosexual relationship. I continued to believe that I could drop my homosexuality at will. When I telephoned her a few weeks later, she said she was pregnant. I did not want to be a father; I told her I could get the name of a doctor who would give her an abortion for £100. I arranged to meet her a few days later at Val's to discuss the money. When she arrived she said she was sorry, she had made a mistake and that her period had been late. I was extremely relieved because I had no idea how I could have raised the money.

I also started seeing my old street mates again. They had forgotten the scandal but I was still despised and rejected by most of the smart people I knew. I wasn't particularly bothered by that. I just wanted to get on with my life, earn some money and live somewhere where no one knew me. It wasn't very easy for me to do, though. I was living at Mark Street and sleeping on a rickety old couch in the kitchen. I was tired all the time. I got home from work after midnight and everyone else was up and about by 6 am.

Bev and her husband had returned to Melbourne and were living in my room. Things weren't working out for them and they now had a baby daughter. He and Bev fought all the time. I became very ill. I didn't know what was happening to me: I felt like I was drowning in my own sweat and my body ached all over. It was finally giving in to all the strain and emotion I had suppressed a year ago during the trial. The articles in the newspapers had distressed me more than I had realised and even though I could escape into fantasy land on the streets at night I could not escape from the reality of what Mark Street and my life had meant to me since I was born. The years of abuse had taken their toll; I spent hours sitting in the back yard crying. I thought about killing myself again. I was still struggling with my belief in God and Catholicism and it was now only the fear of mortal sin and Hell that kept me alive.

I would have totally cracked up had I not received a letter addressed to ACR(M) (Air Craftsman) A311025 Noel Tovey informing him that he had to catch the morning train for Ballarat on 1 June 1953 to commence six months' National Service training in the Air Force. I had been selected to join a special group of eighteen boys to be trained as radio officers. When I finished reading the letter again I said a quiet prayer of thanks to 'Uncle'

Bluey Truscott and then went to find Clarrie to tell him the good news. I had a week to prepare myself for the next six months of my life. They had to be an improvement on the previous six.

I walked to the city and bought some underwear, toiletries and a new pocket dictionary. When I left Mark Street the following Sunday morning to go to Spencer Street station, I told myself no matter what I would never come back here again.

On the train to Ballarat, the boys from Melbourne got to know each other and I remember very clearly how relieved I was not to have to be on guard and how easy it had become for me to say my name was Noel Tovey. Little did I know that I would eventually forget Noel Morton entirely and at age sixty-seven have great difficulty recounting his life and adventures. I told the boys that I was going to be a famous dancer and work in the theatre. No one laughed or called me a poof or Choc or Darkie.

When we arrived at the base we met the other boys and the great thing about our group was that, even though we all came from totally different backgrounds, once in uniform we were all the same. The boy who became my best mate lived in Toorak and had been to Xavier College. There was a boy from the Salvation Army who didn't swear but had his own variety of cussing. His favourite expression was 'flip the flipping thing'. Another boy, Bill, was a confirmed socialist and anti the Air Force Establishment. We became very close and lived in the same boarding house when we finished our six months in Ballarat. Dinny was a first grade tennis player and, without knowing it, very camp in his demeanour. He was often the butt of one of Corporal Coates' bad taste jokes. The corporal was our drill instructor and we spent our first week learning basic drill from him. He was a very loud obnoxious Pommie and considered himself a strict disciplinarian. What he didn't reckon on was getting a group of very single-minded eighteen-year-olds who knew exactly why they had been chosen for this particular course. The first time he said, 'So you all think you're special, do you?' we answered him as one, 'Yes, sir, we do!' We were nicknamed Menzies' Blue Orchids by the regulars because of their rare and exclusive nature.

That evening when we went to the canteen I saw someone I thought I recognised from the city. When he called me over and introduced himself I told him his secret was safe with me. He in turn introduced me to several of his friends on the base—including one of the officers—who also shared the same secret.

Our course consisted of learning to touch-type and code and decode messages that were relayed to us through headsets. A month into the course I got glandular fever. I spent a lot of time in bed and eventually moved out of our hut into the hospital and was given a special diet. As a result, I had a light duties chit: I could go to classes but on no account was I allowed to drill and that infuriated Corporal Coates.

I also got the weekends off. I would go down to Melbourne on the back of my mate's motorbike. Now I was eighteen, I could legally go into the upstairs bar at the Australia Hotel; I still didn't drink but I wanted to show off the new me. I knew most of the crowd: they were window dressers from Myers and Georges. They wore charcoal-grey suits, salmon-pink shirts, drank gin and tonic and thought they were better than everyone else in Melbourne.

I also knew all of the not-so-smart set who liked to drink beer with 'rough trade' in the lower bar. Some of the crowd accepted the change of name but others would say rather tartly, 'Aren't you Noel Morton?' I would smile and say, 'I was.' The first time Mumma saw me in my uniform, she said, 'You've changed, Noely boy.' I think she was pleased with the way I had survived the trial.

My glandular fever didn't improve and I was sent down to the Laverton Base Hospital to have a lymph gland removed from my neck for a pathology examination. While I was still groggy from the anaesthetic I saw a shadowy figure ransacking my bedside locker. When I came to, I discovered my wallet had been stolen. I told the sister and I spoke to the base police but it was fruitless and eventually my empty wallet was found in one of the latrines.

Two weeks later, I returned to Ballarat and finished the course. In December, we had a passing out parade and a grand dinner at a hotel in Ballarat. Bill made a very funny speech of thanks to our warrant officer and I called Corporal Coates darling when I said goodbye to him. I leant across the table and said very loudly, 'Thank you, darling, it was great fun.' I also broke my vow of abstinence that night and got very drunk. We all had terrible hangovers, which made me wonder why people drank in the first place. Next morning, we were ordered to take a cold shower and as we did so our Salvation Army mate played 'The Last Post' on his bugle.

Before I left Ballarat, I wrote to John O'Toole telling him that the six months I spent in the Air Force there had changed my life forever. I told him that I finally had a sense of belonging somewhere and how wearing the uniform filled me with pride and self-esteem and that I was even considering joining the Air Force permanently. In six months, I thought that I had been well equipped for the rest of my life and that I was on the right track. I would never have to answer to anybody about colour, background or indeed anything again. Without realising it, I had replaced one make-believe world with another.

I came out of the Air Force with enough deferred pay to buy a suit and find somewhere to live. Bill and I got a room each in a house in Kew. We had a strange relationship, more than friendship but never quite physical. We tried once, but in the end Bill decided that any sort of relationship other than friendship would be too problematical for him.

Ivor and I spent Christmas 1953 together on St Kilda beach.

We both went over to Mark Street first with some presents. Mumma was sober enough to cook lunch and Ivor had made her a dress for Christmas. I was on edge and restless for most of the time because I knew we were approaching that moment when the next drink could lead to a violent outburst from Uncle Les. When it happened it was a surprise as it came from Mumma. She was serving the pudding on small side plates and I said jokingly, 'What, no sweet coupes, Mother?' She said, '*I'll* give you fucking sweet coupes!' and threw the pudding and the jug of cream at me. That was the appropriate time to leave for the beach. I stayed at Ivor's flat until the end of January.

In the New Year, he introduced me to Deirdre Cash who later wrote two books—*The Delinquents* and *Down by the Dockside*—under the pseudonym of Criena Rohan. It was late summer and Ivor and I were standing on the corner of Swanston and Collins streets at sunset. Coming down Collins Street on the opposite side to us was Deirdre. She was wearing a pink satin Chinese dress and a short white fur cape. Her strawberry blonde hair was piled high on top of her head and she was flanked on either side by two naval officers. They were laughing as they crossed the street and the sun seemed to dance in her hair. She stopped when she saw us and Ivor introduced me to her. She was the image of Danielle Darrieux, the French film star. The three of them were on their way to the Golden Dragon Restaurant in Little Collins Street. Deirdre was the vocalist with a small jazz group who entertained the dinner patrons. She invited Ivor and me to go with them. Eating a mixed grill and drinking sparkling burgundy at the Golden Dragon with two naval officers was very chic in the fifties.

Deirdre and I saw a lot of each other after that night. She decided that with all my mixed blood and a grandmother with the surname McCann and her own Irish ancestry that we must be cousins. I nicknamed her Singapore Lil and she called me

Cousin Noely Boy. She had had classical voice training at the East Melbourne Conservatorium but she preferred to sing jazz to the forces. Her mother, Valerie Cash, was a very promising young singer when she married Deirdre's father but constant touring overseas led to their separation. She introduced me to her father, Leo Cash. Uncle Leo was a button manufacturer but his heart wasn't in it. He was a fiercely Irish, ex-Catholic Marxist and an intellectual. It was a talented family all round. His nephew is a well-known lawyer and the father of tennis player Pat Cash. Uncle Leo wanted to be recognised as a poet and contributed some of his work to the New Theatre in Flinders Street, established in 1935 and committed to social change. Uncle Leo was short and stocky and had been very good looking in his youth. Cousin Lil told me he had had a reputation as a lady-killer when he was a young man.

His ramshackle house was near the corner of Victoria and Lygon Streets, Carlton, and was always filled with the Scrags. The Scrags was the collective name given to the clientele of the Family Swanston Hotel. They were left wing, mainly out of work—the pseudo arty crowd of inner Melbourne. Uncle Leo took it upon himself to instruct me in Irish politics and the importance of Michael Collins. He blamed the British for all the troubles in Ireland and fifty years later I'm not altogether sure he wasn't right.

Cousin Lil left Melbourne for Perth later that year. She said we both needed a change. She was having difficulty writing in Melbourne and she said I needed to do something worthwhile so I got a job at Myers as a trainee window dresser. I moved out of Uncle Leo's house and found a room in East Melbourne. I had one suit, a pair of shoes and two drip-dry shirts. I washed one every night and hung it from the mantlepiece in front of the fireplace to dry. I was definitely going up in the world. Unfortunately, my theatrical flair cost me my job and I was on the way down again very quickly. What happened was that I was asked by my boss to drape a plaster model in the fabric section on the second floor with the new Thai silk. Using pins and staples I created a magnificent crinoline and ruined a whole bolt of very expensive material. My boss was severely reprimanded by *his* boss and we had a row. The upshot was I was out of work again.

Eight

I spent most of my days looking for another job and in the evenings I joined the National Theatre Drama company. I renewed my friendship with Mary Hardy. I had met her previously just before my trial. I think it was at an audition for one of the amateur drama companies that flourished in Melbourne in the fifties. I was eighteen and she was twenty-one.

She was a remarkable person. Born into a large and strict Roman Catholic family in Warrnambool, she grew up in Bacchus Marsh, a small country town west of Melbourne. She didn't swear or drink when I met her. The first time anyone heard her use a four letter word was when she was playing Peter Pan at the Princess Theatre in 1957. She was terrified of heights and the day she put on the flying apparatus and tried it out, she got stuck in the 'flies' and was left suspended high above the stage swearing at the top her voice at the stagehands.

Mary had an individual undisciplined talent, the full range of which was only rarely seen. Had she gone overseas and worked I believe she would have become a major actress. She had a truly wicked sense of humour, like the time when I left Melbourne on my first professional tour. She and another actress, Fay Parsons, came down to Spencer Street station to see me off on the overnight train to Sydney. They made a big fuss, pinning a name tag and a clean hankie on my lapel and giving me a bag of fruit and telling me to be a good boy. I thought it was a big joke and typical of Mary but what I didn't know was that they went to the guard and asked him to keep an eye on me. Mary told him I was retarded and this was my first time away from home. I wondered why he kept coming into my compartment, especially during the night, to ask me if I was all right.

The lacerating tongue for which she was known later in her career and life hadn't developed then. We were having great fun trying to be actors. We shared our dreams and aspirations. I think we only ever spoke about our past once or twice to each other. She had been deeply affected by the death of her father and even more so by the death of her mother from cancer. She once told me she was haunted by the fear of ending her days in a psychiatric hospital. She was very brittle and always on the defensive with people; 'get in first' was her motto.

Mary's brother, Frank, was a well known communist and author. In 1950, he caused a storm with his novel *Power Without Glory*, a not-too-heavily veiled demolition of John Wren, the patriarch of an affluent Melbourne family who was rumoured to be connected to the local suburban criminal fringe. Frank was sued by Wren's wife over certain allegations about her in the book. The trial lasted nine months and was eventually won by Frank. The book became a television series and was later acclaimed as one of the great Australian novels.

Mary and I often turned our fears and complexes into a joke between us. I hated being tall, dark and skinny and she was obsessed about being small and ugly. If I told her I was auditioning for something she would say to me, 'Darling, you're far too tall and far, far too dark.' Likewise, when she told me she was auditioning for something, I would say to her, 'Darling, you're far too short and far, far too ugly.' We saw each other almost every day, meeting somewhere in Collins Street. If we were broke and wanted to go to the pictures I got us in the back way. Mary and I did a lot of amateur and professional work together in revues and television.

The infatuation with Judy Garland that began when she saw her in a film in a hall in Bacchus Marsh when she was a little girl became her nemesis. In 1954, Mary insisted that we went to see *A Star Is Born* every day for the first week of its run in Melbourne. A decade later, when Judy gave her disastrous concert at Festival Hall in 1964 and was so bombed out she couldn't remember the words to anything, Mary was in tears and stood up and called out the lyrics of 'The Trolley Song'.

Thankfully, I wasn't in Australia to witness her demise. I stayed with her at her apartment in St Kilda when I returned to Australia to stage *Oh! Calcutta* in 1970 and again in 1971 when I was invited to Sydney to direct and choreograph a production of *Anything Goes* at the Richbrooke Theatre. I saw what was happening to Mary then. She was very hyperactive, not eating and taking Mogadon for a sleeping problem. The die had been cast, as they say. She was appearing on stage, television and an early morning radio program. She had become the star she had always wanted to be. Everyone knew Mary Hardy and she was in great demand. She won several Logies, Australia's most prestigious TV award, for her numerous television appearances and her brand of comedy opened the door for many of the female comics who are working in Australia today. But, like Judy, Mary was driving herself relentlessly, going to bed after midnight and getting up at the crack of dawn for her radio show.

After 1971, I never saw her again. She came to London several times but I was always somewhere else working. Occasionally she telephoned me from Melbourne. The different pills and drugs she was taking caused her to have psychotic phases and her conversation was for the most part incoherent.

In January 1985, I had the most extraordinary experience; I woke up with a start in the middle of the night. I got out of bed and went to the kitchen and put the kettle on to make a cup of tea. Dave, my boyfriend, followed me and asked me what was wrong. I told him I had seen a headline in the *Sun* newspaper saying 'MARY HARDY SUICIDES'. He said it was only a dream and told me to go back to bed. At about 7 am London time, my ex-sister-in-law, Penny, phoned me from Australia to tell me that Mary had died. She had taken a shotgun into the bathroom of her apartment, got into the bath and blew her brains out. I was devastated. The Mary I knew and loved hated violence of any kind and she was certainly not a manic-depressive in 1960.

When I started writing this book, I asked several mutual friends to tell me about the last years of Mary's life. Their memories of what happened to her differed so much that I went to the Public Records Office and read the inquest report of her suicide. It was a harrowing experience for me to learn about her descent into addiction and what the drugs had done to her personality and brain. She left two notes in a handwriting I barely recognised. At the bottom of one she wrote, 'Give the Logies to anyone who wants them.'

At the beginning of 1954 the National Theatre in Melbourne was preparing for the eighth annual Arts Festival at the Princess Theatre. Every year the festival was a special event but this year was to be extra special: the Queen and Prince Philip were coming to Australia.

Mary, John Truscott and I were cast in George Bernard Shaw's *Caesar and Cleopatra*. John was Porter Number 1, I was Porter

Number 2 and Mary was the Third Woman and had one line of dialogue. She had to run on stage and scream out, 'The Romans are in the courtyard.' During one performance we were talking in the wings—something for which we were always being reprimanded by the stage manager—when Mary thought she heard her cue. She ran on stage and screamed out her line. When she saw the startled looks on the faces of the other actors, she knew she was in the wrong scene and quickly added 'next door' and ran off again. Mary and I were inseparable. We were extras in Offenbach's opera *Tales of Hoffman* and during the Barcarole scene we were acting away on our cushions pretending to be lovers when she looked up to the royal box and said indignantly and not too quietly, 'She's asleep!'

We all wanted to be actors. On Sunday afternoons, we went to Mary's house in Gardenvale for tea and to read plays. John Truscott was performing regularly as an amateur actor and hadn't started designing seriously yet. His Hollywood Oscar for *Camelot* was still to be won. John Muirhead was working in the office of J.C. Williamson and studying voice with Mona Peepiyat and I was taking classes and dancing at the Ballet Guild, which was run by Laurel Martyn. I danced in *The Sentimental Bloke*, a ballet based on the famous poem by C.J. Dennis, and *En Cirque* for the Guild.

Being a member of the National Theatre, I was able to see a lot of operas for nothing. I almost fell out of the Gods with excitement the night I saw Marie Collier play Magda Sorel in Menotti's modern opera *The Consul* at the Princess Theatre. This was a groundbreaking production by Stefan Haag, the one-time member of the Vienna Boys Choir who got stuck in Australia at the outbreak of war in Europe. I felt the same excitement again when I saw Marie stand in for an indisposed Maria Callas in *Tosca* at the Royal Opera House, Covent Garden, a decade or so later. Her brilliant career ended when she fell to her death from the window of her apartment in London.

In 1953, I moved back into Mark Street. I was trying to save money and home life wasn't as stressful. Mumma and Uncle Les were not busting as often as they had in the past. Bev and her husband had gone their separate ways. I got a job at a factory in South Melbourne making ball bearings on a lathe. Every Friday afternoon when I finished work I had a shower, changed my clothes and headed into the city. I couldn't afford to buy the latest zoot suit that all the boys were wearing. It had a single buttoned long jacket with draped shoulders and trousers that were baggy at the knees and very narrow at the cuff. I had all my trousers taken in below the knee by the woman who ran the drycleaners in Melrose Street. I got a crewcut and Clarrie painted a hula dancer on two yellow satin ties for us. We both had a pair of suede shoes with thick crepe soles. We were eighteen and very sharp. Clarrie was the only mate from Mark Street that I saw these days and I didn't see any of my old street mates at all.

For the next year I did nothing but work and have dancing lessons. If I wasn't in an amateur show somewhere, I would meet Clarrie and we would go down to the St Moritz in St Kilda. St Moritz had an ice skating rink on one floor and a dance hall on another. This was the beginning of the rock and roll era. The boys were called bodgies and the girls, in their pencil-slim skirts, bunny wool cardigans worn back to front and hair slicked back into a duck's tail, were widgies. This particular Friday I went to the box office at the Comedy Theatre to get two tickets before meeting Clarrie. Mary and I wanted to see Katharine Hepburn and Robert Helpmann who were touring Australia with the Old Vic Company in *The Taming of the Shrew*.

As I passed the stage door of Her Majesty's Theatre, Janette Liddell came out. She was rehearsing for *Paint Your Wagon*. She and Helene France were the principal female dancers. She told me that Ron Reay, the principal male dancer, had broken his leg that morning, that Kevan Johnston had been given the role and now they needed another boy dancer. Before I knew it she had taken me inside and introduced me to the English choreographer Maggie Maxwell. I did a few high kicks, lifted Janette on to my shoulder a couple of times and got the job and the understudy to Lou Eather who played Rocky and danced the can can sequence with Janette. I was now being paid to dance. At last I was a professional. I started off being paid £13 a week but then everyone went on strike for more money and we were eventually paid £16 a week and I got a little extra as an understudy.

I went straight home; I wanted to tell Mumma the good news. It was November and very warm. Mumma was standing at the front gate talking to a neighbour. I was so excited that I jetted down the hill. Mumma was just as excited as me and made some reference to me being like my father. Then she said, 'What about your tooth?' My tooth! I had forgotten all about it. I had had a front side tooth taken out when I was in Pentridge Gaol and had spent all this time covering my mouth with my hand whenever I laughed. Saturday morning I went to the dentist in Newmarket and explained my predicament and he said he could make me a false tooth by the following Friday.

On Monday morning when I arrived at rehearsals I met the other dancers. They were not very friendly at all. Neither was Betty Pounder who I had worked with at Collins Book Depot. She was now a ballet mistress and working her way up the professional ladder. I had one week to learn the show and no one wanted to help me. I almost gave up and walked out several times during the next few days but I kept telling myself what I had gone through to get here. I was a fairly good dancer now and I deserved to get the job. I had two partners. One was an extraordinarily beautiful girl from Adelaide named Clemence Bettany who later went on to have a successful career as a model in Europe. She was a joy to work with and covered many of my early mistakes. The other was a young girl from New Zealand and the most exciting dancer I had seen. Her name was Joyce Quealy. She understudied Jenny Liddell in the can can and suffered from what I now know was anorexia. She passed out on my shoulder one night in Sydney and was taken to hospital. She recovered fully and I last saw her in London in the late sixties dancing in *Fiddler on the Roof* in the West End.

Paint Your Wagon opened at Her Majesty's Theatre, Melbourne, on 25 November 1954 starring Americans Lynne Lyons, Richard Curry and Australian actor Alec Kellaway. This was a major milestone in my life—my first professional show—and Mumma and Chesca were in the audience to watch me make my debut.

When the curtain went up I was almost paralysed with fear and nerves. I had one line of dialogue. At the beginning of the can can, I had to push Lou Eather out into the centre of the stage and say, 'Go on, Rocky, she means you.' As I pushed him and said my big line, my false tooth flew out of my mouth and across the stage. Luckily, I was able to retrieve it. Then another disaster. In the grand parade at the end of the can can, I found it impossible to lift Dawn Spry onto my shoulder. I was nervous and I was aware of the dancer behind me calling me names. When the final curtain came down I ran off stage and downstairs to the dressing room. I was upset and didn't want anyone to see me crying.

Maggie Maxwell came down into the dressing room to thank the boys and told me that no one in the audience was aware of my mistakes. Clemence consoled me and took me to the opening night party with her. There is nothing quite like the excitement of going to your first, first night party. I've since been to many but the memory of that night and Clemence have always remained with me.

However, the first few weeks of the show were hell for me. Betty came around backstage every night with notes about the evening's performance. Most of them were for me. If it was not my arms, it was my legs. I listened to all her advice with concern and even offered to come in and rehearse on my own time. Despite these setbacks I was now aware of a growing inner strength. I knew this was the better life that my ancestors told me I would find the night they spoke to me in Pentridge Gaol. I wanted to keep this job and once again I was in survival mode. I stood my ground and defied anyone to remove me from it. Perhaps I became too arrogant for my own good. Being nervous all the time was my biggest problem and contributed to the mistakes I was making at every performance. I was constantly hounded by the older boys in the dressing room but I refused to give in. Where there's a will, there's a way.

I spoke to an old trick of mine who was a doctor. He gave me some pills called Dex (amphetamine) and told me to take one an hour before the performance. They certainly worked. I flew through the show without making a mistake. My friend had only given me ten pills and I swallowed the last one before the Saturday matinee. By the evening performance I was starting to feel very strange and began sweating and shivering; in fact, I was having the same reaction to the pills as I had had after three days on bennie cocktails. I just got through the performance and took a taxi home. I stayed in bed all day Sunday and most of Monday. When Mumma asked me why I was feeling so crook I told her about the pills. She hit the roof and said I was a bloody fool for taking them. 'Do you want to end up like your father?' she yelled at me. 'It'll be the booze next.' I was feeling fine again by the time I reached the theatre and I knew I could get through the show without the pills.

Eventually I was accepted by some of the girls. I became friends with one of the singers, Tony, and his girlfriend, Bev, who was a show girl at the Tivoli. I also got to know a couple of the minor principals, Bobby Healey and Graeme Bent, who were kind to me. Then, just when I started to feel comfortable in the dressing room, one of the boys told me rather bitchily that Betty Pounder didn't like me and had wanted Maggie to take another dancer instead of me. She had already told him that the part was his. The same boy told me that the older boys who had organised the hatchet job on Ivor and got him sacked from *Kiss Me Kate* went to Maggie and told her they didn't want to work with me because I was a notorious homosexual and that I'd been in gaol.

Maggie refused to sack me. Instead, she offered to let *them* go. Twenty-five years later, I was able to repay her kindness. I was appearing in the original production of *Oh! Calcutta* at the Roundhouse Theatre in north London. I was also the assistant to the director Clifford Williams and the American choreographer Margot Sappington. A year after we opened, Clifford asked me to restage the production in Paris and Hamburg with him. I needed a good ballet mistress to take care of the London show, which had now transferred from the Roundhouse to the Royalty Theatre in the West End, so I asked my agent, Myrette Morven, to find out what Maggie was doing. I heard that she had been out of work for some time. I hadn't seen her since 1963 when I was principal dancer for her in a production of *Red Riding Hood* at the Theatre Royal Windsor. Myrette knew her very well and I asked her to offer Maggie the position of ballet mistress.

I decided that if I was going to be happy dancing in *Paint Your Wagon* I would have to have it out with the bullies. I wasn't going to be intimidated for the next year by a bunch of sissy ballet boys so I had to tell them that I knew what they had said to Maggie. I waited until the next bitchy remark came my way then I rounded on all of them. I had over the years acquired the same acidic tongue as my mentor Brian Finemore and I used it. I told them what I knew and exactly what I thought of them. I said that I did not want them to say anything to me at all unless it was an apology. Things settled down after that and, with the exception of the ringleader, who I sat next to in the dressing room, I got on well with everyone and I started enjoying my work.

Mary Hardy got her first professional job with J.C. Williamson's that year too. She played the maid in a production of *Charley's Aunt* starring the popular English actor William Hodge.

Mirka and Georges Mora opened Cafe Mirka in Exhibition Street, the heart of Melbourne's theatre district and a block from Her Majesty's Theatre. The opening was performed by the French singer Jean Sablon who was appearing in his own show at the Tivoli Theatre. The guests were our leading lady, Clemence and me, and the usual assortment of socialites and models. Mirka and Georges had emigrated from Paris to Australia in 1951. They were like a breath of fresh air to us with their French food and their continental way of life. In no time at all, the café became a magnet for all the writers, artists, actors and dancers in Melbourne. Mirka was in her twenties and strikingly beautiful. She typified the word 'gamine', being short, slim and olive-skinned with luscious dark hair that fringed her sparkling eyes. For me, she brought with her the very essence of the Bohemian Paris I had imagined when I worked at Collins Book Depot. I spent a lot of time at the café practising my French in between ballet classes. I was doing two a day, one in the morning and another before the performance.

Mirka's husband, Georges, was fifteen years her senior. He appeared to be the more serious and academic of the two. Together, they galvanised the Melbourne art scene of the fifties. I went with them to many Contemporary Art Society meetings and they took me to David Wynn's big house on the river in Hawthorn. David's family owned Wynvale Wines and his brother Alan was married to Sally Gilmour, who I had first met in 1948 when she was the principal ballerina with the Ballet Rambert. She was considered by the critics of her day to be one of the finest interpreters of

Giselle in the classical ballet of the same name. I thought so too and I had waited outside the stage door of the Princess Theatre to get her autograph.

Paint Your Wagon had a very successful season in Melbourne and I was looking forward to my first tour of Australia. However, the show was not the success in Sydney that it had been in Melbourne. I think the Empire Theatre where we played was too big for the production. Richard Curry left the show at the end of the Melbourne season and returned to America. He was replaced by Bill Newman, a young good-looking minor principal player with a pleasant voice. He went on to have a long and successful career with 'The Firm', as J.C. Williamson's was affectionately known.

Even though the trouble I had had with the boys at the beginning of the season in Melbourne had long since disappeared, I didn't want to share accommodation with any of them. I was still a loner and preferred to live by myself. I found a flatette for thirty shillings a week at Santa Fe apartments in Kellett Street, Kings Cross. It was the favourite place for theatre people to stay when they were on tour and it was only a short tram ride from the city. The Cross in the fifties was Sydney's equivalent of New York's Greenwich Village. Bohemian in every sense, artists, homosexuals, writers and oddballs of all kinds could live there side by side without being harassed. The prostitutes were the best-dressed girls on the street. Their trademark was their white gloves and handbags. They were indeed 'ladies of the night' of both sexes. The drugs and crime that gave the Cross its bad reputation were so well controlled that I was never aware of them and I never felt threatened wandering around late at night. I knew several operators from my street days in Melbourne and I could have had entree to any of the illegal clubs that were hidden away in the back streets but I had put all that behind me several years before.

Local artist Rosaleen Norton, nicknamed 'the witch of the Cross', spent most of her time sitting in the Casbah Coffee Lounge in Macleay Street chain-smoking and making her satanic drawings. Further down Macleay Street was Mrs Smith's Café. Like Mirka's in Melbourne, everyone gathered at Mrs Smith's after their evening performance.

There were nine, very active live theatres in the city area of Sydney in 1954. My favourite was the Phillip Street Theatre. I saw my first intimate revue there. Bill Orr, the founder and artistic director, came from England in the early fifties and brought intimate revue with him. It became the rage in Sydney and all the top actors wanted to perform at Phillip Street. The stars of those early revues were Bud Tingwell, Ray Barrett, Lyle O'Hara, Ruth Cracknell, Barbara Wyndon, Dolore Whiteman, Gordon Chater, Paula Langlands, June Salter and Jill Perryman.

Mary followed me to Sydney with *Charley's Aunt* and moved into Santa Fe. We spent our days exploring the city and drinking a lot of tea in all the smart tea shops. We loved going to David Jones department store. On Friday mornings, after being paid, we went shopping. I wore my new suit and Mary wore her overcoat from La Louvre in Collins Street, Melbourne. She had saved up for months to buy it. We would have a coffee and then set about terrorising the woman behind the information desk at David Jones. She disliked us and visibly winced whenever we approached. She was incredibly tall, wore too much make-up and had a rich, plummy and totally affected speaking voice that she used very loudly to give directions. She behaved as if she owned the store. Mary and I knew she also sold stamps, which she obviously thought was beneath her dignity. We would wait until there were several people at the desk then Mary would say, 'Excuse me, miss, could I have a penny stamp, please?' She knew better than to ignore us so she would have to stoop down and bring out an old-fashioned tin box from under the counter and give Mary a stamp. Mary always gave her a two shilling piece to prolong the torture. We then took the lift to the fur department. Mary went straight to the minks and I settled down in a very comfortable armchair and took out my pipe. John Pease had given me this for my nineteenth birthday and I thought it made me look intellectual and sophisticated.

John and I had met the previous year at a supper party given by an acquaintance of mine to introduce him to her Melbourne friends. He was a television technical director and had been brought to Melbourne from England via New Zealand to help set up Channel Seven in Melbourne. He was some years older than me and very shy. I was very loud in those days and always wanted to be the centre of attention. I was still very shy but I had learnt to cover it up, just as I did with many of my other frailties. John looked quite out of place in these surroundings. Without anyone noticing, I slipped my hand underneath the table and found his. He looked at me and smiled and by the time the dessert arrived he'd asked me to stay the night with him. This was the beginning of a long but not always happy relationship. I wanted everything that the theatre and life had to offer but I didn't know how to respond to genuine friendship and love. I was surprised that he still wanted to talk to me after I practically ignored him when he came up to Sydney to see me during the run of *Paint Your Wagon*.

Anyway, to get back to David Jones. The saleswoman who was attending Mary was getting very excited at the prospect of a large commission. Mary tried on every mink coat on the rack and after she had asked me for the umpteenth time which one I wanted her to have I took out my cheque book and with a flourish signed a cheque. I gave it to her saying, 'I've had enough of this, darling, make up your own mind,' and walked out. She followed me, saying to the astonished saleswoman, 'All I wanted was a warm coat.'

The season in Sydney was drawing to a close and we were all happy to be going on to Brisbane. Brisbane was stinking hot when we arrived. Luckily we only played a very short season there. The only memory I have of that time is the trams and the conductors who wore hats like the legionnaires in an amateur production of *The Desert Song*. My best friend in the company was Lynne Lyons, our leading lady from America, and by the time the short Brisbane run had finished everyone thought we were having an affair, even the management. When they found out that we were going to share a flat in Adelaide, they called her into the office and told her it was not the done thing in Australia for a visiting leading lady to live with a ballet boy. She told them it was none of their business. She was actually having an affair with someone else in the cast and I was the only one who knew about it.

Adelaide was not the straight and conservative city most people had expected it to be. I went to some pretty wild parties up in the hills. I remember seeing a well-known society hairdresser walking down Rundle Street, with his pet poodle and his mother, all with the same colour hair.

Adelaide was in every way the major turning point in my career. When we arrived at the theatre there was a notice on the board from the company manager telling everyone that the next production by the Firm was to be the current Broadway hit *Can Can*. Elanore Treiber was coming out from America to choreograph the production and play Claudine. We were all asked to audition for her. I was the only member of the chorus who failed. The dancer Betty Pounder had wanted for *Paint Your Wagon* got the role and I never worked for J.C. Williamson's again.

I was desolate and I spent the rest of the day sitting by the river asking myself the same negative questions that I always did when things didn't work out for me. What had I done to make so many people dislike me? Why didn't I fit in? I had to force myself to go to the theatre for the evening performance. I wanted to run away but I knew that if I did my career in the theatre would be over.

I managed to put on a brave face when I walked into the dressing room. To my relief there were no bitchy remarks and I think some of the boys were genuinely sorry for me. In an effort to cheer me up our stage manager told me that the Princess Theatre in Melbourne was holding auditions for the musical *Kismet* and suggested I go.

I had only been in an aeroplane once before when I was doing National Service training and I was terrified of flying but the only way I could get to Melbourne and back in one day was to go by plane. One of the dancers I had been having a romance with loaned me some money and so I was able to buy a ticket. I was given a seat by the window and the air hostess, sensing I was nervous, chatted to me for most of the flight. Once in Melbourne I went straight to the theatre and presented myself to Lisa Brionda, the English choreographer. I failed that audition too. Lisa was very gentle when she told me I didn't have the right shape to be a Nubian slave and dance naked from the waist up. It was true. Although I had the height—I was six feet tall—I was still very skinny.

I was pretty miserable when I returned to Adelaide. Lynne took me to dinner after the performance and told me that what I was going through was par for the course and I had better get used to it or look for a different job. To comfort me she told me how she almost gave up her career. It was in the early days of American television when commercials were performed live. She had been chosen from a number of young girls to do the Budweiser beer commercial. Dressed in a Latin American costume, she had to walk to a rumba rhythm saying, 'If it's beer, it's Buds.' As she started to walk towards the camera nerves took over and she began to shake. She dropped the tray she was carrying, breaking the glasses and spilling the beer, and ran off the set in a flood of tears. We both laughed so much that night that I forgot my immediate problems and we had a great time for the remainder of the season in Adelaide.

One of dancers I met in Adelaide was Robina Beard. She was rehearsing for *Can Can* and was an extraordinary dancer, actress and comedienne. We have since worked together many times and she has been my best friend and critic for nearly fifty years. She was my assistant and danced the tango in *The Boy Friend* in 1968 and stole the show in my production of *Anything Goes* in Sydney in 1971. She later became famous for her part as Madge in a Palmolive washing-up liquid commercial that aired for nearly twenty years. When we were working together on a production for the Adelaide Festival 2000, we drove out to the hills one Sunday morning for breakfast. The owner of the café where we stopped looked at Robina and said, 'And what brings Madge to Hahndorf on a Sunday morning?'

Paint Your Wagon returned to Melbourne for a brief farewell season at Her Majesty's. By then Mirka had closed her café in Exhibition Street and taken her confit and other exotic French food to a new address in East Melbourne. A short time later the old café reopened with a new name, the Danish Delight, and a new owner, Bims Gunness. Her open sandwiches became as popular with the theatre crowd as had Mirka's pâtés.

Working in the kitchen at the Danish Delight was my close friend Margaret Clucas. With the exception of Clarrie, who I still saw quite frequently, all my best friends were girls. Margaret lived in a boarding house in Punt Road, South Yarra. She had a very small bungalow at the back of the main house and Mary and me and Margaret's friends would cram into it with a flagon of wine and listen to records of the latest Broadway musicals.

John Pease lived in a flat in the main house and I often stayed there with him. He knew that I really cared for him but I still wouldn't commit myself to a serious relationship with him.

Playing at the Comedy Theatre opposite was a very bad English production of *White Cargo* starring June Sylvane, daughter of the well-known film comedian Vernon Sylvane. It was from this show that I got my nickname. June played Tondalayo, the island temptress. Even though she wore black body make-up there was no mistaking her posh English accent, particularly when she spoke the play's most famous line of dialogue, 'Me Tondalayo. Me make tiffin for you.'

I saw a matinee performance and thought that even *I* could have played Tondalayo better. I went back to Her Majesty's, found an old black wig in the wardrobe, blacked out two of my front teeth, made a sarong out of the curtains and hung a sign that said, 'Me Tondalayo. Tiffin 3 pence,' above the dressing room where I made the tea at interval. The boys fell about laughing when they arrived for the evening performance and saw me in my Tondalayo costume. The name stuck. Everyone started calling me Tondalayo, even Mumma, who abbreviated it to Tondo which my close friends still call me today.

Another friend I made in those days was Maureen Grant, a friend of my old friend John O'Toole. I replaced a dancer at the Tivoli Theatre in the Weir Brothers show for three weeks and that was the first time I worked with Maureen. She was a platinum-blonde beauty and had no intention of becoming a dancer as she was at art school. But Fate had other plans for her. She went to the theatre with a friend of hers who was nervous about auditioning and sat in the wings, sketching. Ginger James, the producer, saw her and asked her to walk across the stage. He offered her the job and her friend missed out. Although she never had a dancing lesson, she worked at the Tivoli for the next ten years and even learnt to skate for *The Ice Follies*.

Just before Christmas, I made a major and what I thought

would be a life-changing decision. I moved into a house in Gardenvale with John Pease. It was life changing for me inasmuch as I learnt a whole lot about myself that I didn't like: that the world didn't revolve just around me and that saying you cared about someone was not enough. It took many, many years for me to deal with these issues. As much as I loved John, and with the best intentions of making it work I was emotionally immature and too scarred from my childhood to have the kind of relationship I knew he wanted. He was very patient with me and hoped that I would settle down. He'd been married and expected a similar kind of bonding in our relationship. I behaved very badly; I was very demanding and selfish. I was out of work and I became bored and restless. I felt marooned and isolated in Gardenvale. Our relationship was all about me. John became exhausted by my tantrums and temper. Eventually he told me he wanted to end our friendship and that he was giving up the house we were living in. I felt pretty bad for quite a while after this experience; my pride had been hurt and I knew that I had deliberately destroyed a relationship that I needed and wanted. On reflection, that relationship was the first stage of the dismantling of the protective walls I had built around myself. That I actually cared as much for John as I did and admitted it to myself was a major breakthrough in my becoming an adult.

After we broke up, I stayed with Ivor for a few days. Then I made a reappearance at Mark Street temporarily. It was always temporarily. Mumma asked me why I was unhappy and I told her what had happened with John. She said perceptively, 'Maybe you're growing up at last.'

Mumma gave me a watch for my twenty-first birthday. It was gold and had small fake ruby and emerald numerals. I didn't really like it but I didn't want to hurt her feelings. I knew that she had saved up for the whole year to buy it. I waited until the New Year and then I asked her if she would mind if I changed it for something simpler in design. I told her I was afraid someone might steal it if they thought the rubies and emeralds were real.

Mumma was getting older and no longer able to drink as much as she had in the past. Her binges now lasted days instead of weeks and were not as destructive. In fact, we had our first sober Christmas at Mark Street that year and I got a glimpse of what life might have been for all of us in a world without alcohol.

Nine

In 1955 the *Herald* began running a series of articles telling everyone why they should invite a foreigner into their homes the following year. There was a fear that there would not be enough hotel rooms in the city to accommodate all the expected crowds for the Melbourne Olympics.

That year also saw the emergence of a housewife from suburban Moonee Ponds who was destined for fame and fortune. Her name was Mrs Edna Everage aka Barry Humphries. Barry and Noel Ferrier did an hilarious send-up of the *Herald* articles in a sketch called 'Olympic Hostess' in a University revue that year. I think this was Edna's professional debut. There was not one Australian who didn't have a relative or know someone 'just like Edna'. No one who saw that first airing of Edna has ever forgotten it. It transcended drag. We were all watching a real person. This was when I first met Barry. Not that we became friends, but the theatre scene being as small as it was in Melbourne, I saw quite a lot of him. Later on, I danced with both his first and second wives and appeared in a revue for ABC television with him. In the seventies he collected Art Deco and was a client of my gallery in London.

Ray Lawler's play *Summer of the Seventeenth Doll* premiered at the Union Theatre that year. It was a huge success. After years of listening to fake British and American accents, the audience heard actors who sounded just like them as they told their story of ordinary Aussie blokes and sheilas.

The big event in Melbourne in 1956 was the Olympics. They wiped the world news off the front pages of all the local newspapers. We only heard about the Hungarian uprising being put down by the Russians when their respective water polo teams had a bloody battle in the Olympic pool. The Tivoli Theatre staged a big glittering revue called *The Olympic Follies* starring Darval and Julia, an acrobatic duo. It was the first program televised live by Channel Seven.

Kismet was well into rehearsals at the Princess Theatre and a friend of mine was one of the dancers. She sneaked me into the Gods to watch a dress rehearsal. It was by any standards the best production of a musical I had seen. American director Burry Fredrik and Lisa Brionda, who had been the ballet mistress for the London production, faithfully re-created the original. I was totally in awe of Hayes Gordon's acting and singing as Hajj the beggar. I had seen him in *Kiss Me Kate* at Her Majesty's Theatre in 1952 and was impressed but that day I thought he was phenomenal. At the end of the rehearsal while I was waiting at the stage door Hayes came out. I went up to him and said, 'Excuse me, I want to act like you. Where can I learn?' If I had thought about it beforehand my shyness would have taken over and I would not have approached him. He asked me what I did. I told him I was an out of work dancer and he said he needed a dresser. He added that if I worked for him he would teach me. I went to the Wardrobe and introduced myself to the wardrobe mistress,

Madame Beddoes, and told her that Hayes had asked me to be his dresser.

Hayes was a disciple of the Stanislavsky method of acting that was made popular in America by the Group Theatre and Lee Strasberg at the Actor's Studio. The Method, as it was nicknamed, involved being able to totally recall past events in one's life and use the emotions that the memories evoked to prepare for whichever part one was to play. It was ridiculed by comedians and quite a few well-known actors. The comics did bad impersonations of Marlon Brando's mumbling performance in Tennessee Williams' *A Streetcar Named Desire* and the actors said they didn't need it. I did: it opened so many doors in my subconscious that not only helped me to become a better actor but also made me think a great deal about my life and myself.

Once again I thought about the night my ancestors spoke to me in Pentridge Gaol. I could hear them telling me to be strong and to wait. Having found the life they spoke to me about in *Paint Your Wagon*, my meeting Hayes confirmed their words of advice and I knew that whatever happened from now on this was all I wanted to do. If I failed to make the most of the opportunities that were presenting themselves to me I would have no one but myself to blame. For the next four years I was consumed with a passion to learn as much as I could.

Hayes told me many times that this was only one method of learning to act, and that I needed to have my voice trained properly. I started having singing lessons with Joan Arnold at the Melbourne Conservatorium. She was very encouraging and I enjoyed our lessons but I was extremely nervous singing for an audience. Even after I had made my debut as a singer in the West End in 1966 I was still never comfortable singing at auditions. I think it was the memory of my father singing and what he represented in my life that impeded the development of my singing career.

Subconsciously I would judge and execute myself before I walked on stage.

Lisa Brionda, the choreographer, gave the dancers a ballet class every day that I was allowed to attend and twice a week she worked with me on my speaking voice. I was treated more like a member of the company than a dresser and I got on very well with Mrs Carroll, wife of the theatre's owner, Garnet Carroll. As Kitty Elliot, Mrs Carroll was a well-known juvenile performer. In the 1920s she changed her name to Kitty Stewart and appeared in many musicals including *Rose Marie* with Stephanie Deste and *Show Boat*. She was more or less responsible for me working on and off at the Princess Theatre for the next five years. The day I auditioned for *Bells Are Ringing,* I heard her say to the English director Stanley Willis-Croft, 'Take the tall dark boy on the end; we always use him.'

My acting lessons with Hayes were different to what I expected. There was no emphasis on elocution. The lesson began the moment I walked into his dressing room. After I laid his costume out he made me sit down and watch him prepare. I was not allowed to talk. He explained to me that this was where his performance began. First, he did a series of vocal exercises and physical stretches. Then he applied his make-up. I saw him gradually change. He would ask me questions as his character and I quickly learnt to improvise the answers. By the time I had helped him into his opening costume he had literally become Hajj the beggar. He introduced me to the plays of Chekhov and chose whole scenes for me to study as homework. On matinee days in between shows, he gave classes for the dancers. This way of developing a character came easily to me and I had no trouble letting 'it all hang out' but a lot of people had great difficulty opening themselves up. In the class situation we were encouraged to criticise each other and this often led to tears and bitter arguments. Hayes was having a live-in affair with Clarissa Knipe (her stage name), one of the speciality dancers in the show. Her background was as a contortionist in circus and vaudeville. She was in love with Hayes and his 'method'. She became a reasonably good actress and played Mick Jagger's mother in the film of *Ned Kelly*. She later married British actor James Mason.

Hayes was my Svengali; once under his spell I became an acolyte. He had an immense ego but unlike a lot of other egos in the theatre he had an immense talent to go with it. He was very demanding, almost to the point of eccentricity. He expected perfection and total professionalism from all his fellow workers, including me. He hated alcohol and he had many heated arguments with his American leading lady, Morgan St John, when he smelt it on her breath. He often talked to me about growing up in Boston and the tough times he and his family went through when he was a young man. I think this is why he understood the complexity of my personality at that time. He became very passionate when he talked about his mentors Lee Strasberg and Sandford Meisner and he was even more passionate when he talked about politics in America. He was in a production of *Show Boat* when he found out that members of the black chorus were being paid less than their white counterparts. He complained to Actors Equity. Furthermore he had refused to sign the loyalty oath in the post war forties. I asked him why. He said it was a matter of principle; he could not and would not name any of his friends that may or may not have had leftist sympathies. This almost certainly ended his career on Broadway. He gave me the plays of Clifford Odets, one of the founders of Group Theatre, for my birthday.

Hayes founded the Ensemble Theatre in Sydney in 1958 and many of Australia's leading actors owe him their careers. All my work with him helped me considerably with my first audition as an actor in London. I read for a small part in *Oh Dad, Poor Dad* by Arthur Kopit. The director Frank Corsaro had worked with Lee Strasberg at the Actors Studio in New York, and the leading lady was the legendary Stella Adler. After several auditions, which were all improvised, I got the part and I became the assistant to the movement director Lee Becker. Lee had played Anybody's in the original production of *West Side Story* on Broadway. I met another young actor named Steven Berkoff at the auditions. He, too, had been successful.

When I returned to Australia in 1991, I heard that Hayes had suffered several heart attacks and was not very well. I telephoned him and said that as we had not seen each other for thirty years, it would be great if we could get together again. He replied, 'We won't get maudlin about the past, will we?' We never did get together again and he died in 1999. He was a great humanist and a great teacher.

After *Kismet* opened, I moved out of Mark Street and into a house in Hoddle Street, Collingwood, with my friends John Taylor and Joyce Bruce. John and Joyce both worked in the office of the Princess Theatre and had been friends when they were both younger and lived in Adelaide. We rented the top floor of the house from Tina Bethel, a well-known writer of radio plays and serials. Tina was crippled from the waist down. She chain smoked and drank endless cups of instant coffee. The walls of her part of the house were covered with works by all the then well-known but not yet famous painters. Laurie Hope, who recently had a retrospective at the Heide Gallery and who lived at one time in Uncle Leo's house in Carlton was one I remember. She gave me a painting of a woman and baby by Ian Fairweather to hang on my bedroom wall. She had a succession of young lovers, mainly rough trade and my imagination ran wild as to how they made love.

Ian Westcott, an actor writer and radio presenter, was co-writing a serial with Tina. He was tall, flamboyant, outrageous, arrogant, wildly promiscuous and utterly charming. An inveterate gambler, he used to take me to the races with him on Saturdays when I wasn't working. We had known each other since my street days. He too had a penchant for rough trade and street boys. Bunney Brooke and I were in a serial he wrote for radio called *At Noon on Saturday*. Later, he wrote many revue sketches for Mary and me.

When *Kismet* ended its very successful run we gave up the house in Hoddle Street. John went to England to work for producer Robert Stigwood, Joyce returned to live in Adelaide and I found a room in a house in St Kilda. I got a small part as the court stenographer in *Witness for the Prosecution* at the Princess Theatre starring English actors Philip Stainton, Noel Howlett and Sir Donald Wolfit's daughter Margaret. The play only lasted until November and then I was out of work again. I was having private ballet lessons, tap lessons, singing lessons and I needed to pay for them. I needed to get a job quickly.

I found a job at 'Macs, The Happy Home Furnishers' on the second floor of the Astoria building in Flinders Lane. I enjoyed the work enormously. My boss told me that I was being considered for a junior executive position and in a short but dazzling career I was promoted to Dispatch Manager. A very old friend of mine Bruce McBrien, who was the manager of the kitchen, carpet and lino department wrote to me recently and said he remembered me dancing from his department, to mine. Everyone has a story to tell about my dancing. I don't think I ever stood still in those years; I danced everywhere, I was free, like a bird on the wing. My life was bubbling along very smoothly: I had a job, a room, some money, clothes and I had apologised to John Pease. We were trying again only this time we thought it best not to live together. He had a small flat in South Yarra.

I joined the Cid Elwood amateur operatic company in Moonee Ponds. Cid gave me the part of Rafaello Carboni in his musical about the Eureka Stockade called *Strike It Rich*. Cid was very likeable. He owned a catering business that freed him up to do the things he really loved doing—teaching singing, and performing. He taught a number of good singers in Melbourne and almost everyone in his company had either worked as professionals or wanted to. Some of the artists to have gained their early experience with the company were Betna Pontin, winner of the Sun Aria competition, Justine Rettick and Robert Simmonds, who both went on to have successful operatic careers, and Nance Grant, winner of the highly prestigious Mobil contest for 1957. Winning this same competition in 1950 set a young Joan Sutherland on her dazzling road to stardom. By its tenth anniversary the company had donated more than £10 000 ($30 000) to the Burwood Boys' Home, Essendon Rotary, the Lions and other local charities. Cid wrote, directed and performed in a number of his own shows. I would never have got the opportunity to play a role as big as Carboni in a professional production. The part was a challenge for me and I flung myself into it with great enthusiasm. The company also performed the standard repertoire of operettas for amateur companies, *Maid of the Mountains, Desert Song, Lilac Domino* and *Rio Rita*. Occasionally asked to direct for a professional management, Cid would cast it from members of his company, which consisted of some fifty performers and an orchestra. That happened with *Show Boat*, which he directed for the National Theatre at the Tivoli Theatre in Melbourne in 1963. I was home from London at the time and Cid asked me to be in the production.

I made a lot of friends in Cid's company. Judy Hooke was one. A plumpish jovial girl and a natural comedienne, she had recently moved to Melbourne from Geelong, where there was a thriving amateur theatre scene, a light opera and musical company with an orchestra and several straight theatre groups. Judy, who wanted to have a career in the professional theatre and television, got a job at Woolworths on the cosmetics counter. I convinced her that she would look great with a streak of colour in her hair. A month later, she was a platinum blonde. I met her mother and sister Pat who also came down to Melbourne. They were very kind to me and I knew I could always stay at their house when I was broke or out of work.

I charmed everyone in the company, particularly the women, who seemed to know I always needed feeding and vied to make my favourite cakes. For one reason or another I sensed I was still a threat to a lot of the male members of the company. The wives and girlfriends of the cast made the costumes for Cid's productions and their men built the sets. Consequently the standard of the production values was always very high. We rehearsed three nights a week for three months. The show played at the Essendon Town Hall in August for one week and another week at the Box Hill Town Hall in October.

That December Mary Hardy landed the leading role in the Rodgers and Hammerstein version of *Peter Pan* at the Princess Theatre. Midway into rehearsals the rights were withdrawn. John Carroll, son of Kitty and Garnet, collaborated with his secretary, June Lansell, and together they wrote a new book with new lyrics almost overnight. Bruce George was engaged to write the score. 'Never Never Land' was only one of the memorable songs he wrote for Mary. Bruce, his wife, Peg, and I were good friends. After Peter Pan, he wrote *Ballad of Angels Alley*, an excellent musical about Melbourne at the turn of the century. We started rehearsing a production of it at the New Theatre in Flinders Street but we had money and cast problems and it never got off the ground. We last met when he played the piano for a night club act John Muirhead and I were in on the island of Ibiza in 1967.

Mary had a big success in *Peter Pan* and got rave reviews but at the end of January she was out of work as the show only ran for the holiday season. She got a job at Berlei, the manufacturers of ladies' lingerie. Her office in Degraves Street was a stone's throw from my office. We met every morning for coffee and spent most of the day on the telephone to each other. We were both very happy with our day jobs and doing amateur work at night. We were in a production of *The Heiress* for Eddie Clements. His little company was probably the number one amateur group in the inner suburbs. This was the way we all learnt our craft. In those days there were no drama schools like NIDA (National Institute of Dramatic Art) or the VCA (Victorian College of the Arts). You just got on stage and did it. With so little paid theatre in Melbourne, amateur companies were reviewed by the newspaper critics in a highly professional manner.

I saw Barry Humphries and Peter O'Shaughnessy in *Waiting for Godot* at the Arrow Theatre. Barry was hypnotic on stage; he had the ability to hold an audience indefinitely during the long pauses in the dialogue. He was also hypnotic off stage. In fact, he appeared to be performing all the time. When he spoke his eyes seemed to pierce your head and his voice cut through the air. He was the first male I knew to wear his hair long at a time when short back and sides was the fashion.

The year of 1957 was hailed as a milestone in the Australian theatre. *Summer of the Seventeenth Doll,* co-presented by the Australian Elizabethan Trust, won the critics' award in London and put Australian theatre on the world map. Visiting actors from overseas also came to Australia. I saw Margaret Rutherford, Dame Sybil Thorndike, Sir Lewis Casson, Emrys Jones, Leo McKern, Jessie Mathews and Margot Fonteyn. They fired my imagination and my desire to go overseas. Paul Rogers played Hamlet in Hugh Hunt's production for the Elizabethan Trust. He so impressed me that I bought the collected works of Shakespeare and learnt two of the long soliloquies. The Elizabethan Trust was formed in 1954 to commemorate the royal visit. Its aim was to present the best of overseas opera and drama to an Australian audience and also encourage Australian writers. The first production was Terence Rattigan's *The Sleeping Prince*, an English play with an English director and cast. So much for encouraging Australian talent.

I was totally obsessed with the theatre and didn't have time for much else. I went everywhere and saw everything. I was making up for lost time.

The highlight of 1957 for Mary and me was the arrival in Melbourne of Sydney actor Edward Brayshaw. He was extremely good looking and an actor of exceptional talent. He made his Melbourne debut at the Little Theatre in *One Bright Day*. It didn't take very long for Teddy to be the most sought-after young actor in town and he was snapped up by Wal Cherry for the Melbourne Theatre Company. He had a great personality and was charm personified. Mary had a huge crush on him that I think lasted her entire life. For his work in *Traveller without Luggage* he won the 'Agon' award for best performance of the week. Agon was the theatre critic for the *Listener in TV*, a weekly newspaper that listed the radio and television programs and all the usual gossip about the stars. He headed his review 'Brayshaw Arrives'. Mary and I sent Teddy a telegram that said 'BUT THERE WAS NO ONE THERE TO MEET HIM'. He didn't think it was very funny and it took us a week to convince him that we were only joking. He went to England in the early sixties where he had a moderately successful career. We saw each other quite often, usually at the actors' dole office in Chadwick Street. He died from an AIDS-related disease in the late eighties.

In February 1958, Mary telephoned me from her office to tell me that open auditions for the American musical *Bells Are Ringing* were advertised in the *Listener in TV*. We took the afternoon off to go to the auditions at the Princess Theatre. The director was Stanley Willis Croft from England and the choreographer was ballet dancer Rex Reid. Mary and I thought both of them were wrong for this production. How right we were.

Mary was given the understudy to the highly talented English singer and actress Shani Wallis, and I played one of the dancers and understudied Noel Hardres, the principal dancer. After the auditions Mary and I went for tea and congratulated ourselves for being so talented. We also wanted to discuss how we were going to give notice at our respective jobs. I decided to tell my boss that my family were going to Sydney and that they wanted me to go with them. Mary gave a different version of the same story to her boss. The manager was very understanding and I felt a little bit guilty taking the farewell present from the staff and the letter of reference from my boss.

The rehearsal period for *Bells Are Ringing* went smoothly enough and I was given the part of the Hollywood actor Paul Arnold. Shani was not Mrs Carroll's idea of a glamorous visiting star, even though her credentials were impeccable. She 'stopped the show' as the princess in *Call Me Madam* at London's Coliseum Theatre and starring opposite Sam Wannamaker in *Finian's Rainbow.* However, her appearance and attitude off stage were more East End than West End. The first night was a total disaster. The opening scene was set on a revolving stage. The front half was a New York subway with some of the chorus and dancers and the back half was a party in the apartment of the leading man with the rest of the chorus and dancers. The opening number went quite well but in the blackout the revolve got stuck. The orchestra played the lead-in music for the party scene several times and in the silence that followed all the audience heard was, 'I'll turn the fucking thing.' It was big Jack, one of the stagehands. He gave the stage a shove and it turned so fast that it flung the furniture and the cast onto the stage and nearly into the orchestra pit. The audience applauded very loudly but each scene change was more disastrous than its predecessor and by interval most of them had walked out. They should have stayed.

The big party scene with all the girls in white evening gowns posed around a fountain was the highlight of the show. The orchestra played the intro and the lights and fountain were timed to come on at the same time. They did, only the force of the jets in the fountain was too strong and sprayed everyone on the stage before it could be turned off. I could hear the audience laughing but I couldn't see what was happening. I was standing behind the door waiting to make my big entrance. As I walked on stage and said my one line—'Hey Miss Scott, it's great to be here'—the set collapsed. By the time we got to the final scene, Shani was in tears but the audience loved her and when she sang the opening line to her last song—'I'm going back to where I can be me'—everyone in the theatre stood and cheered.

Mumma was in the audience. She came to all my first nights and was not beyond giving me a little advice: 'Smile more, don't get lost in the background, make more of your dialogue,' etc. She already knew Mary and some of my other friends in the theatre and felt comfortable with them. I could tell that she was very proud of my achievements. Sometimes the atmosphere would prompt memories of the past and occasionally she would drop little bits of information about my father: 'When your father danced he glided across the floor,' or 'Did I ever tell you that he was one of the first people to demonstrate the tango in Australia in the mid twenties?' Other times one of my old street mates who had given up his former life would arrive at the theatre with his wife or girlfriend and we would go out for supper.

Bells Are Ringing closed after a few weeks but luckily I was asked to be in a new production called *On the Move*. This was the first live industrial show to be produced in Australia and was designed to introduce and and sell the new Massey Ferguson MF 67 tractor. Stanley Willis Croft devised the scripts and directed the show and we were allowed to use the costumes from *Bells Are Ringing*. Each weekend we were flown by Ansett, who advertised the new tractor on their inflight menus, to a different capital city to perform. It was great fun but very hard work. Massey Ferguson took over the Hilton Hotel or the equivalent in each city for their two hundred guests—the farmers and tractor sales people in each state. We arrived on Friday morning, had a rehearsal in the theatre, checked the sound in the ballroom and then prepared for the action. This started with a cocktail party where we met all the MF people, as we called them, and was followed by dinner and a few speeches.

The girls wore their white cocktail frocks from *Bells Are Ringing* and I wore the white tuxedo I had worn as Paul Arnold. I felt very suave and sophisticated. In each of the guest's room was the schedule of the weekend events and a bottle of fake laxatives with a label that said 'On the Move with Massey Ferguson'. Next morning at 7.30 am, Jeannie Ross and I greeted the guests by singing 'Good Morning' to them as they came into the dining room. After breakfast, they were taken by bus to the theatre where we performed a series of sketches about the new tractor.

Ken Warne and I had great difficulty keeping a straight face during our sketch. He played my father and I had to say to him, 'Dad, I'm having a lot of trouble with my big end,' and he had to reply, 'Massey Ferguson are here to take care of that son.' Shani was furious when she discovered that the tractor was billed in the program as the star of the show and it took a lot of talking from Stanley to stop her from walking out.

In the afternoon, the men were taken to a field and given a demonstration of the new tractor and their wives were taken to a fashion parade. Another cocktail party and a formal dinner where we entertained with a cabaret ended the festivities for me in Perth. I flew back to Melbourne on Sunday afternoon because on Monday morning I had to go to an understudy rehearsal at the Princess. I had been contracted to understudy one of the leads in *Salad Days* which followed *Bells Are Ringing* into the Princess.

Mary was also an understudy. I don't know what would have happened if the actor I was covering had been ill while I was in Perth. No one had thought about that possibility.

That was the year my passion for football almost got me the sack. It is impossible to be born and raised in Melbourne and not be interested in Aussie Rules football, a hybrid of Gaelic football and rugby. Every Saturday afternoon during the winter months, Melbournians in their thousands armed with beer and meat pies doused with tomato sauce head for the football ground. There is nothing to compare with the sound of eighty-five thousand voices all calling for the death of the umpire.

We were scheduled to have a matinee on the same public holiday afternoon that my team, the Demons, were to play their arch rivals Collingwood. My barracking for the Demons started when I found out that Bluey Truscott had played for them before World War II. Mary knew that I would try almost anything to get to the game and warned me not to do it. I ignored her of course. I went to the stage manager and told him I wasn't feeling very well. He asked me to wait until all the cast were in the theatre and then told me to go home and rest up for the evening performance. I waited until the half hour call and made sure everyone was in. Then I left the theatre and went straight to the Melbourne Cricket Ground where my friends had saved a seat for me. These were people I had met during my amateur days and others who I saw every Saturday afternoon.

It was a great game and a minute or so before the final whistle the Demons were down by five points. Defeat was staring us in the face when Bluey Adams passed the ball to our hero, the legendary Ron Barassi; he kicked a goal and we won by a point. In the excitement I jumped up on my seat and started waving my scarf. That evening when I arrived at the theatre I was met by the stage manager who was holding a copy of the *Herald* with a photograph of me at the game on the front page. Had this been any city other than Melbourne I would have lost my job but here, where football is a religion, I got off with a warning.

Salad Days was very successful and a second company was formed to tour country Australia. I stayed in Melbourne because *Anniversary Waltz*, starring Richard Arlen, was coming to the Princess Theatre and I was asked by Mrs Carroll if I would like to be Mr Arlen's dresser and look after him. Richard Arlen had been a famous Hollywood star of silent films. He was absolutely charming, still very good looking and appeared to be a lot younger than he actually was. Looking after him meant keeping him off the whisky during the performance.

The first thing he would say to me when he came into the dressing room was, 'Gimme a belt, Noel.' After a while I started watering the whisky down, which helped considerably. He would talk to me for hours in his hotel room after the performance. He loved to tell me about the early days of Hollywood and I loved to listen. He always ordered a large supper for me and a bottle of whisky for himself. I heard all about his affairs with Lupe Velez, the 'Mexican Spitfire', and Clara Bow, the 'It Girl'. Eventually he would pass out and I would go home. *Anniversary Waltz* was a slight frothy bit of nonsense. In the cast were Pat McDonald, Ian Westcott, Bruce Wishart and comedienne Barbara Wyndon.

Barbara had been one of the stars of the Phillip Street revues and won the Sydney Critics' Award for best female musical performer in 1955. She liked to party and this was very much a party cast. She introduced us all to a friend of hers who she referred to as the Baroness or Madam. I learnt in time that Madam was the more appropriate title. She was English, very tall, beautifully dressed and wore a turban. She told me that she had been an alcoholic during her modelling days in London. Now she was addicted to Relaxa Tabs, a 'downer' that could be bought anywhere. So many uppers and downers that are considered dangerous today could be bought at chemists without prescription in the fifties.

She often nodded off when we were all at the club. Alcohol was still illegal in most restaurants but we knew places like Johnny the Greek's café in Londsdale Street where we could order a special coffee laced with brandy. It was such an icon that I'm sure the police turned a blind eye to what was going on.

The Baroness and Pat had their eyes on Mr Arlen but he was not at all interested in either of them. He had been very happily married for many, many years. Madam offered me the spare room in her flat in South Yarra rent free. This would help me save some money to get out of Australia.

I had learnt quite early on that being a dancer or an understudy would not get me very far in my career and I knew that would be my lot if I stayed here, especially with my background. I doubted very much if I would ever be accepted by the Melbourne theatre establishment. Some people still made remarks about my trial while others either ignored me or put me down. My reaction to this was to be louder and more insulting than they were. I knew I had to go somewhere where I wasn't known and England seemed the most logical place. There, I could continue my studies and be totally accepted for my work.

I became very fond of Madam. She told me something of her past, which was bizarre. As improbable as it sounded I hoped it was true. If it wasn't, I thought it deserved full marks for invention. She said her real name was Fiona Pitt-Rivers and that she been educated at Rodean, a very posh English girls' school. When she was seventeen she became pregnant to the son of her mother's gardener. To save her reputation, her mother married her off to an impoverished British aristocrat whom she divorced a few years later. She then became a model for the fashion designer Norman Hartnell and married another impoverished aristocrat, Baron von Dyjas. She said she was so drunk on her wedding night that she got into bed with the best man by mistake. The Baron was a freedom fighter and pilot and was killed towards the end of the war. She emigrated to Australia in the mid fifties.

I soon discovered that she was a high class courtesan. Some people would have said prostitute but she had too much class to be called that. She told all her friends that I was her nephew and that she was raising me. I don't know how old they thought I was but one 'uncle' from the bush always brought me a cricket bat or a football and sometimes he would leave an envelope under my pillow with a pound note in it for my pocket money at school.

She told me she needed help with one of her friends. She called all her clients 'friends'. After she explained the situation, I told her Ivor was the ideal person for the kind of help she needed. I introduced them and they got on like long-lost sisters. He had become very spiritual and was preparing to go to a Buddhist monastery in Ceylon. Whenever I complained about something he would say, 'Take a deep breath and transcend it, dear.' Her 'friend' was a leading Melbourne barrister and a cross dresser. Every Friday he would arrive at the flat in his big chauffeur-driven car. Once inside he would change into whatever new creation Fiona had bought for him. Usually it was something very expensive from Magg of Toorak, owned by Zara Holt, wife of the prime minister to be, Harold Holt. Once dressed, the 'friend' and Ivor, who had also dressed for the occasion, would be served tea by the maid, played to perfection by Fiona. Then the three of them would go for a chauffeur-driven ride through the Botanical Gardens. Only when they returned to the flat and changed their clothes was I introduced to the friend, but not by his real name. Fiona would say, 'Darling, I want you to meet a good friend of Aunty's.' Part of the arrangement was that she got to keep the clothes. Although I knew what was going on, I never saw anything untoward happening in the flat and Fiona never discussed her business with me. When she was temporarily broke she would say to me, 'Darling, Aunty needs some red or blue paper' (meaning ten or five pound notes). 'Do you have any?'

She went into a private Catholic hospital to have her breasts lifted. On the second night she rang me at two in the morning and asked to bring her some Relaxa Tabs. I had to climb the fire escape to get to her room and avoid the nuns at the same time. She was certainly given to eccentric behaviour. She had this habit when she was stoned of putting on more and more eye make-up, nodding into the mascara as she did it. We had a Spanish woman who came twice a week to clean the flat. One morning she couldn't come and sent her sister in her place. When the young woman arrived at the flat she rang the door bell and Fiona, who had just showered, opened the door and stood there stark naked and said, 'Yes dear, and what can I do for you?' The girl shrieked, crossed herself and fled.

In the meantime, *Anniversary Waltz* was forced to end its season earlier than expected at the Princess because of Mr Arlen's 'illness'. The theatre had arranged for his wife to meet him in Hawaii. I put him on the plane at Essendon airport and I was really sad to see him go.

I wasn't out of work for very long. Lisa Brionda stayed on in Melbourne after *Kismet* closed to create the choreography for a major television spectacular on Channel Nine called *The Hit Parade of 1958*. Number one on the hit parade that year was 'Jamaica Farewell' sung by Harry Belafonte and Lisa asked me to perform it. I had to sit on a rum barrel on the deck of a banana boat against a back projection of Montego Bay and mime his recording. Rehearsals were running overtime and I didn't have a final run-through. When it came to my spot the soundtrack was turned on and everyone in the studio started laughing. At first I thought they were laughing at me until I looked up at the monitor and saw that the stagehands had forgotten to place the prow of the boat on the set and it looked like I was sitting on the rum barrel bouncing up and down on the waves in the middle of the bay. This was live television and there was no stopping and starting again. Thankfully the cameraman had the sense to move in and I finished the number in a tight close-up shot of my head and shoulders.

Ten

The year 1958 was a relatively good year for me. I worked a lot but for very little or no money and my savings disappeared fast. I was living at Mark Street again and enjoyed being home with Mumma. I auditioned for the part of Crooks the negro in John Steinbeck's play *Of Mice and Men* at the Union Theatre. The Union Theatre Repertory Company was established at Melbourne University in 1953 under the direction of John Sumner . . . Wal Cherry was arguably the best director in Australia at that time and I really wanted to work for him but I was far too young for the part.

The famous black American dancer Katherine Dunham and her troupe came to the Tivoli in a revue called *Tropical Holiday*. I was stunned by the Afro–American music and dancing. The vitality and expertise of the dancers in everything from voodoo and folkloric to contemporary American jazz was a revelation to me and I wanted to learn how to do it. I also wanted to meet the dancers. They were all very beautiful and I could tell from their demeanour that they had no problems with their blackness. I presented myself to Miss Dunham the same way I had to Hayes Gordon. I waited at the stage door for her and when she came out I told her I wanted to learn her style of dancing. She asked me about my background and I told her as much about my black inheritance as I knew at that time. She invited me to take her classes. She called me her 'high yaller' friend, an Americanism for mixed black and white blood. I did classes every morning with the company. Mary Hardy insisted that I looked like a young Miss D and that was why she let me take her classes.

Katherine Dunham was the first black dancer to achieve personal fame and elevate black performing arts in America. She appeared in several films in the thirties and forties with Lena Horne, Dorothy Dandridge and other black film stars. In 1945, she opened the first Dunham School of Dance and Theatre in the heart of the New York theatre district. The school also offered classes in Spanish, French, Anthropology, West Indian Folk Culture, Music, Semantics and Design. Although past her prime technically as a dancer, when she performed here she still had a very commanding presence on stage and a magnificent partner in Vanoye Aitken.

Bruce Wishart, the actor who played Mr Arlen's son in *Anniversary Waltz*, took over the lease on an old church hall in Blanch Street, St Kilda, and called it the Arlen Theatre. Apparently Mr Arlen had promised to help Bruce financially with the project but the cheque he gave Bruce bounced. The cast of the first revue, *Off the Beach*, was Mary, Bruce, Paul Karo, Beris Sullivan, John Muirhead, Margaret Horsely, daughter of the well-known singing teacher, Josie Keen and myself. Bruce was the director, I was the choreographer and John Michael Howson and Ian Westcott wrote most of the sketches. Friends helped to make the costumes and the sets were very minimal.

I had a big row with Mary the first day of rehearsals. I was setting the opening number and she said, 'I can't do that.' I mimicked her voice and replied, 'Can't, can't can't. That's the story of your life!' After a few heated exchanges mimicking each other everyone became hysterical and we all collapsed laughing.

The critics weren't very kind to us. Their reviews ran from 'New theatre opens with a misfire' to 'Talented cast in patch play'. None of us were being paid. John Muirhead had kept his job at Robertson & Mullens Bookstore but Mary and I were broke. Judy Hooke joined us at the Arlen for the second revue, *Further off the Beach*. We did our own publicity: we borrowed a flat top truck, put a piano on it and drove around the shopping centres in St Kilda performing numbers from the show. This fared better with the critics, but we still weren't making any money.

However, we were nothing if not resourceful. The big hit on television was a team show called *Having Fun with Charades* on Channel Seven. Mary, Judy, John Muirhead and I formed the Arlen Team to challenge the winners. We won and became the longest surviving team. The very small fee we were paid each week fed us. Bruce was writing a lot for children's television and he used the cast from the Arlen as much as he possibly could. He wrote a series called *Madelaine's Music Box* for Madelaine Burke, presenter of children's television, Young Seven. I was in the first program, 'Momma'.

I had been appearing regularly on children's television since 1957. Many of Melbourne's actors got a lot of their early experience working on children's television. Barry Humphries played the legendary Australian monster, the bunyip, on one program.

Live television was nerve-racking. I had two very alarming experiences. The first was in a production of *Beauty and the Beast*, which Bruce had written. I played the father, Mary and Judy played the stepsisters, Paul Karo played the Beast and Beris Sullivan was Beauty. In the first episode I had to make a long speech to Beris about 'being carried away on the wings of the night wind'. I was halfway through it when Beris started crying and ran off camera, leaving me to improvise her dialogue as well. Our English director, David Baker, was completely unfazed. Instead of getting angry with her he told her he was looking forward to the next episode. Nothing fazed him. I think he would have done a children's version of *Ben Hur* if he'd thought of it. Not only was he unflappable, he was friendly—he called everyone buddy—and open to new ideas. I suggested to him that I could dramatise six Aboriginal legends for Young Seven if I had an actor and eight dancers. He loved the idea. Anne Frazer designed one backdrop for the six episodes. Dave filled the studio with the branches of gumtrees that he chopped down himself. In one story I needed a boy's face reflected in a billabong or small waterhole. Dave improvised with one camera on a baby's bathtub filled with water and another camera on the boy's face. These were exciting days for all of us. Everyone was experimenting.

I was cast as the juvenile lead in a play for ABC Television by Alun Owen called *The Hot Potato Boy*. Making her Australian acting debut and playing an Asian servant was a young girl who had recently arrived from England named Julia Blake. She has since had a long and distinguished career in Australia, winning many awards for her stage, film and television performances. Like most of Alun Owen's plays this one was about class. The plot was about a young British naval officer (me), son of an admiral, marrying the daughter of a merchant sea captain. During the engagement dinner on board ship the candles in the floral arrangement in the centre of the table burnt down and set fire to the plastic flowers. When the captain made the toast to the young couple the cast raised their glasses then ceremoniously emptied the contents onto the flames and put the fire out. Once again, clever camera work helped enormously to cover the blaze.

The cast of the Arlen were invited to appear as part of a

charity evening in aid of the Actors' Benevolent Fund at the Little Theatre in St Martins Lane, South Yarra, to celebrate its twenty-eighth anniversary. The set for the evening was the opening scene from their current smash hit, *Dr Jekyll and Mister Hyde*, starring the irrepressible and idiosyncratic Melbourne actor Frank Thring. John Truscott, who had given up acting, had created the design, a replica of Victorian London.

We were the first half of the program and the second half was the English star of the thirties Jessie Matthews who had first come to Australia for a production of *Larger than Life* at the Princess Theatre in 1952. Standing under one of John Truscott's East End gaslights, wearing a glittering red evening gown, with fog covering the stage floor, she gave one of the most memorable performances I have ever seen. She sang all the songs she had made famous when she was the darling of British stage and film.

After seeing her performance I embarked on a serious study of period musicals and plays. This interest led me to being asked to create the choreography for Sandy Wilson's twenties' pastiche musical *The Boy Friend* in 1967 and later open my gallery, L'Odeon, in Chelsea.

Frank Thring was one of Australia's best known and most flamboyant actors. Born into a wealthy Melbourne family, his father was F.W. Thring, an important entrepreneur in Australia's entertainment business. He was responsible for building eight Hoyts Regent theatres, including the palatial Regent in Collins Street where I and my alter ego Rohan Scott-Rowan spent many happy Saturday nights. Frank began his career as a radio actor and later performed at the Little Theatre. He founded the Arrow Theatre company in Middle Park in 1951 and by the time the company closed in 1954 he had staged twenty-two productions. He was outstanding as Herod in Oscar Wilde's *Salome*, a performance he re-created at the Q Theatre at Kew Bridge in London. The production later transferred to St Martins Theatre in the West End. He joined the Royal Shakespeare Memorial Theatre Company and appeared in Peter Brook's production of *Titus Andronicus* with Vivien Leigh and Laurence Olivier. He was the ideal choice for the roles he played in such epic films as *Ben Hur, The Vikings* and *El Cid*. He was a great party giver and host and had a way of saying '*Darling*' that engulfed everyone within earshot.

I did a lot of revues in and around Melbourne; I even did one at the Woomera rocket range in the desert of South Australia with well-known Melbourne actor John Finlayson. I had previously worked with John in various musicals at the Princess Theatre. He wrote a sketch about two camp astronauts knitting in their spare time. We thought it was very funny, but when we performed it no one laughed. At the reception afterwards I asked a woman standing next to me why no one thought the sketch was funny. She turned to me and said under her breath, 'We have some of them up here and we don't think they're funny at all.'

I was enjoying the work I was doing and I was delighted that I was making real friends in the theatre. But I was still uneasy about who I was. I thought about it all the time. What if these people knew the real me and my origins? Would they still accept me? When I looked in the mirror I didn't see an 'Abo' or any other black man for that matter. Outwardly, I had distanced myself from all things Aboriginal and black, yet I still harboured a deep resentment in my heart for everything that white Australians stood for. I couldn't forgive all those people who had abused, misused and called me a little black bastard.

Then something happened that year that made me aware of the rumblings of dissent among certain Aboriginals. It was only a whisper but I heard it. There were many Aboriginals of my colouring who passed for white and were prepared to blend into society. Why be ostracised and abused if you don't have to be? I was very aware of my own black heritage and what I felt for

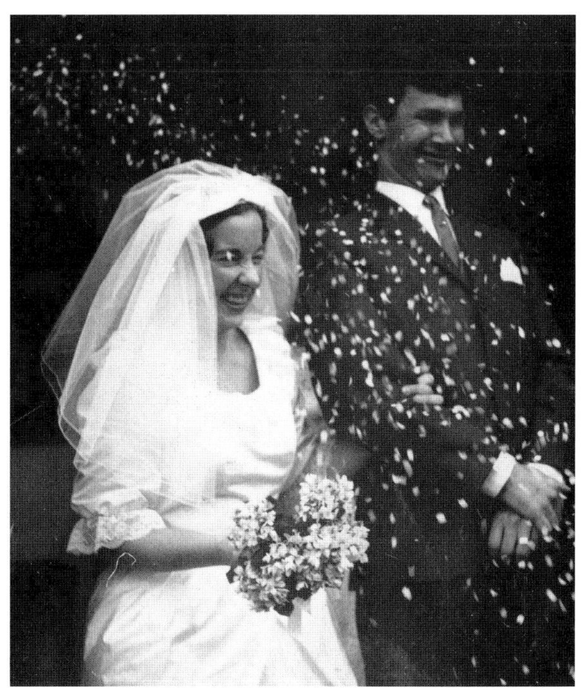

On our wedding day — August 1960.

My mother with Barbara, Station Pier, Melbourne, 1960.

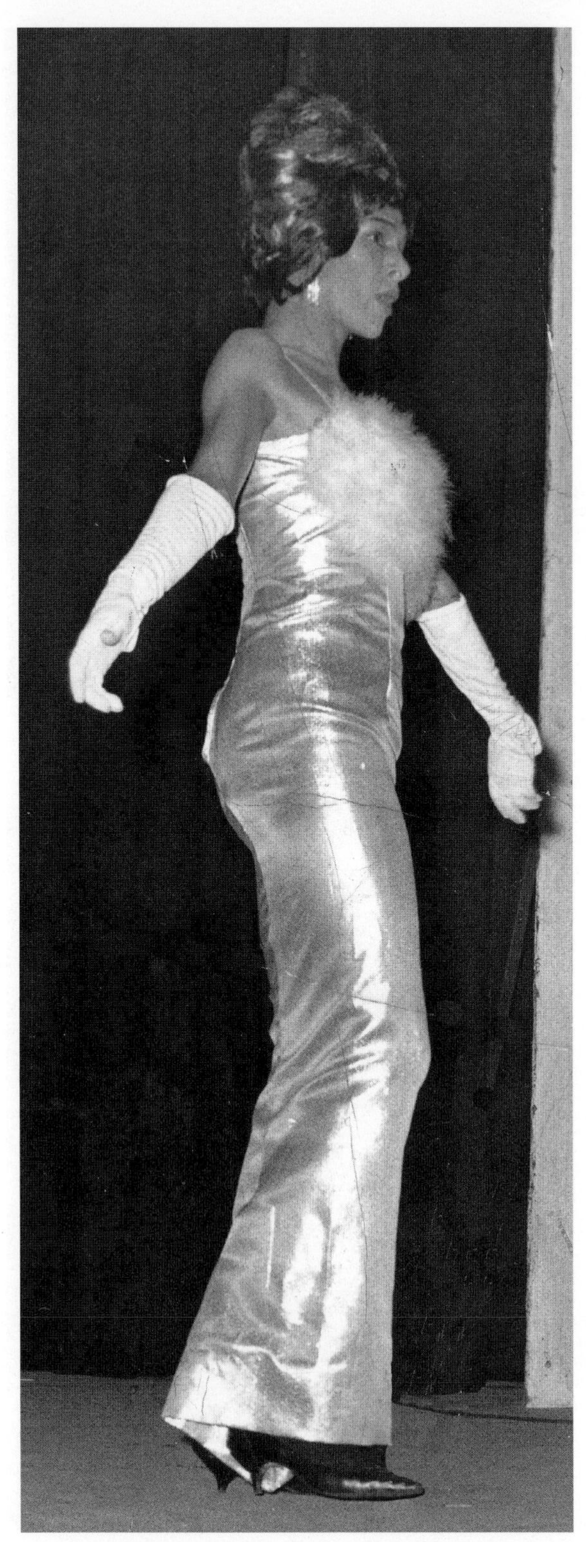

As Shirley Bassey in *Shush*, London, 1961.

A long way from Burren Junction — in London, 1961 (Princess Margaret's house is in the background).

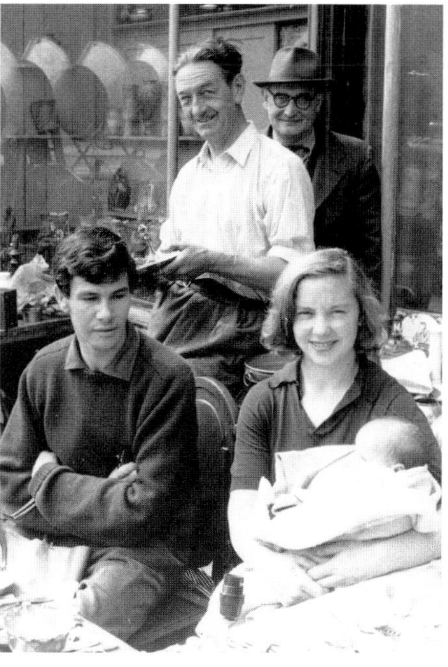

In Bob's Second Hand Shop, Clapham Road, London, 1961. Barb (and Felicity) and me in the front, Bob standing behind us.

With Dave and Pattie Harrison in the early 1970s.

Ice skating in Austria — 1967.

With Camilla Powell at her coming out party, 1961. Julia Box on the right.

With Trish, announcing our engagement backstage at the Comedy Theatre, London, 1967.

Dave and dogs in Wales, 1982.

My brother Frank in 1983.

The last Christmas photo before Mumma died. From left: Damian, Bev, Mumma, Fred, Greta and me.

Photo of the cast and team of *The Aboriginal Protestors*, Sydney 1996.

Congratulating Larissa Berendt on receiving her law degree from Harvard University (the first Aboriginal to do so) in 1999. Justine Saunders is on the right.

Making the keynote address on the steps of the Opera House to launch the Gay and Lesbian Mardi Gras in 1996.

Portrait taken by Michael Brogan for the Festival of the Dreaming, 1997.

what white Australia was doing to its first peoples was only exacerbated by what I read in the newspapers. Other Aboriginals were defying the law and behaving like they were human beings or, even worse, Australian citizens. Well-known Aboriginal artist Albert Namatjira was arrested in Alice Springs for supplying alcohol to other Aboriginals and sentenced to six months' hard labour. He fought the case in both the High Court and the Supreme Court. He lost the appeals but his sentence was reduced to three months in Papunya Native Reserve. He was granted remission for good behaviour and spent two months there.

Albert was born in 1902 into the Arrente community at the Hermannsburg Lutheran Mission in the Northern Territory. He was initiated at the age of thirteen and became a full law man. He met Australian artist Rex Battarbee in 1934 when Rex visited Hermannsburg. Namatjira accompanied Battarbee on his painting trips around the area. On one of these trips Albert did a landscape painting using Battarbee's watercolours and a mug of cold tea. Battarbee was convinced that Albert could be a fine artist and began tutoring him. With the help of his friend and tutor Albert had his first exhibition in Melbourne in 1938. The exhibition was a sell out. This led to others in Sydney and Adelaide. Albert now had money; first he tried to buy a cattle station, then he tried to build a house in Alice Springs but could not get around the Aboriginal's Ordinance Law. Here was a man whose work was admired by the Queen of England, considered an important Australian artist, treated like a celebrity and yet not allowed to own his own house because he was an Aboriginal. He was probably the first Aboriginal to be recognised by white Australians. Come the 50s his work had been denigrated by the art of printmaking and bad prints of his work appeared everywhere. In 1957, he and his wife became the first Aboriginals to be granted full citizenship rights. He could now vote, live where he wished and was able to purchase alcohol. All too late: after two months in prison he had lost the desire to live and he died in 1959.

When I read his obituary in the newspaper I was sad and bitter. I didn't identify with him but it did make me wonder if this was the sort of racism that my father would have been subjected to. Intellectually, I wasn't equipped to deal with my feelings at all, so I repressed them. I told myself, forget them and they'll go away.

Come November, I began rehearsals for the pantomime *Aladdin* at the Princess Theatre. The star was Graham Kennedy, the unchallenged king of Melbourne television and host of the popular series *In Melbourne Tonight* on Channel Nine. He'd already had a very successful radio program and his transition to television was equally successful. Graham had a genius for comedy. *In Melbourne Tonight* ran for many years.

There is a scene in *Aladdin* when Widow Twankey rubs the magic lamp for the first time. The genie appears and asks her what her wish is. In our production she replied, 'I'd love to see *In Melbourne Tonight* dear.' In a flash and a cloud of smoke a giant cut-out of a television set appeared with Graham and his sidekick, Joff Ellen, behind it. They did a half hour comedy spot. That was Graham's first and only stage appearance in his long career.

I was doing two performances a day playing one of the comic policemen in *Aladdin* and the revue at the Arlen in the evening. Life was really good for Madam Fiona and me. She had a very rich Japanese lover and John Pease and I had discovered a suitable level on which to enjoy our relationship. I was certainly more adult and he understood me a lot better. I saw him whenever I was working at Channel Seven and we would go out for a meal somewhere. I was still very fond of him; he was solid and sensible, the complete antithesis of me at this time—I still spent most of my earnings on clothes instead of saving—and I could talk to him about whatever particular problem I was having that day. Physically, he was the only male I had found it comfortable and compatible to be with.

At the end of the final performance of *Aladdin,* I had a rather heated row with John Carroll on the stage. The cast list for the next production, *Auntie Mame,* had been put on the noticeboard just before we all went on stage for the finale. Several members of the cast who thought they would be in it were not on the list. It didn't concern me because I was preparing for another revue at the Arlen and my tap teacher, Betty Meddings, had offered me a job with Channel Seven television to appear in *Sunnyside Up,* a weekly variety program she choreographed. While John was making a very pompous speech of thanks to the cast for *Aladdin,* two girls standing next to me were crying. I told him I thought he had no feelings and that I wasn't interested in his speech and walked off stage. Everyone assumed I would never work for him again.

Just after Christmas, Fiona told me she was giving up the flat and going to Sydney for business. She asked me to go with her but I wanted to stay in Melbourne. I saw her again two years later after a performance of *Music Man* at the Princess Theatre. She arrived at the door of my dressing room with an American naval officer who introduced himself as 'your new Uncle Bud'. We had supper at the Florentino restaurant and she told me that they were going to live in Seattle. That was the last time I saw her.

Ivor went to a Buddhist monastery in Ceylon and I didn't see him again until 1969. I had devised, directed and choreographed the first professional drag revue in London for club owner Paul Raymond. The show, which I called *Birds of a Feather*, was quite spectacular as Paul had given me a huge budget and carte blanche. All my early movie going in Melbourne and my love of movie musicals influenced my style. I engaged Bobby St John Roper and Todd Kingman to design the sets and costumes and I had more stairs and feathers than *The Ziegfield Follies*, which is exactly what I wanted my show to look like. Bobby and Todd had both designed for the Palladium and The Talk of The Town revues. I had eight of the top drag acts from Europe and America. The star was American Riki Renee. There were twelve 'chorus girls' and my own group of boys who were known as the Noel Tovey Dancers. The production singer was Kenny Day and I engaged a relatively unknown comedian named Larry Grayson. The show made him a big star. We opened at the Royalty Theatre in the West End to very mixed reviews. I thought it was judged morally and not artistically.

One reviewer in the evening papers said, 'I'll never forgive Noel Tovey for making me believe there were twenty beautiful girls on stage at the Royalty Theatre last night.' Paul and I both knew the show was way before its time and that it would be a big gamble for him. Ivor read about the show in a gay magazine in San Francisco where he had become some sort of guru. He came to London to see me, looking like Edith Sitwell in his kaftan.

When Fiona went to Sydney I moved back to Uncle Leo's. He hadn't changed at all since I lived there several years ago. Cousin Lil taught me to play some Irish songs on the ukelele and we sang duets. Uncle Leo took me with him on his button rounds and introduced me to his clients. Cousin Lil spent all her time writing. I think she knew then that she was seriously ill but she never said anything to anyone about it.

The first time I had any inkling about her health was when she wrote to me in 1961 and told me that she was bringing Leonie and Otto to London to discuss the possibility of a film being made of her book *The Delinquents*. It had been published by Gollancz and received very good reviews in the English press. Kenneth Allsop writing in the *Times Literary Supplement* said, 'It was a minor *Tristan and Isolde*'. I was working at the Olympia

Theatre in Dublin at the time. After they found a flat in North End Road, Cousin Lil came to see me. We climbed the hills and ate soda bread, stood on the O'Connell Street bridge and visited the post office, which still bore the scars of the Easter 1917 uprising. Just after she returned to London, she was admitted to hospital for more tests and a few weeks later the family returned to Melbourne. She died from cancer in 1963, aged thirty-six.

1959 was a momentous year for me and many other Australians: Edouard Borovansky died and Aboriginal actor Robert Tudawali was imprisoned in Darwin for six months for providing a fellow Aboriginal named Moses with alcohol. In a written statement Judge Kriewaldt said, 'I have had the benefit of evidence from Chief Welfare Officer Mr Evans, that Tudawali had been in contact with whites most of his life and has lived in Darwin since childhood. He must have been fully aware that he was breaking a law not only supplying Moses with liquor but also in drinking it himself. The evil the legislature is trying to suppress is the consumption of liquor by Aboriginals.' His statement ends with, 'There was no blood or tribal relationship between Tudawali and Moses so the compliance of an Aboriginal custom (*sharing all possessions*) can have little bearing.'

Tudawali had been discovered by film director Charles Chauvel who cast him as Marbuck in *Jedda* in 1955. The film was a serious attempt at telling a story about two fullblood Aboriginals who are in love but separated by their own culture. Tudawali was acclaimed for his performance but he had great difficulty coming to terms with ordinary life after the success and fame he found as an actor. In 1965, he moved from Bagot Reserve to Wave Hill in the Northern Territory. He worked there as a stockman and became the spokesman for the Gurinji people when they went on strike for better living conditions and pay. He died in 1967 in a grass fire lit by a cigarette that fell from his hand while he was asleep.

I was more disturbed by that article than I was by the news of Boro's death. Every time I read something like this I went through emotional turmoil. My anger was directed at white society in general. I still couldn't understand their treatment of Aboriginals. The draconian alcohol laws that targeted tribal and traditional Aboriginals were not enforced in the same way on urban Aboriginals. Anyone with a mixture of white and black blood like me was not officially considered Aboriginal. We were called half caste, octaroon and quadroon.

I got a part in the musical *Once upon a Mattress* at the Princess Theatre. Everyone in the cast knew about my row the previous January with John Carroll and they all expected me to get the sack when he returned from England. To his credit the first thing he did when he arrived at the theatre was to come on stage at the break and tell me in front of the cast how happy he was that I was there working for the family again.

Playing the role that made Carol Burnett a star on Broadway was Gloria Dawn. She was the consummate performer, a huge talent and a superstar. There was no big ego or nonsense. She would sit in the stalls of the theatre with her blonde hair in curlers knitting something for the baby. She looked like any suburban housewife until the moment she was called on stage. Then it was like the big overhead crystal chandelier had been suddenly switched on. There was absolutely nothing Gloria couldn't do. It takes a lot of talent to totally command the attention of all one's fellow performers and she did just that at every performance. In the cast playing the court jester was Johnny Hunter who I had last seen as a female impersonator in the Kiwis at the Comedy Theatre in 1948.

George Carden, who had left Australia when he was a young dancer, came home from London to direct and choreograph the production. He was now the choreographer for the London Palladium and independent television. It was George who encouraged me to go to London. Mary and I were in a late night revue at the Arts Theatre in Richmond. George came to a performance on Friday night. At rehearsal on Saturday morning in the coffee break he told me that I reminded him of a young Jack Buchanan, the English revue star, and added that he thought revue was definitely my métier. He suggested I go to London and look for work and even promised to give me a job. London in the fifties was the Mecca of intimate revue.

Joy Mudge, an actress and producer, opened the tiny Arts Theatre with a very successful production of *The Male Animal* by James Thurber. Phillip Stainton, with whom I had worked in *Witness for the Prosecution,* was the director. He was very well known in England and had appeared in some forty-five films in various character roles. He opened the first bona fide drama school in Australia at the theatre.

Ian Westcott was the brains behind the supper revue venture and it was this that really put the theatre on the must-go-to list. This is how it was described in an article in the *Listener in TV* in October 1959:

> *. . . murky Richmond side Street and up a dim lit double flight of stairs go some of the top names in TV and show business each Friday night. After supper and some gossip in the small lounge they file into a 90 seat theatre, stalls only, and take their place among the audience. It's the stars' favourite night for relaxing.*

Ian wrote a very funny sketch for Mary and me about an extremely bad act we had all seen at the Tivoli. Mary's line, 'I'm the lovely Pilita Ole', became a catchphrase around town. Wynne Austin wrote a solo for me called 'A Little Piece of Thring', a wicked send-up of Frank, who was now the theatre critic for the *TV Times*. Frank had a very distinctive voice that I could mimic perfectly. *Beauty and the Beast* had been such a success that it was screened again while we were rehearsing for the revue and Frank wrote in his column:

> A tiny word of praise for David Baker of HSV7 for trying to inject a little originality into that company's children's session. It is a little early to be repeating *Beauty and the Beast* but it was and is very good, and accompanied by a slight musical sketch featuring David Mitchell, Paul Karo and Noel Tovey with Mary Hardy thrown in for good measure, it certainly gave the show a lift.

The Arlen Theatre closed before *Once upon a Mattress* opened. By this time we had built up a small audience of regulars and we were making enough money to pay ourselves a salary. Bruce hired a friend of his to look after the box office but instead of paying the bills she and the takings disappeared. Mary, John Muirhead and I were on stage doing a sketch the night a truck pulled up outside the theatre and four very large men started repossessing the seats. The audience remained and sat on the floor.

We had a very successful season of *Once upon a Mattress* at the Princess and I was resolute in my effort to save my fare and go to England.

When the show closed I got a job working for Bunney Brooke and her girlfriend Dodie in their coffee lounge, Prompt Corner, at the top end of Collins Street. I was their cook. The menu was very basic. Apart from the usual toast, crumpets and pastries, there was steak and chips with a salad, Wiener schnitzel and, on Friday, fish and chips. Bunney was pregnant at the time and there was much speculation as to who the father was. I never did find out and the interest waned after the baby was born. Dodie made coffee that was truly appalling. She filled a large stockpot with cold water and when it reached boiling point, she threw in a few handfuls of coffee. The pot sat there simmering all day with Dodie adding water and coffee from time to time. Every Sunday evening Bunney held play readings. Admission was the price of a cup of coffee. Many actors, including myself, got the opportunity to read a lot of parts we would never have been cast in. A number of articles have been written about the various talents of Germaine Greer—indeed, she has said and written a lot about herself—but I have never seen anything written about her outstanding acting ability. Had she chosen, she could have been a fine actress. We did a reading of *Tea and Sympathy* one Sunday night and she was terrific. I saw a lot of her at that time. Lusillo and his Spanish dancers were performing at the Comedy Theatre and I was lucky enough to be allowed to take flamenco classes with the company. Germaine had a crush on one of the dancers and was never very far from the theatre. She and Mary had many similarities and they knew each other very well. Both of them lived in Gardenvale near the convent where Germaine went to school. They both had razor-sharp tongues and spared nothing or no one to get the last laugh. I saw her intermittently when I was in London. She came to the first night of an all-Australian revue I was involved in and I saw her demolish the American right wing politician William Buckley in a live televised debate from Oxford College shortly after I arrived in London in the very late sixties.

Bunney somehow got enough money to form a production company and took over the small National Theatre in East Melbourne. The first production was *Frenzy*, starring Frank Thring. Bunney asked me to be in the second production, Carson McCullers' play *Member of the Wedding*. Mary played Frankie the fourteen-year-old. A young John Stewart played John Henry and Bunney played Bernice the negro housekeeper in a black face. I played the negro junkie Honey Camden Brown and John Truscott designed a superbly realistic set. Rehearsals were fine with both Mary and Bunney keeping their egos and tempers in check.

On the opening night everyone gave outstanding performances, particularly Mary and young John. The critics heaped praise on both of them, John Truscott's set and the production. The *Listener in TV* review 4 September 1959 said: 'Bunney Brooke's production of Carson McCullers' prize winning play *Member of the Wedding* at the National Theatre is something that every lover of good theatre should see.' I got very favourable notices for my role too. One reviewer said, 'Noel Tovey as the young restless negro Honey rises splendidly to the one powerfully dramatic moment that comes his way.' When I read that I felt that at long last I had arrived as an actor on the Melbourne theatre scene. But how ironic that it should be playing a negro.

Bunney was also well reviewed but she was clearly not as happy and excited as we were when she came to the theatre for the second performance. I think everyone telling her how great Mary had been the night before seriously disturbed her. She called Mary and me into her dressing room and said very sarcastically, 'Don't let the reviews go to your head, my dears!'

From that moment on it was daggers drawn between Mary and Bunney. They tried to upstage each other at every move. During Mary's first long speech, Bunney crossed her legs and jiggled the slipper on the end of her right foot distractingly. In her second long speech, Mary picked up the carving knife on the kitchen table and held it so close to Bunney's face that she had to sit quite still. Had it not been so tragic it would have been funny. What should have been a success and an enjoyable venture turned into a bitter, acrimonious affair.

That production was the turning point in Mary's career. Director John Sumner came to see her playing Frankie and asked her to join the Melbourne Theatre Company at the Union Theatre. She gave several splendid performances there. She was outstanding in *Moby Dick Rehearsed* by Orson Welles, playing opposite Frank Thring, and the newspapers hailed her as the new Zoe Caldwell.

Bunney gave up her production company and returned to Prompt Corner. A young girl named Barbara worked there part time in the evening washing dishes. She became my best friend and confidante. I told her about my ambitions in the theatre and introduced her to John Pease who was a regular at the café.

Our relationship was slowly coming to an end but we were still close friends. I was very comfortable with who I was now and grateful to John for all his input into my life. Barbara introduced me to her friend Chris Pearl; his mother was a cooking expert and his father was the editor and author Cyril Pearl. Most of Barbara's friends were pretty young homosexual men from Toorak and South Yarra. Her mother and father had divorced and both had remarried. She told me that she wasn't happy living at home, which is why she was working in the evenings. She worked during the day as a stenographer for a law firm in Collins Street. I suggested she come with me to England. She agreed but said it would be difficult to arrange. Planning our escape reminded me of the days Bev and I planned our escapes from Burren, only this time I knew I could do it.

In January 1960 I was in a revue for radio station ABC TV called *Once More with Fooling*. I was paid £22, my biggest pay packet yet, and most of it went into my escape fund.

When *Once upon a Mattress* closed I was employed by John Carroll for the new American musical *Music Man*, which was to open on 4 March at the Princess Theatre. I gave up working at Prompt Corner. Barbara stayed on washing dishes. We saw a lot of each other and continued to make plans for our big trip to Europe. On Sunday afternoons we met in the city and walked to the Botanical Gardens. On one of our walks I said I thought we should get married. She agreed. I knew she cared for me and I certainly cared a lot for her. We had a great deal of mutual trust and affection for each other. I had no compunction about taking her to Mark Street to meet Mumma. They became very fond of each other. I simply assumed that I could make our marriage work and I gave no thought to the hidden demons still lurking within me.

We decided we would leave for England later in the year on an Italian boat the *Aurelia*. That would give us enough time to get married and save £98 each for the fare. I was indefatigable; I ran everywhere. Barbara made me some shirts for the voyage. In a few months we would be gone, away from Mark Street and Australia and into a new life in Europe. I was so elated and optimistic that it never occurred to me that we would arrive in England practically penniless. Everything that I and Rohan Scott-Rowan had ever dreamt about or imagined when we were young was about to come true. I still said my prayers in the evening. Maybe God had finally heard.

The stars of *Music Man* were Americans Carolyn Maye and Ted Scott. The choreographer, Harding Dorn, was also American. He had been contracted to play the sixteen-year-old character Tommy. He was far too old to play the part and his thinning dyed black hair didn't help. On Monday morning the dancers arrived early at the rehearsal studio. He arrived late. There were none of the usual pleasantries of the first morning ritual. He began the day using extremely foul language and by mid morning he had reduced most of the girls to tears with his insults. I was the deputy for Actors' Equity. I had been a member of Equity since the day I started work in *Paint Your Wagon* and I experienced my first strike when the chorus and dancers demanded more pay. From that time on I was aware of politics and the rights of the chorus. So I wasn't going to let my friends and fellow union members be spoken to like that by anybody. I didn't care who he was. We all grew up in the theatre in Australia believing that anyone imported was automatically better than us. Everyone except me, that is. I had known too many fakes and I still had a very cocky attitude towards people who thought they were my superior.

I called a halt to the rehearsal. I turned and said to him, 'I don't know how you treat your dancers in America but here in Australia we don't swear at them the way you are swearing at us. Either you apologise to the girls or we are leaving right now.' I asked everyone to collect their things and we stood our ground and waited for him to make the next move. Sweating profusely; he was very nervous. He made a big show of apologising and I made a joke about him playing a sixteen-year-old. Everyone laughed and the ice was broken. By opening night, we had all become friends. And this was the happiest company I had worked in so far. There was only one hiccup which I had forgotten about until just recently.

It was a matinee day and I was making tea. The boys were discussing the Sharpeville massacre in South Africa, in which police had opened fire on a black crowd demonstrating against apartheid laws. I pretended I wasn't listening because I didn't want to betray myself by showing my true anti-white feelings. They only showed themselves at times like this but they were always there not too far from the surface. Growing up hadn't changed anything in that respect. One of the male singers said rather facetiously, 'Kill them all!' I turned on him and in a violent show of anger I threatened to throw the jug of boiling water I was holding over him. A few months ago in 2002, he saw me being interviewed on *The Message Stick* program and wrote me the following letter

> Seeing the impassioned account of your childhood, and seeing the way you have risen above adversity and developed into the respected, talented and distinguished gentleman you are, has prompted me to express how pleased I am to have known you and to have shared those mostly happy times in *Music*

> *Man.* There is something that has always been of some concern to me, and I have often hoped to set the record straight. It was the day of the Soweto murders and I started to say, in a sarcastic criticism of those events, 'That's right, shoot them down and you will reap a blood bath in South Africa.' Unfortunately, I only got the first five words out and you shouted, 'Shut up Ames, you are lucky you didn't get this jug of boiling water over your head.' You would not listen to any further explanation and stormed out of the dressing room. As you can see, I have always been sorry for this misunderstanding, and whether or not you even thought about this matter again or not, I wanted you to know I did, with sorrow.

Mea culpa. I include this letter because it has illustrated for me the number of years that I spent hearing only what I wanted to hear. I was so defensive and protective of my black inheritance that I thought everyone was against me because of it.

The understudy to Carolyn Maye was Maureen Howard. She was a biggish girl with the highest beehive hairdo in Melbourne and a very strong Australian accent. The first time she went on for Carolyn we all rushed into the wings to watch her performance. We were all curious as to how she would cope playing a role that was so American. There were quite a few who thought she couldn't do it. We witnessed the complete metamorphosis from suburban chorus girl to star. Out of her mouth came a singing voice so glorious that we were shocked into silence. Maureen became one of Australia's leading sopranos with the fledgling Australian Opera Company and one can only speculate as to what her career might have been had she too gone overseas.

The year 1960 was a great year for singers and dancers in Melbourne. The chorus, always considered the minor members of the business, were nevertheless the backbone of every musical production. All in all, more than a hundred of us were employed that year in *My Fair Lady* at Her Majesty's, *Lions, Ladies and Laughter* at the Tivoli and *Music Man* at the Princess.

Each company had a social committee that organised functions where everyone met up. These outings and functions were an antidote to the boredom that can creep into a long-running production. By now I was no longer shy or backward in coming forward and I was on our committee. We arranged a crazy hat party that we held at a church hall in East Melbourne after the second show on a Saturday night. It was great fun and everyone made a big effort with their hats. Mine won first prize. It was a mad confection that I called 'Ladies night out'. I found an old black picture hat and a pair of elbow-length gloves that I stuffed and sewed onto the brim. I attached a champagne glass and a very long cigarette holder, complete with smoking cigarette, to one hand and some playing cards to the other.

Every so often during the evening I noticed a dancer from *My Fair Lady* sitting at the piano. He didn't seem to be enjoying the festivities at all. I went over to the piano and introduced myself to him. He said his name was Peter and that he was from Sydney. He was painfully shy, which is a strange affliction for a dancer but one that I understood very well. That meeting led to a friendship that has lasted more than forty years. I took him to South Africa in 1969 as my assistant on a production of *The Boy Friend*. It was his sense of humour and ability to make a mockery of the apartheid laws that kept me focused on the job at hand and the success of the production.

After that first encounter he asked me to meet him on Monday morning. Over coffee I asked him if he knew about my trouble with the police in Melbourne. He admitted he'd heard the boys in the dressing room talking about me. Apparently my notorious reputation was still with me. He said he wasn't happy living in Australia, nor was he happy in *My Fair Lady*. Some of the same boys who had given me a hard time in *Paint Your Wagon* were in his dressing room. I gave him a long talking-to about how to deal with them. My advice was, take no nonsense and strike first. Almost instantly his attitude changed. Confidence is an elusive quality to acquire but once caught and harnessed it can work miracles. My years of hard work and my belief in my abilities as a performer, as well as the advice of my ancestral spirits had made me quite confident. Peter told me many years later that he felt like I had let him out of prison.

I know he walked into the dressing room that evening a changed person. He told the boys and one or two of the girls what he thought of them. In his diary he wrote, 'Noel Tovey was right, slap first and they'll respect you.' I told him Barbara and I were getting married and asked him if he would like to be my best man. A few weeks later we asked him to come to London with us. He said he didn't have enough money so we offered to pay the deposit on the ticket and I told him he had several months to save the rest.

We saw a lot of each other over the next few months; he was as excited about going away as Barbara and I were. Most nights we would meet Mary Hardy and Teddy Brayshaw at the Danish Delight for supper. Teddy was also planning a trip to London but Mary was on the crest of a big wave and wanted to stay in Melbourne.

We were coming home from yet another party at Ian Westcott's flat a couple of Saturday nights later when it started raining. We ran to the nearest bus shelter and while we were waiting for the rain to stop Peter said, 'I have something to tell you.' I recently asked him to write in his own words what had happened to him. These are his words:

> I wanted to go to the loo. When I walked into the brightly lit lavatory on the concourse of North Sydney station there was only one other man there. He was about twenty-six, in a shirt

> that was fashionable then. It was 'Guy Mitchell Blue' and he wore it outside his pants. I glanced at him briefly as I stood there. He was about three urinals away. He was tanned and good looking. He gave me an intimate smile, then pulled back and showed me what he had been concealing behind the porcelain wall—his big excited member that he was stroking. The fear that went through me was greater than any desire and I pulled quickly away from the urinal and crossed the room to the wash basin. He walked up to me and said, 'Vice Squad, you're under arrest.' I was taken to North Sydney police station and charged with 'behaving in an offensive manner' and my fingerprints were taken. On Monday morning I went to court and when the judge asked me how I wanted to plead, I said, 'I don't know. I didn't do the things they said but I think I'm homosexual.' I was fined £5 and advised to see a priest and my doctor and have treatment.

He became very upset as he recounted his story. I assured him that homosexuality was no longer a crime in England and that he would be able to live whatever sort of life he wanted to there. He laughed when I told him that I thought that we were the only two Australians who weren't fucked up.

I didn't want to leave Melbourne with any unfinished business so I tried to get in touch with the people who had been important to me over the years, to say goodbye. I had lunch with John Pease and thanked him for his years of love, friendship and support. He was genuinely pleased that Barbara and I were getting married and leaving Australia. I wanted to contact Chesca to tell her that in a few months I would be sitting in a café on the Left Bank of Paris, but I no longer had an address for her. She moved away from Melbourne shortly after *Paint Your Wagon* opened and we lost touch with each other.

For all my flamboyancy and apparent indiscretions there was

one secret I kept hidden from everyone in Melbourne. My friendship with Kenn Brodziak was a long, happy, sometimes intimate and always amusing one. We first met when I was in *Paint Your Wagon* but we didn't get together until I started working at the Princess Theatre. He invited me home for supper after a performance of *Kismet*. In 1956, I stayed the night and our secret relationship began. It had to be secret because he was the director of Aztec Services and Garnet Carroll's business partner. No one would have understood our friendship even if it had been a straight one. He was as passionate about food as he was the theatre. He always returned from London and New York with tins of exotic food for me and recordings of all the latest musicals on Broadway. I had dinner with him before I left Australia. We laughed a lot as we always did. Half-jokingly I said to him, 'I won't see you again until I make it.' Thirty-five years later I saw him at the opening of *Miss Saigon* in Sydney. He looked at me and said, 'Well, you said you'd do it, and you did.'

Barbara introduced me to her family. We went to her grandmother's for Sunday tea. She shared a large thirties' mock Spanish house with her sister Vi in Kew. It was very big inside—four bedrooms, dining and living rooms and a large kitchen. I learnt later that they didn't get on and only spoke to each other when they had visitors. Her younger sister, Penny, was also there. None of them knew that we had planned to get married. Muzzie, the girls' nickname for their grandmother when they were little, was extremely pleasant; she smoked a lot, drank endless cups of tea and ate very little. Our first meeting went smoothly enough. After tea, we were joined by two old friends of hers, Uncle Chas, a Catholic priest, and his sister, and we played penny poker.

I met Barbara's mother once when she picked me up from the airport in her Singer sports car after I'd returned from a job in Sydney. She was a pretty woman with long auburn hair. She had obviously lived the good life and looked the quintessential

Melbourne socialite in her little black dress, pearls and a mink coat. I was a bit alarmed when she opened the glove compartment of the car, took out a bottle of whisky and swigged it while she was driving. Barbara had told her we were getting married and her reaction was, 'You *sleep* with boys like Noel. You don't *marry* them.' Barbara's father did not like me at all; one meeting at his flat in Toorak was enough for both of us. He was very tall and reminded me of one of the detectives who arrested me on that fateful night in 1951.

Now that everyone knew our plans, life did not get easier. My brother Fred had his first short story published in the *Bulletin* and I was very proud of his achievement. I took a copy of the magazine to Muzzie's to show them. They noticed that we had different surnames so I had to explain our illegitimate beginnings and the reason why Fred had changed his name to our father's by deed poll.

The following week Barbara's stepfather and mother gave her a dossier on me. They had hired a private detective who obviously found nothing under the name Tovey but a search under the name Morton revealed all. Barbara explained to them that I had told her everything there was to know about me and my family. Of course, there were parts of my chilhood and early teens that I didn't tell her about. I thought at the time that I would never have to talk about those days again to anyone. The dossier contained mostly the articles about my trial. I was still considered by many to be notorious seven years after the event and I can't deny that I contributed to this popular belief by my arrogant, free-wheeling behaviour and scathing tongue. However, I had put the trial so far behind me that I had temporarily forgotten it. Barbara's parents tried to dissuade her from going ahead with the marriage but to no avail; we were far too busy with inoculations and passports and arranging the wedding to let anyone bother us or interfere with our plans. Luckily, Reuben Fineberg stepped in to help when it looked like our wedding would be a disaster. He was the associate musical director of *Music Man,* and our friend. He had studied the piano with Yascha Spivakovsy and was something of a prodigy. He invited us to his parents' house for dinner. They were charming and Reuben offered to give Barbara away and they even held a reception for us in their home.

Barbara had asked her friend from work, Kay, to be her matron of honour. She and her husband, Don, said we could stay with them for the few days after the wedding before our boat sailed. I bought a new grey suit and Bars had a short off-white silk dress made. All was set for the big event.

On 4 August 1960, Rueben and Peter walked me to the church of St Thomas Aquinas in South Yarra where Barbara and I were married. The church was filled with all our friends from the different theatres. Not one relative was there. Mumma had busted the week before and was feeling crook, I hadn't seen Bev for several years and Barbara's family were not in the least interested. Her father must have felt that I had handed him the ultimate insult. Not only was his daughter marrying me, but she was about to be given away by a Jew in a Catholic church.

After the wedding and the reception at the Finebergs, we returned to Don and Kay's flat. A few days later we took a taxi to Mark Street and collected Mumma, who insisted on coming down to Port Melbourne to see us off. I have a technicolour memory of the moment the taxi turned the corner to enter the port. It was a cold late spring morning, the sky was pale blue and reflected in the water, which was as flat as a mirror. The *Aurelia* was docked at the pier. Everything was so still it reminded me of a painting. Suddenly I was woken from my reverie by the hustle and bustle of the crowds. I felt like I had swallowed a whole bottle of Dex tablets; I couldn't sit still. All I could think of was, this is it, I'm getting out and leaving twenty-six years of abuse, intolerance and racism behind me. Peter almost missed the boat. He had to go the Taxation Office before coming to the pier. There was a mix up with his papers and he almost didn't make it.

Our cabins were in the bowels of the boat. This was a one class tourist ship and we had paid the cheapest fare. We came back up top and found a taxi for Mumma and said goodbye. I've never liked farewells and I didn't want her to stay down at the pier by herself. I think she was upset and pleased, both at the same time, to see us leaving. We could see quite a few people we knew on board and a lot of people had come down to Port Melbourne to see us off. We were very loud and very theatrical. Everyone was calling each other 'darling'.

Also on board was a group of young English boys returning home who were taking great delight in calling us a bunch of poofs. Peter said that he thought they could be a nuisance once the ship got under way. I went up to the loudest of them and asked him to follow me. His friends thought it was a hoot and made all the appropriate remarks and innuendo. I took him behind the smokestack and in the vernacular of my street days I told him that if I heard him or any of his friends call me a poof once more I would beat the shit out of all of them. Once again, the tactic worked and they became part of our mob and helped us carry out all sorts of pranks on the rest of the passengers and crew.

Jane Casson, an actress I knew, and her mother, Patricia, were on board. Jane had been in a production of *The Chalk Garden* with her grandmother, the famous English actress Dame Sybil Thorndike, at the Comedy Theatre. Between us, we organised everything on board: the concert, fancy dress ball, the deck games competition and who sat at the captain's table for dinner.

We had a great time on the ship and got up to all sorts of pranks. Teddy Brayshaw and Mary Hardy had given me a box with a 'don't open until on board' label on it. In the box was a starting pistol in the shape of a revolver with a box of blank shells. The card with it read, 'If it doesn't work out in London, use this.' Our best prank was one evening when we waited until we thought everyone was in bed. Jane called out, 'Don't do it, John. I'm sorry.' I fired two rounds of the starting pistol, Peter screamed at the top of his voice and then we hid. No one found out that we were to blame for the late night search of all the cabins.

I remember we were standing on the deck very early one morning and I turned to Barbara, Peter and Jane and said, 'Africa is over there. I can feel it.' The mist lifted and there it was rising out of the sea, the land of my paternal ancestors. After four weeks on board, the sun had turned me the colour of one of them. That evening at dinner Jane summed up the first twenty-six years of my life when she very innocently said, 'Noel, I think you've gone too dark!'

Part Three

The Journey Home

Eleven

December 1990, I came home to live, much to the bewilderment and consternation of all my friends in London and New York. They couldn't understand why I was giving up L'Odeon, the gallery that I had opened very modestly in 1970 and which by 1980 had become one of the top galleries in London specialising in twentieth-century decorative art. My clients and friends ranged from royalty, movie stars and rock idols to all the best museums and art galleries in America, Europe and Australia.

In 1976, I had published a very successful book on ceramic artist Clarice Cliff written by Kay Johnston and Peter Wentworth Shields. Kay was working as film director Stanley Kubrik's secretary when we first met. She and Peter collected Clarice Cliff ceramics. They were cheap at that time; Clarice had her heyday in the thirties but had fallen into obscurity after World War II. We decided to reinstate her. I held a retrospective exhibition of her work in the gallery but no one wanted to publish the book.

I borrowed the money from the bank and published it myself in a limited edition of fifteen hundred copies. Just to give you an idea of how Clarice has gone up in value: a ceramic vase that we sold at the exhibition for the then outrageous price of £50 in 1971 sold at auction last year for £10 000. Many books have since been written on the ceramics of Clarice Cliff. The latest one, by Leonard Griffin, the founder of the Clarice Cliff Collectors' Club was published to celebrate the centenary of Clarice Cliff. The foreword, by Kay and Peter, gives a flavour of the sort of life I was living then:

> We first met Noel Tovey and David Sarel at their stall on Kings Road. We bought and talked Clarice Cliff, became good friends and had some heady times together. One evening Dave was due back from a buying coup in Scotland with boxes of Clarice in his car. We waited with Noel into the night for his triumphant arrival. We were not disappointed. Newspapers flying and with cries of astonishment we unpacked each new treasure. We spent many a spirited dinner either at their place or ours, gloating over new finds and pondering the depths or shallows of Clarice. Noel was a gifted cook and many evenings were enriched by a baked Alaska. He threw fabulous Thanksgiving dinners with Kay and a friend dressed in backless Puritan maid costumes. By now Noel and Dave had opened L'Odeon, their famous gallery and shop in Fulham High Street.

Eventually Dave got to know the real me as few had done before. The caring, vulnerable, sensitive, strong-willed, giving me. He also knew the not so real me—flamboyant, gregarious, untrusting, suspicious and bad tempered. He understood both very well.

I met him in 1970 when I was in the much publicised production of Kenneth Tynan's nude revue *Oh! Calcutta* at the Roundhouse in North London. He had come down from Yorkshire for a job interview and bought an overpriced ticket from one of the touts outside the theatre. We met briefly in the bar before the performance and he waited for me at the stage door after the show, so I invited him home for supper. He returned to Yorkshire next morning, and over the next few weeks wrote me a stream of love letters, but he never included his address. He told me later that he was working things out. I was his first homosexual experience, and I was totally smitten by his innocence and honesty.

I had just finished a long and happy relationship with the well-known actress and singer Patricia Michael. I had first worked with her in a production of *Grab Me a Gondola* at the Gaiety Theatre in Dublin in 1961. She was quite beautiful with a lovely singing voice and went on to play many leading roles in the West End. We had the same agent and singing teacher and were very close friends. We had been living in a flat in Holland Park since 1967. Considered the couple most likely to succeed in the press, we announced our engagement when she joined the cast of *The Boy Friend*. The newspapers ran big headlines like 'GIRLFRIEND FINDS REAL BOYFRIEND IN THE *BOY FRIEND*'. We enjoyed all the publicity and the parties but we both knew that we were never going to get married and that eventually we would have to move on, which we did. We are still very good friends.

Dave got the position he'd been interviewed for and three weeks later he came down to London. We rented the top floor of a house belonging to an agent friend of mine and moved in together. His new job didn't last too long. I wanted to show him off to all my friends and he wanted to be part of my social whirl. I got him a job as my dresser at the theatre in the evening but he couldn't keep up the hours and he resigned from his day work. He was the reason I opened the gallery. I had always been a collector, ever since the day I bought a small tortoiseshell purse at the old Eastern Market in Exhibition Street when I was a kid, and I was particularly interested in twentieth-century decorative art. I had amassed quite a collection by the time I met Dave. I said to him, 'You like what I collect, so why don't we sell it?' We opened a stall in Antiquarius, a market on Kings Road in Chelsea.

Our first customer was Hollywood actress Debbie Reynolds who bought a classic 'T42' ceramic teapot. We were only there a few months when a shop became vacant in Fulham High Street. The rent was £350 a year. I was doing a lot of work in the theatre and could well afford that even if the shop failed. What I didn't have then was enough money to compete with the top dealers but I did know that Art Deco wasn't just a passing fad. I would have to find my own niche market. I bought every book and magazine on the Decorative Arts that I could find and I studied and memorised all the important names. I aimed my sights at the top museums and galleries who were eager to acquire name pieces for their collections. We specialised in ceramics and glass at first. Ten years later, we moved to Fulham Road, Chelsea. The rent was now £20 000 a year and when I closed the gallery in 1990 the rent had tripled.

Dave had a broad Yorkshire accent that he wanted to lose. I taught him all of Miss Cullen's voice exercises and made him read the newspaper out loud to me. In no time the accent disappeared. The other thing he was always slightly embarrassed about was his nose—he thought it was too big—so for his birthday I made an appointment with a cosmetic surgeon and he got a new nose. It was rewarding for me to watch him grow in confidence and enjoy all the things we could now afford.

These were, for the most part, good years. Dave was my anchor. With him I thought there was nothing I couldn't achieve. One morning we had a phone call from a woman saying she had a glass cabinet for sale. We drove down to Ascot and when I saw the cabinet I nearly fainted. I couldn't believe our luck. It was the cabinet designed by the famous French designer René Lalique for the autumn Salon Exhibition of 1928. She told us the price she wanted for it and I wrote out a cheque. When we got ouside Dave reminded me that we were already over our limit at the bank. This didn't deter me. I rang the bank manager to borrow the money and assured him that the debt would be paid by the end of the month. So sure was I of the worth of this rare example of decorative art that I telephoned Roger Berkowitz, the curator at the Museum of Art in Toledo in the United States and he purchased it, sight unseen. The cabinet is now part of their collection of fine twentieth-century glass.

Dave and I now had more money than we had ever dreamt of and we spent it freely. We went to all the best restaurants and were welcome at all the smart and exclusive bars and clubs. We were on everyone's party and opening night lists. We went to auctions in New York, Munich, Paris and Monte Carlo and we knew everyone on the London scene. In the late seventies a top London fashion magazine published a list of the ten most interesting men in London and I was number ten. I think Mick Jagger was number one. *Vogue* magazine published a photograph of me teaching Patti Harrison, wife of Beatle George, to tapdance. These were heady days for both of us but all that ended in February 1986 when, after sixteen years together my friend, partner and lover, died of an AIDS-related brain infection.

I gave up my work to care for him as he developed severe dementia and loss of all bodily control, knowing that there was nothing anyone could do for his condition. I spent nine months watching him die. On more than one occasion I found him crawling around the flat on all fours in the middle of the night defecating on the carpet. That meant bathing him, putting him to bed, then cleaning the carpet. I was not as strong as my friends thought I was and I had many moments of desperation. The telephone became my lifeline. I would call the Samaritans, a counselling service for people who were desperate, and talk to them until dawn.

I was exhausted from lack of sleep and extremely angry at the prejudice I saw during this time. It was as bad as the racial prejudice I had experienced as a child. Some of our best friends wouldn't visit the flat and his mother refused to drink tea from our cups when she finally came to see him. Such was the fear and ignorance surrounding HIV AIDS. It didn't occur to me that I could get infected. I never had time to put on the prescribed rubber gloves before handling him.

There was one beautiful moment, though, that made up for all the months of pain we both shared. The night Dave died, Penny, a close friend and principal dancer in many of my productions, brought her baby who was only a few months old to the hospital to see Dave for one last time. To everyone's amazement, including my own, she lowered the baby quite close to Dave's face and said, 'Kiss goodbye to Uncle Dave.'

For the last week of Dave's life, I sat beside him in his room in the hospital. He was in a coma and on a morphine drip. I wrote on a piece of paper: 'Das Geheimnis der Liebe ist grösser als das Geheimnis ders todes' and placed it in his hand. Everyday the nurses washed him, but they never took the note out of his hand. When he was placed in his coffin and taken to the crematorium, the message was still in his hand. The translation is the dedication to this book.

Two years later, and only after the recurring nightmare of watching him die I was tested for HIV. I had an anxious wait for the results but I wasn't surprised they were negative. It was not my time.

Three months after Dave died, my sister telephoned and told me that Mumma had joined him in the Dreamtime. I came home for the funeral, stayed a few weeks and returned to London feeling lonely and depressed. I had seen Mumma the year before. She was living in a nursing home and had looked very frail but I wasn't prepared for her death. I always hoped we could have one last conversation about the past. I couldn't and wouldn't grieve properly for either Mumma or Dave. I no longer wanted my gallery or to work in the theatre. I was tired and very resentful of the world and God. Earlier that year I had an operation to remove some nasal growths that were high up in my head. My doctor warned me about the anxiety attacks I was having and which had become more frequent. He suggested I return home to recuperate and to think seriously about the future. I took his advice and arrived in Sydney just before Christmas.

I went to the beach every morning very early. I needed space to think; I knew I couldn't keep running away from my responsibilities. The sea at Bronte one particular morning was flat and calm; suddenly, from out of nowhere a 'whirly whirly' wind came off the water. It circled me and in the whirling sand I heard voices, the same voices I had heard many years before when I was a young boy in Pentridge Gaol. They were saying, 'Come home, Noely boy, it's time to come home.' And it was. Hearing those voices again gave me time to reflect on just how fortunate my life had been, all things considered, for the past twenty-seven years.

My theatre career really took off in the mid sixties. I was sitting in Sandy's Bar in the tiny village of Santa Eulalia on the island of Ibiza when Sandy told me there was a telegram from London for me at the post office. It was from my agent Myrette Morven of Fraser and Dunlop and it read: MICHAEL CODRON WOULD LIKE YOU TO CHOREOGRAPH THE WEST END REVIVAL OF SANDY WILSON'S MUSICAL *THE BOY FRIEND* LOVE MYRETTE.

I had gone to Ibiza with a group of actors I knew to perform a night club act. When we arrived there we found that the club was still being built. We soon realised that the whole venture had been a mistake. Everyone except me returned to London. I decided to stay and be a hippie. There were no big clubs on the island, then and only one holiday resort on the other side of island. In the sixties Ibiza was the place to tune in, turn on and drop out, it was the time when most young people like myself who were born between two great wars and lived through several more decided there was more to life than blowing each other up. We smoked dope, experimented with acid, listened to the music that changed the world and searched for Nirvana.

My friend and mentor from London, author Robin (Lord) Maugham, nephew of Somerset Maugham, had a beautiful villa on the island. I met Robin in 1961 at a dinner at the house of artist Keith Vaughn. He was absolutely charming and we became good friends. He took me under his wing, taking me to many first nights at the theatre and to all the important art gallery openings. I stayed with him for a few weeks then I moved into La Pilarica the only boarding house in the village. It was a small white villa at the end of the plaza facing the sea. The landlady was a very old Ibizenca woman who always wore black and spent the entire day wandering around the house saying her prayers. When my money ran out I became the nanny to all my friend's children. Actor Terry Thomas's son Tiger, director Mike Nichols's daughter Daisy, the Pulitzer prize winning playwright Howard Sackler's two children, Denholm and Susie Elliot's children, the children of Spanish artist Manolo Mompo and several American artists I knew.

I borrowed the key to Es Moli, the only disco in the village and there I gave the children basic dancing and story telling lessons, then it was off to the beach for swimming lessons. The children were all characters in their own right and I was very fond of them. One day I invited Molly Sackler, age five, for lunch at the best restaurant in the village. The waiter handed us both a menu, Molly held hers upside down and when I asked to order for both of us she turned to the waiter and said with all the panache of a Hollywood Hostess 'dos hamburgers and dos dry martinis por favor'. Her martini was a coke in a martini glass.

I earned enough money to stay on the island but I didn't have enough to pay my fare back to London when the telegram arrived from my agent. Terry Thomas and his wife Belinda took care of it for me, and at a special lunch the children presented me with a set of six antique gold Ibizenco dress buttons.

After the success of *The Boy Friend* at the Comedy Theatre, I staged the numbers and created the choreography for several new musicals including *Dean* at the London Casino Theatre, *Bakerloo to Paradise* for a national tour, *Charley's Aunt* for BBC TV and *The Streets of London* at Her Majesty's for Australian director Diane Cilento.

I was invited back to Australia three times. First to choreograph *The Boy Friend* in Sydney, then to direct and choreograph the ill-fated *Oh! Calcutta* in Adelaide. The producers had been assured by Don Dunstan, the 'with-it' premier of South Australia, that they would have no trouble from the police, but what he didn't reckon on was the power of the Church. They printed and distributed a small book titled *No! No Calcutta* and the show closed before it even opened. I returned to London and a few weeks later was invited by the same producers to direct and choreograph a very successful production of *Anything Goes* starring Toni Lamond, Ronnie Frazer and Robina Beard in Sydney. By 1981, I had directed and choreographed different productions in Australia, Germany, Paris, South Africa and Denmark.

I had also become politically very aware and deeply concerned with what was happening in the world around me. I had finally found my voice and I wanted everybody to be free and equal and able to live their lives without all the shit that I had endured as a child and young person. I attended anti-Vietnam rallies outside the American Embassy in Grosvenor Square and joined in anti-apartheid demonstrations. I avidly followed the news from America about the freedom marchers in the South and the rise of the Black Panther movement.

It was at one of these demonstrations that a very close friend of mine asked me why I fought for every black in the world except my own blacks. I can't remember my reply, but her question set me thinking. Who *were* my blacks? My blacks were the drunks who starved and abandoned me when I was a small boy. They were the faceless, nameless urban minority of 'Abos' and other blacks who were vilified by white Australians. They were the people I had long ago distanced myself from. But why did I think they were different from all the other blacks in the world who had been disenfranchised from their land and culture by white imperialism? After all, hadn't I been to Soweto in South Africa and seen for myself how apartheid had wreaked havoc among the Africans?

Over the next few months, I felt guilty, angry and ashamed of myself whenever I thought about Australia. In my personal struggle to survive I had left behind my roots. What would it take for me to feel proud of who I was? Would I ever be able to find my way back to the real me? Or had I built too many walls around myself? How many Noels were there? Armed with these questions and many more I embarked on a ten-year study of my blacks, their culture and the colonisation of Australia.

None of my friends in London except Dave knew fully about my childhood and background. If I was pressed for information I would make up elaborate stories. Sometimes I was part Spanish, other times part Jamaican or part American negro. I always stressed the word 'part' but I never mentioned the word Aboriginal. I never felt white but on the other hand I didn't particularly feel Aboriginal either. I always felt black.

Part Four

Home

Twelve

It is now twelve years since I returned to Australia to live and the journey I've taken to find myself and my place in the indigenous community has been a long and at times arduous and painful one. My obsession with searching for artistic self-expression had been tempered by time and past achievements and I seriously thought that maybe I should retire from active participation in the theatre and concentrate on my study of indigenous art and politics.

I needed to do something with my spare time. I offered my services to the AIDS Trust. I had had quite a lot of experience raising money for AIDS in London. Not long after Dave died I was asked to be part of the first AIDS training clinic, set up by a young New Zealand psychologist, David Green, and Alana MacCreaner, a nursing sister from the STD clinic at St Mary's Hospital. The aim was to dispel all the myths and paranoia surrounding AIDS.

Ita Buttrose was the chairperson of the AIDS Trust and totally committed. She knew how to press all the right buttons to get the support the Trust needed. By the early nineties, supporting AIDS charities was very fashionable and everyone who was anyone wanted to be seen doing their bit and wearing a red ribbon. It was at a Trust function that I met restaurateur Jennice Kersh. She and her family had had a long association with Aboriginals and she was the first person I spoke to who told me about the difficulties they were still facing on a day to day level.

She took me to an art exhibition at Eora, the Aboriginal College of Visual and Performing Arts. The school was a revelation to me. It was fully equipped to teach all the arts and had cost the government several million dollars to build. I decided that if I had anything to offer it would be here, teaching, passing on all the experience I had gained in a career spanning more than forty-five years. It would also give me an opportunity to work face to face within the Aboriginal community.

I hadn't had contact with any Aboriginals for fifty years or more. Having lived in Europe and America for thirty-five years I had to all intents and purposes become reasonably well off and middle class. I wondered how I would fit in and what I would feel. It didn't take me long to find out.

I sent in an application for a teaching post, together with my CV. At the beginning of the next term I was called for an interview and got the job. I didn't know what to expect when I arrived on the first day of the new term. I hoped that I would work with a group of people who had the same ambitions that I had when I was their age—people with the same guts and determination I had seen in black performers in other countries.

What I got was a group of about fifteen young adults who, with the exception of two or maybe three, had no idea of how to learn or even if they really wanted to. Nonetheless, it didn't take long for me to see that they all had natural talent in abundance but absolutely no drive. By lunchtime, I thought I had made a big mistake coming here and by the end of the day I was tempted to throw in the towel. However, I decided to give it a week's trial. I spoke to Chris Sainsbury, the head music teacher and told him that if we were going to achieve anything we had to have a properly constructed course that included a literacy strand.

I was also on a learning curve: all my knowledge about Aboriginal culture and modern community life was secondhand. I had to stay focused on why I had come home, and why I was at the college. It was up to me to bridge the gap between myself and the students, and the only way I could do that was by telling them there were things they could teach me about life in the community. So I told them that I had never lived in an Aboriginal community as such. I also told them that I had been in denial about my black inheritance for more than thirty-five years and why, and that now I felt very proud of who I was and how at home I felt in their company. I agreed to take one class a week in Aboriginal studies.

It was in this class that I became aware of the bitterness and hatred that still exists in many Aboriginals today. A mature student, probably the same age as me, said, 'I still hate the white man for what he did to me.' I pointed to the young boy sitting next to him and said, 'I can understand that in people of our generation, but do you want him to grow up filled with hate as well?' This led to a heated debate about a lot of issues that I was still coming to grips with myself. I myself had stopped hating 'the white man' by the time I was eighteen because it was too negative and I was obsessed with having a career.

The new drama course consisted of dance, voice, improvisation, script analysis and music. At the end of the first term, I did a production of *Murras* by Eva Johnson, a play about white mistreatment of black Australians. The students flung themselves into it with all the enthusiasm I had expected from them the first day I arrived at the college. I saw them grow in stature at rehearsals as they realised their own potential.

One of the tasks I had set for the students who were not in the play was to write something themselves to be performed as part of the end of term program. The best piece was written by the last person I expected it from. Chris was the student who had given me the most attitude and trouble on my first day. He handed me several sheets of handwritten paper and said, 'This is for you, Uncle.' I asked him to read it for the class. He said he didn't read very well. I told him that was not a problem, just to tell us all in his own words what he had written. He walked onto the stage with the arrogant, cocky air we all knew and started to tell us a story about a boy in gaol. As he got deeper into the story we knew he was telling us about himself. The arrogance disappeared and we were treated to a very moving account of his experience, told with all the natural ability of a great actor. I thanked him and asked him if he would like to work with me on it and perform it at the end of term evening.

The quality and standard of the production surprised the representatives from TAFE (Technical and Further Education) who saw it. What they didn't see were the problems I was having with non-attendance and dope. I was repeatedly told by various teachers to take it my stride. That was just the way it was. Presumably what they meant was, that's the way it was in Aboriginal schools. But that was not the way for me.

I did another production but my heart wasn't in it. I was fighting a losing battle, not only with the apathy of some of the teachers, but also my own attitude. I was finding it difficult to contain my true feelings. This culminated with me throwing three girls out of my class for coming back after lunch stoned. I had had my baptism into the community by fire. I knew and understood the reasons for the disenchantment the students felt with their lives but condoning dope was never part of my agenda.

The principal asked me to see the counsellor from TAFE, who wanted me to take the girls back but I wouldn't relent. My only option was to go. I was sad to leave because I knew all the good work that Chris Sainsbury had achieved would mean nothing. The college which could and should have been the 'jewel in the crown' of indigenous learning, is no longer the Aboriginal College of Visual and Performing Arts. Now it is simply the TAFE College of Aboriginal Studies.

Although I had discovered for myself the difficulties facing many young Aboriginals, I was convinced that the performing arts could offer them the same salvation as I had found. I became determined to speak out about their plight at every available opportunity. I deliberately started networking all the right people and in no time I was invited to sit on many committees and boards representing indigenous arts.

At first, I wasn't aware of the problems my strategy was creating. But gradually I learnt that by speaking out as I had at Eora, I distanced myself from the community. A well-known indigenous artist told a friend of mine that I wasn't accepted by the community because I wasn't in Australia during the years of 'the struggle'. To me, that sounded the same as one Jew blaming another Jew for getting out of Germany before the Holocaust.

Generally, this sort of attitude didn't affect me. I only became concerned when I heard some of the gossip and lies about myself. I didn't particularly mind being called 'a flash black', but I objected to being called 'a coconut': the inference being, brown on the outside and white in the middle. I saw Lydia Miller, daughter of magistrate Pat O'Shane, at the opening of a show at the Art Gallery and asked her why I was having these problems. Her answer—that '*they* didn't like my entrepreneurial ways'—completely bamboozled me. How else was I going to be able to push my agenda forward and create more work in the mainstream theatre for young indigenous actors playing non-indigenous roles?

I could see no alternative but to do the same as I had done when I began my career: let my work speak for itself and close my ears to any unwanted opinions, advice and gossip.

When Lydia became the new CEO of the Aboriginal and Torres Island Arts Board for the Australia Council for the Arts, she asked me if I'd like to take over a project that she could no longer carry out because of her position. She sent me the script of a play called *The Aboriginal Protesters Confront the Declaration of an Australian Republic on January 26th 2001 with the Production of* The Commission *by Heiner Mueller* with a note saying she thought it was very dense.

The idea of a group of Aboriginals performing a play by Heiner Mueller as part of a protest was Gerhard Fischer's, Associate Professor of German Studies at the University of New South Wales. He invited Aboriginal author Mudrooroo to write a play based on this concept. They had a workshop reading of the script at Belvoir Street Theatre in 1991. It was directed by Brian Syron, a gifted actor and director. In 1995 Gerhard received a $38 000 grant from the Theatre Fund of the Australia Council for the Arts to have an extended workshop and reading. Lydia's remark that it was very dense was an understatement. What I read was a splendid academic thesis but not a play.

I met Gerhard and agreed to direct the workshop on the condition that I could cut and rework the text. First I had to accept the implausible and improbable premise that a group of Aboriginal students would perform any play by Heiner Mueller, considered by many to be the most important German playwright since Brecht. I selected from his play '*Die Auftrag*' subtitled '*Memory of a Revolution*' those extracts and speeches about slavery in Haiti and the Emissary who had been sent from France to incite the slaves to revolution that I thought would resonate with contemporary indigenous issues. I didn't know where to begin on Mudrooroo's text; it was well written but it was obvious from his ideas of staging that he had had very little practical experience of writing for the theatre. In the end I retained that part of his script which articulated and related to Mueller's play so well and cut out all topical references. I choreographed a semi-classical pas de deux to the final speech of First Love, one of Mueller's characters which Billy Mac underscored with his didjeridoo and I placed the action of the play in the now demolished Black Theatre of Redfern.

Not long after I began the reworking process I saw emerging a very interesting and important piece of theatre. I telephoned Gerhard and told him that I would prefer to do a full production of the play instead of a reading. He shared my excitement and enthusiasm and introduced me to the artistic director of the Performance Space, Angharad Wynne-Jones. I applied for the additional funding needed for a production from the Aboriginal Board of the Australia Council but the application was rejected. This was my first brush with Aboriginal politics. I had no idea about Aboriginal politics. I'd heard a lot of gossip and bitching but at the time I didn't pay any heed to it at all. In the end there was no funding money from the Aboriginal Board of the Australia Council in my production.

Angharad arranged a meeting with Anthony Steele, director of the Sydney Festival and I outlined my vision of the play to him. He agreed to take it into the Festival and gave us the additional $45 000 for a full production. Andrew Raymond designed a wonderful set for which he won an award. Joe Mercurio designed the lighting, Chris Sainsbury composed the music and Robina McKellar was the assistant director.

I got together a cast of fine actors: Rachel Maza, Justine Saunders, Kevin Smith, Gary Cooper, Billy MacPherson, Glenn Shea, Victoria Kennedy (a former pupil from Eora) and two dancers, Jason Moore and Sue-Ann Williams. I was very nervous the first morning of rehearsals; I was confident that the script would work but I had not directed a professional indigenous cast before. When I'm nervous I waffle, and that's what I did for the first hour. I talked about everything except the play. But I shouldn't have worried. The cast were exactly the same as every other professional cast I had worked with. Within a couple of days I felt that I was accepted as an equal by this part of the community. Everyone called me Uncle, a sign of respect in Aboriginal culture.

At the end of the first week I had to ask Gerhard not to attend rehearsals. I discovered that he was giving the cast notes about their characters when I wasn't around. Why do dramaturgs want to be directors?

The play opened at the Performance Space in January 1996 and was a resounding success for all concerned. Angela Bennie's review in the *Sydney Morning Herald* was glowing: 'This production is a cry, a call to arms, for all of us as people; but it is also a call to our theatre, to show where it might go. Tovey and Mudrooroo and indeed Gerhard Fischer, whose concept it is, have shown us.'

The production won two inaugural Performing Arts Awards, I was nominated for Australian of the Year in a poll in the *Australian* newspaper and I received an invitation from the German government to bring the production (all expenses paid) to the Weimar Arts Festival in Germany.

As a result of an indigenous company performing a play by the legendary Heiner Mueller, The Goethe Institute in Sydney had arranged for the theatre critic from a top German newspaper to review our production, which he did brilliantly.

While we were negotiating with the directors of the Weimar Festival the directors of the Performance Space assumed that they owned my production. This was a big mistake on their part and could have had very unpleasant consequences for all of us. I engaged the best arts lawyer I could find and, supported by Mudrooroo, proved that I owned the intellectual rights to the play and production.

The season was a sell-out in Weimar and Munich and we were all surprised at the genuine interest by the public and the critics in our work and their reaction to the messages in the play about slavery, dispossession of land and genocide.

In the last scene in the play, the cast, having decided that Mueller's voice is not their voice, take off their masks, smear their faces and upper torso with white ochre, and one by one turn to the audience and recount the horrors of the massacres, the spreading of disease and the two hundred years of suffering by indigenous Australians under the yoke of white imperialism.

On the opening night in Weimar, I made a speech thanking the festival director and the audience. When I finished a woman stood up and said, 'Thank you, Herr Tovey, for bringing your play to Germany. Now I can grieve for my family who perished in Buchenwald.' The notorious concentration camp is on the outskirts of Weimar.

On our return to Sydney I was asked by the actor John Howard to play the grandfather in a production of *Somewhere in the Darkness* by Ray Kelly that he was directing for the Sydney Theatre Company in 1996. The last time I had performed on stage was in London in 1970 and I really enjoyed the opportunity to tread the boards again. This was the first time I had been asked to play an Aboriginal.

My agenda meanwhile was panning out just as I had planned. More and more I was being sought after for my input on indigenous arts and theatre issues. Aboriginal Education Officer Angela Martin asked me to give a series of sixty lectures to three thousand American students at the Art Gallery of New South Wales and I was invited to sit on the board of the National Playwrights' Conference.

I was the face of Aboriginality that was acceptable to many people. I had a high profile, a good speaking voice and total command of what I was talking about.

I agreed after much careful deliberation to launch the Sydney Gay and Lesbian Mardi Gras. In front of 23 000 people who had gathered on the steps of the Sydney Opera House, I made a long and impassioned speech about my early life in Australia, racism, HIV AIDS and the growth of the gay community throughout the world. If no one had heard of me before the speech, they certainly did after I finished it. I was inundated with requests to be interviewed by all the media.

While I was rehearsing at the Sydney Theatre Company, Wayne Harrison, the artistic director, asked me if I would like to direct a play there for the festival of the Dreaming in 1997, the first of the Olympic Arts Festivals. I told him I would like to do a production of *A Midsummer Night's Dream* with an all-indigenous cast. He said he was hoping I would choose a classic and immediately put all the infrastructure of the company at my disposal. He also acted as my dramaturg. Apart from some of the usual cuts in the text we didn't change any of the dialogue. I wanted all the Aboriginality and cultural references in the production to come from the sets and costumes.

I engaged two designers, Andrew Raymond, again, and Julie Martin. I needed to have a set that was a combination of a solid structure and a computer-generated animation of the Dreamtime. Julie designed and built the animation but we couldn't find a suitable projector. She had friends who worked for a company in England that had just what we needed, only there was no money in the budget for hiring anything from overseas. She telephoned her friends and explained our situation, the cultural importance and the Olympic significance of the production. They offered to send us their latest projector and a technician at their expense for a credit in the program and to be able to demonstrate their projector during the day to potential Australian buyers. Wayne agreed to their requests but there was a snag. As the company wasn't an official Olympic sponsor we couldn't give them a credit. I overcame this by thanking them profusely in my director's notes on the first page of the program. I was in the position to offer several newcomers their first professional jobs. I gave the part of Titania to a beautiful young woman named Tessa Rose Leahy. She had been in one of my drama classes at the National Aboriginal and Islander Dance Association. She arrived at the first rehearsal knowing all her lines and was a superb Titania. It was the cast's innate sense of the Dreamtime and storytelling that created the magic.

The rehearsal period was not without its problems but I had learnt that the best way to resolve Aboriginal problems was in an Aboriginal way. At one rehearsal, a good friend who had worked for me before lost his temper for no apparent reason and ran amok. I ordered everyone except the cast out of the room. When he finally calmed down I made him sit on the floor and asked the cast one by one to tell him what they thought of his behaviour. A young actress said she expected this sort of violence at home but not in the theatre. That did it for me: I said they could decide if I should keep him or replace him. He apologised to everyone and we continued the rehearsal and remained friends. Wayne would have been alarmed had he known what was going on. Luckily, I managed to keep all the cast problems from him. At one dress rehearsal an actor was so stoned he said to me, 'I've had enough of this rehearsal shit, Uncle, let's just do it.'

I gave several interviews in the weeks before we opened. One that sticks in my memory is of a very young reporter asking me if 'they [Aboriginals] would understand the language?' I replied, 'What language am I speaking to you in?'

The performance was an unqualified critical success. However, I was having serious second thoughts about my agenda. Why did I expect more from my own people than I did from non-Aboriginal actors? I have been known to replace non-Aboriginal actors for a lot less. Why did I feel so hurt and betrayed by their lack of commitment and loyalty? A young actor, Lee Willis, said, 'You have to stop looking at us through rose-coloured glasses, Uncle Noel.' He was right, but I wanted to know the answers to my questions. Had I been away from Australia for too long? Why did I so desperately want to be accepted? I had set myself a near impossible task. I became very depressed and my doctor at that time jokingly advised me 'to think white for a while'.

Kate Cherry, the associate artistic director of the Playbox Theatre and daughter of Wal Cherry, the best director in Australia in my youth, asked me to devise a series of workshops to be held in Melbourne at the theatre in conjunction with the Koori students from Swinburne College and Ilbijerri, a local Aboriginal theatre company.

While I was in Melbourne, Aubrey Mellor, the artistic director, asked me to direct a play called *Stolen*. It had already been workshopped by a good young director named Andrea James for Ilbijerri. My first reaction to the play was that it really wasn't well written but it did have enough emotional content based on the history of the Stolen Generation. With a lot of rewriting and a good cast it could be made to work. I was also concerned about the intellectual ownership of the stories the play was based on and if the owners were to be compensated in any way.

I submitted a list to Aubrey of the actors who I wanted to audition for the play. He told me I could cast who I wanted but he didn't tell me that part of his arrangement with Ilbijerri was that only Victorian actors would be used. It took several months of correspondence for me to work out what was going on and when it became obvious that I could not have the cast I wanted I dropped the production.

For all the progress we had achieved at the New South Wales Ministry for the Arts in the area of arts protocol for indigenous artists I still had to listen to bureaucrats and arts people on other arts committees being oh so careful to say the 'right' thing. They didn't realise they were being just as offensive as if they had said the wrong thing. (I was recently interviewed on Darwin radio, and the first thing the interviewer said to me was, 'You don't look like a black fella to me—how black are you?'). Once I was at an opening night, standing behind the head of an arts institution, and actually heard him say 'we have a lot of trouble with them [Aboriginals] when they come here.' I was, and still am convinced that racism is alive and well in the halls of Federal and State government, albeit couched in a polite and patronising language.

By the beginning of 1998 I was feeling hemmed in and restricted, and I couldn't do anything about the tell-tale signs—that I knew so well—of the onset of a deep depression that was heading my way. My doctor prescribed medication and gave yet another warning about the way I was pushing myself. I was also having very worrying family and personal problems. One of these was to do with my daughter. Barbara and I had separated less than two years after we left Melbourne. Our daughter, Felicity, was born in London. A year after we arrived Barbara received news of the sudden death of her mother. She returned to Australia, taking Felicity with her. I stayed in London; I was under contract to the Palladium for the Christmas show but as the weeks passed it seemed that war was looming between the United States and Cuba over the Cuban missile crisis, especially after President Kennedy's speech to the nation, and I didn't want to be stuck in Europe if that happened. I wrote to Barbara and told her I was coming home. I was released from my contract and arranged to have the contents of our small flat in West Kensington shipped to Australia. I followed on a Dutch passenger liner, the *Wilhelm Ruys*.

We lived at Barbara's grandmother's in Kew. I more or less took up where I had left off. I got work in television and in Cid Elwood's production of *Show Boat* at the Tivoli Theatre. It was while I was doing a revue that I became friends with our stage manager. She and her husband had a son Felicity's age, and Barbara and I spent a lot of time with them. I didn't like being back in Australia at all. This was not the way I saw my career developing and I suggested to Barbara that we return to London. We agreed that I should go first and find a flat. Once again, I said goodbye to Mumma and all my friends and sailed off on another Dutch liner, the *Oranjeboom*, for Europe.

I had no sooner arrived in London when I received a letter from Barbara telling me that something had happened at home and that she would not be returning to London as planned. Using the last of our savings, I set sail again on the *Wilhelm Ruys* for Melbourne. I broke a bone in my right foot while teaching four very large football players the Dance of the Little Swans for the ship's concert and spent most of the five weeks it took to get to Australia immobilised.

Once home in Kew, Barbara told me that she and the husband of my stage manager friend had fallen in love and that they were leaving us. I was so angry, I lost my temper and struck her. For the next few weeks I behaved appallingly. I was beset by many of the demons that had plagued me when I was young. My self-confidence had deserted me and the ghosts of the past were giving me all the wrong advice. My manic temper returned and I ran amok. When I calmed down we went to Adelaide and stayed with some friends. Barbara was genuinely sorry for what had happened and finally she gave me enough money to return to England. It took me many years to understand that my pride had been hurt once again and that being good friends is not the basis for getting married, particularly if one of the friends is homosexual. I was saddened at the thought of leaving Felicity behind, but there was no way I could have taken care of her when I could barely take care of myself at the time.

I used to see Felicity whenever I returned to Australia for work or a holiday. When she was seventeen, I received a telephone call from her asking me if she could come to London and live with me and Dave. She enrolled in a modelling course and I introduced her to all my friends, including Princess Mariam of Johore, who I had met at the Queensway Ice Rink in the early sixties when I started skating again, and she was a young girl. Mariam took her shopping and to all the 'in' restaurants. Felicity and Dave got along extremely well and I was very happy. It wasn't until a few weeks later when I heard her screaming at her mother down the telephone that I realised that they had big problems and that she had come to London as a result of one of their fights. That night, she asked if I would pay her fare home and she left London at the end of the week.

The next time I heard about her was a year or two later from a hospital in Melbourne asking me if I would pay her medical bills. It was a 'drying out clinic'. I agreed to but only until the end of the month. I wrote to Felicity and told her that if she had inherited anything from me, it was the will to survive. Several years went by before she wrote and thanked me for the good advice I had given her. She told me that she wanted to marry a boy she had met at AA. I came home and arranged the wedding. It was a grand affair and cost a great deal of money, but I thought it was worth it to see her get her life in order. The marriage lasted less than a year. I came home again to see her, we had a huge row and I returned to London a very sad father. I knew then I would never have the relationship with her that I had always wanted.

Her life since has been all downhill. Last year, ten years after we last spoke, I got a call from her, somewhere in Queensland. She sounded intoxicated and was very abusive. 'I don't want to be a boong,' she said. 'Anyway I only called to tell you that you are a grandfather, and guess what? Your granddaughter has blonde hair and blue eyes.' I replied that life would have been easier for all of us if we had been born with blonde hair and blue eyes.

On top of all this I received a series of telephone calls that even now sounds like they were written for a film script. Mark, a close friend of mine who had had an enormously successful career in England and Australia was just getting his life back on track after years of alcoholism told me he had lung cancer and was going into hospital for chemotherapy. My brother Fred rang me from Melbourne and said he was dying from mesothelioma, a lung disease caused by inhaling fibrous plaster particles. That same night I had a call from London. It was Victor telling me that his boy friend Peter, who I employed to run the gallery after Dave passed away, did not have long to live. This was in a curious way my immediate salvation. I had no alternative but to galvanise myself into action and do whatever I could for my two friends and my brother.

Mark's chemo didn't work and he asked me to move him into St Vincent's Hospice. I visited him every day and together we arranged his funeral. When he slipped into a coma I said goodbye to him and flew to Melbourne. I arrived there too late to say goodbye to Fred, he was already in a coma. I no longer had any need to stay in Melbourne. I explained to my niece and nephew that I had to go to London, that I wanted to see Peter before he died. That same evening I flew to England. I was quite exhausted by the time I went to the hospital to visit Peter. He was mentally quite unstable and I found it most distressing to see him going the same way that Dave had. I was shattered but resilient. I stayed in London for the rest of the week then I flew to New York where I totally collapsed. When I had recovered enough to go out I immersed myself in the theatre and the warmth and affection of old friends who had known me for many years. A month later, in 1995, I returned to Sydney with regenerated vigour and fresh ideas.

For my next project, I arranged a partnership between the Riverina Theatre Company in Wagga Wagga and Tandanya, the Aboriginal

Cultural Institute in Adelaide, to jointly present a production of Tony Strachan's play *State of Shock* in Wagga and Adelaide for the youth festival. Once again I had a great cast: Trisha Morton-Thomas, a pupil of mine at Eora and one of the stars of the film *Radiance*, Lee Willis, another former pupil of mine and a fine young actor, and the vastly experienced Jim Holt.

The play is mainly about domestic violence and drinking problems in an Aboriginal community in Queensland. It also deals with the diaspora of the indigenous people of that State from their native lands, the widespread instances of glaucoma and trachoma, and racism. I wanted young people to come to the theatre and stay after the performance to discuss the issues raised in the play with the cast.

When we were rehearsing in Sydney I was invited by the New South Wales Benevolent Society to take the members of their Sydney Leadership program for a day of Aboriginal cultural studies. In ten years I had acquired quite a reputation for making speeches and giving lectures, most of which were politically based. I never pass up any opportunities to talk to and educate non-indigenous Australians about indigenous culture but I am always a little apprehensive to begin with. For most people, all they know about Aboriginal culture is what they read in the papers or see on TV. The lack of knowledge about Aboriginal culture in the wider community still amazes me.

The Leadership Program is a group of people who are at the top level in their particular field. At one point during our discussion on alcohol-related violence I told them that I was rehearsing a play that dealt explicitly with these problems in an Aboriginal community in the far north of Australia. I invited them to come and watch a run-through of the play the following day.

Next morning they came to our rehearsal room, which was so small we had to perform the play twice so they could all see it. When we finished, Roger West, the former NSW Community

Services Minister, asked me if we were having a season in Sydney. I told him we only had enough funding for Wagga Wagga and Adelaide. He and the other members of the program collected $26 000 between themselves and their friends that enabled us to play for two weeks at the Stables Theatre in Kings Cross.

While we were in Wagga, I got permission to take the cast into Shepherds Park detention centre. We performed the play for the young indigenous inmates without any set, lights or sound. I knew some of the boys from my previous visits there and I was interested to see their response to the play. They laughed at the violence. In fact, the more violent the action, the more they laughed. I am not a psychiatrist, but I knew that this was the only way these boys could deal with the mirror image of the violence they had all experienced at one time or another. It still saddens me to know that there are no adequate safety nets to catch these young people when they get out of such places as Shepherds Park. The production of *State of Shock* and the actors received outstanding notices wherever we played.

> Sydney Morning Herald: *Here's a play that gives you back your breath, reminds you of it and of your context in no uncertain terms [and] confronts unacceptable realities that leave you tingling with indignation.* State of Shock *is as tight as a tourniquet and stings like salt in the wound.*

> Sydney Observer: *Noel Tovey creates compelling theatre.* State of Shock *moves both beyond the facts and beyond the spite and creates a compelling piece of theatre . . . The play has the emotional pitch of an intensive care ward.*

When I was on the board of the National Playwrights' Conference in Canberra I workshopped a play by Merrill Bray, a feisty, brittle Aboriginal woman from Adelaide. She had had enormous problems while growing up and was inclined not to trust anyone until I came along. Her short play, *Mechanics for the Spirit,* was provocative and well written. I found it stimulating and challenging to work on. I told her that one day I would do a full production of it.

The opportunity to do this presented itself in 2000. Tandanya wanted me to mount a play for the Adelaide Festival. I thought a production of Merrill's play and Ray Kelly's *Somewhere in the Darkness* on the same program under the title *Spirit, Time and Place* would be an ideal project. They both dealt with a depth of Aboriginal spirituality that is seldom seen in the theatre.

I asked Merrill to apply to the Australia Council for funding; I explained to her that for the same amount of money I could do both plays. I didn't ask Ray to apply because it would have been almost impossible to split the funding between two separate applications. Besides, we were all close friends and they both stood to benefit enormously from having their work seen in the festival. My fee for directing and designing was being funded by a corporation in Adelaide.

Merrill's application was successful and Tandanya received the money. I flew to Adelaide, designed and had the set—an outback gaol—built for her play. There was no set for Ray's play, only light and sound. I got together a cast, including three actors I had used in *State of Shock*, that I knew would do us proud in the international milieu of the Adelaide Festival.

Several weeks before rehearsals began I received a telephone call from one of the actors, who was having some problems and needed money. This didn't alarm me; I had given money to a number of people for all sorts of reasons over the years. The first day in Adelaide everyone showed up except this actor. That made me feel just a little uneasy. The same day Merrill dropped a bombshell. She told Tandanya that she didn't want Ray's play on the same program as hers. Someone had got to her and told her that all of the funded money belonged to her. She had also disagreed with my use of the word 'gin', a term used by white Australians in a derogatory fashion to describe certain Aboriginal women. She had misunderstood my intention because the context I used it in was the reclaiming of our language. The word itself is *dyin*, meaning woman, or *dyjinuragang*, meaning old woman in the Sydney language. The director of Tandanya, Kirstie Parker, advised Merrill to write to the Australia Council and ask for a variance of funding to include Ray's play. The next day Merrill sent us a fax stating that she had been advised not to do so by a member of the Aboriginal Board. This was 'payback' for me, politics again. I had not agreed on many issues during my three-year term on the funding committee. Merrill withdrew her play, insisting that only her actors be paid and not the two actors in Ray's play. Legally and technically, she was right. The cast of Merrill's play were paid. Then I asked them if they would perform *Somewhere in the Darkness* for nothing. I offered to pay any additional fees myself. As I expected everyone agreed.

Another problem that went unnoticed while I was trying to sort out Merrill's issues, now caused me serious anxiety. One of the actors never arrived on time in the morning and spent his lunch break in the pub. On those occasions when he was together, he gave a brilliant interpretation of his part. However, he was having difficulty learning the lines and time was not on our side. I hung in there. I knew what he was capable of doing if I could keep him in one piece. He is one of Australia's best actors and I was torn between my feelings as the caring Uncle and the professional director. He was wracked with emotional pain and in the clutches of his demons but I also had eight other people to think about and I was fast running out of ideas. The end came the morning of the opening night. I had told the cast the previous evening that we were having three rehearsals before lunch and another three in the afternoon. I wanted to keep him focused and he agreed to do them.

At the first break, hoping to make him feel better, I gave him a large envelope that had just arrived—a first night gift of some sort, I assumed. He ripped it open and turned it upside-down. Hundreds of pieces of torn-up photographs fell to the floor. He went berserk; I've never witnessed such a violent outburst anywhere. Jim tried to calm him down but he became even more violent and abusive. Jim was extremely distressed and wanted me to call the police. In his long career he had never had to deal with anything like this. I turned around and saw Sarah de Jong, the composer of the soundscape, sitting in the stalls in a catatonic state. Tears were streaming down her face. I blew my stack and threw the actor out of the theatre, called a halt to rehearsals and went for a walk in the park.

I was absolutely wiped out; I could not comprehend any of the scene I had just witnessed. I had worked my balls off getting this project up and running only to see it destroyed by two individuals who had pushed their self-destruct buttons. I have never subscribed to the popular adage that 'Aboriginals are set up to fail'. I would have failed myself years ago if I believed this. I had a job to do: I had to minimise the fallout from the morning's events, save face for Tandanya, the Australia Council and our place in the Festival. I also had to ignore the fact that someone I trusted had contributed to this behaviour by repeating certain things I had said in professional confidence. I returned to Tandanya and called everyone together. The first thing was to cancel the evening performance. We told the press it was due to a sudden illness in the cast. Then I asked Jim, Trish and Lee if they would re-rehearse *State of Shock*. Jim agreed on the condition that we had a security guard in the theatre. I designed a new setting with no set or costumes, only a few props, which Cali, our stage manager, knew where to get in a hurry as she had worked with us on the earlier production. Joe re-created his lighting, Sarah returned to Sydney that afternoon, sent us a CD of her original sound design and we opened two nights later, ironically to even better reviews than we got the first time around.

I not only lost all my fees on the project and the money I had given to the actor, but I also lost my desire to direct any more indigenous plays or projects. I returned to Sydney and retired from all the committees and boards I was on. The questions that I had agonised over for most of my adult life had all been answered. Yes, I told myself, I *had* been away too long—not only the thirty years I had spent overseas but the more than sixty years I had lived away from my people. No, I didn't really fit into the indigenous community and now it no longer mattered. I had made several close friends who respected me for who I was, not where I came from. There's more to being indigenous than colour. Spiritually, I feel very much at home. The scars of the past may never fully heal but I wear them on the outside now.

Ultimately, I achieved what I had set out to do: I proved my point that indigenous actors can hold their own on any stage. Many of the writers, dancers and actors I have taught or worked with have consolidated their careers. More young Aboriginals are now going to drama schools and having proper training.

I hope the time comes when everyone, particularly in the arts, will have the guts to stop 'pussy footing' around indigenous politics and the major issues and tell it how it is. The next decade could be very exciting if the shackles of community thinking—black and white—are thrown off and our leaders lead by example.

Last year, I was asked to give a lecture on *Othello* to several hundred high school students. I based my lecture on the racism inherent in the text. This enabled me to broach the broader issues of racism and by telling them about my early childhood I could debunk the myth that you have to be well educated to understand and appreciate Shakespeare.

If this new millennium is, as we are told, the 'Golden Age' for indigenous Australians, then we must be sure to make the most of every opportunity that is on offer. The future of indigenous Australia is in the hands of our young people. We must prevent them from walking down the same paths of self-destruction that many of our friends and families have done. We must tell them that in all four hundred Aboriginal languages that existed before colonisation there were no words for suicide, drugs or Welfare. It's time to forget being stereotypical black men and women. There are numerous Aboriginals who have achieved success in their chosen fields. Let's make *them* the stereotypes. It won't be easy, but it is possible. I'm certainly looking forward to the time when I can work on productions with well-integrated casts, where colour-blind casting is the norm and not the exception.

Not long after I started writing my book, I asked my cousin Libby Gleeson, herself a writer, if I could read to her what I had written so far. I sat with Libby on the board of the Sydney Writers Festival and I had previously met her husband Euan Tovey when I was the guest lecturer in indigenous art at the Art Gallery of New South Wales. We joked about having the same surname and their daughters called me Uncle Noel. When I finally received Mumma's family tree from New Zealand, I telephoned Euan and told him that we were blood cousins. Libby sensed that I was feeling negative and wanted some feedback. I read her the passage about the tram ride and she said I should tell the story myself on stage. Heeding her advice, I extrapolated a theatre piece from this book and I performed it at the old Carlton Courthouse. The building has been preserved in its original state and is now used as a theatre under the auspices of La Mama, Melbourne. In my dressing room was the very dock that my father stood in 1941. The show opened on 9 March 2003. The following is an extract from the review in the *Age* newspaper: 'Tovey's performance is gripping and intensely moving . . . A remarkable story and performance of great cultural and historical importance.'

My tram ride has come full circle.

I am so filled with optimism for the future that I cannot understand why I tried so hard and endured so much trying to prove to everyone, including myself who I was when all the time I knew. I am me. I am genetically engineered by a hundred thousand years of indigenous and African culture mixed with the genes of French, English and Celtic migrants. I am grateful to the spirits of all my ancestors who heard my call for help that night in Pentridge Gaol when I was seventeen years old. They are the reason that I have survived.

Epilogue

Now that I am seventy years young and have finished writing my story and relived the past there is no one more amazed or surprised than me that I am still here. I achieved more than I ever dreamt was possible in the theatre, with my gallery and as a person. I never thought I would be invited by a bank manager to a private box at Lords to watch the cricket, but that happened the day my overdraft hit £100 000, or that I would be a director and choreographer in the West End of London.

Coming from a broken-down terrace house and a very dysfunctional family in Barkly Street, Carlton, to a flat in one of the most exclusive blocks in Sydney, surrounded by works of art and furniture from my days in London, and many happy memories to balance the scales, I know that my survival has been more than coincidence. Every part of my journey was a learning curve. I spent too many years blaming Mumma's drinking habits for all my mistakes. My teachers were my spiritual ancestors and that power that is beyond them. They were there to pick me up whenever I fell off the tram. I was down many times but I never hit rock bottom. They cushioned my fall. I have always believed in their existence and I still do.

I never imagined that one day I would be able to have a loving and fulfilling relationship but that's what happened with Dave. Whenever I now have a problem or I've had a particularly good day I have a yarn with him, not in my mind but out loud. To care for someone and be able share their life is a great gift but to share that moment when they die is even greater. This is what Dave taught me, among other things. Knowing my own shortcomings and frailties has enabled me to counsel others in need.

I think about the inner strength I was given when I was born. I come from a long line of survivors. I agree with whoever it was who said, 'If you are born black, you are born political'. You have to be. Either you successfully defend your identity or you let the opposition win. I didn't know how to fight when I was young, but I learnt. I still don't like the opposition to win and I never will. There were times in my later life when I didn't believe what I knew had happened to Bev and me and I am grateful to my ancestors for giving me the courage to open my own 'Pandora's Box'. I am fearfully proud of who I am.